Table of Contents

CHAPTER 4: SEAFOOD

The Ultimate Ninja Foodi Cookbook

1000-Day Fast & Delicious Air Fry, Broil, Pressure Cook, Slow Cook, Dehydrate, and More Recipes for Beginners and Advanced Users

Nancy C. Jackson

Chapter 1: Breakfast

Butter Cookies

Prep time: 5 minutes | Cook time: 15 minutes | Makes 6 biscuits

2 cups self-rising flour, plus extra as needed
½ cup (1 stick) cold unsalted butter, cut into small cubes, plus 3 tablespoons, melted
¾ cup buttermilk
Cooking spray
¼ teaspoon kosher salt

1. Remove the inner pot from the Foodi and add the flour and cold butter cubes. Use a silicone-coated potato masher (so you don't scuff or scratch the pot) to mash the butter and flour together until there aren't any pieces of butter larger than a small pea (you may have to push the butter off the potato masher occasionally).
2. Add the buttermilk to the flour-butter mixture and use a silicone spatula to stir until it makes a sticky dough.
3. Coat your hands in some flour and work the dough in the Foodi pot, adding more flour as needed to prevent sticking to the pot, until the dough is just barely holding together. Turn the dough out onto a lightly floured work surface, lightly flour the top of the dough, and use the underside of the Foodi pot to flatten the dough into a ¾-inch-thick disk. Then use your hands to press the dough until it is about ½ inch thick. Wipe off the bottom and the inside of the pot, and lightly coat the inside of the pot with cooking spray. Insert the pot back into the Foodi.
4. Dip the rim of a drinking glass or biscuit cutter into a bit of flour and then cut 6 biscuits from the dough, flouring the cutter after each cut. (You can gather the scraps, press them together, and cut out 1 more biscuit.) Arrange the biscuits in the pot (it's totally fine if they touch), brush with the melted butter, and sprinkle with salt.
5. Drop the Crisping Lid and set the Foodi to Broil for 15 minutes, or until the biscuits are golden brown. Let the biscuits cool for 5 minutes before lifting the lid and removing them from the pot.

Raspberry Jam

Prep time: 5 minutes | Cook time: 8 minutes | Makes 3 cups

12 ounces (340 g) frozen raspberries
1 cup sugar
Juice of 1 lemon
1 tablespoon cornstarch

1. Add the raspberries, sugar, and 1 cup water to the Foodi's inner pot. Lock on the Pressure Lid, making sure the valve is set to Seal, and set the Foodi to Pressure on High for 2 minutes. When the timer reaches 0, quick-release the pressure and carefully remove the lid.
2. In a small bowl, whisk together the lemon juice and cornstarch and add it to the pot. Drop the Crisping Lid and set the Foodi to Sear/Saute on High for 6 minutes, cooking the raspberry mixture until bubbling and thickened and coats the back of a spoon, lifting the lid to stir often.
3. Transfer the jam to a container and refrigerate uncovered until cool and thickened, about 3 hours. Once cool, cover the container and store in the refrigerator for up to 1 month.

Tropical Fruits Steel-Cut Oats

Prep time: 5 minutes | Cook time: 10 minutes | Serves 4

1 cup steel-cut oats
4 allspice berries
½ teaspoon kosher salt
½ cup whole milk or your favorite milk alternative
2 tablespoons light brown sugar
Sliced tropical fruit, such as kiwi, mango, pineapple, and toasted coconut, for garnish

1. Place the oats, allspice, salt, and 3 cups water into the Foodi's inner pot. Lock on the Pressure Lid, making sure the valve is set to Seal, and set to Pressure on High for 10 minutes. Turn off the Foodi and allow the pressure to release naturally for 15 minutes. Then quick-release any remaining pressure and carefully remove the lid.
2. Remove the allspice berries and stir in the milk and brown sugar. Divide among bowls and serve topped with fruit.

Sour Cream Scrambled Eggs

Prep time: 5 minutes | Cook time: 9 minutes | Serves 2

6 large eggs, lightly beaten
3 tablespoons cold butter, cut into small pieces
½ teaspoon kosher salt
Cooking spray
1 tablespoon sour cream
Lemon wedges, for garnish
Freshly ground black pepper, for garnish
Chopped chives, for garnish

1. Add the beaten eggs, butter, and salt to a medium bowl and stir to combine (the butter will stay in small pieces).
2. Generously coat the Foodi's inner pot with cooking spray. Drop the Crisping Lid and set the Foodi to Air Crisp at 390°F (199°C) for 9 minutes to preheat. After 1 minute, lift the lid and add the egg mixture. Drop the lid again and resume cooking, until eggs are fluffy and set.
3. When the timer reaches 0, lift the lid and stir in the sour cream. Serve the eggs with a lemon wedge, a sprinkle of pepper, and chives.

Eggs and Mushrooms Casserole

Prep time: 10 minutes | Cook time: 18 minutes | Serves 4

1 tablespoon unsalted butter
2 medium shallots, minced
8 ounces (227 g) button mushrooms, sliced
1 teaspoon minced fresh thyme leaves
1 cup baby spinach leaves
½ teaspoon kosher salt
Freshly ground black pepper, to taste
1 tablespoon plus 1 teaspoon finely chopped fresh chives
4 large eggs
4 slices Swiss cheese
4 pieces baguette, sliced on a bias
Cooking spray
Zest of ½ lemon

1. Add the butter to the Foodi's inner pot and set to Sear/Saute on High. When the butter has melted, use a silicone spatula to "paint" the bottom of the pot with the butter. When the butter starts to foam, after about 5 minutes, add the shallots and cook until they begin to soften, about 3 minutes, stirring occasionally. Stir in the mushrooms and thyme, and cook until mushrooms begin to soften, about 7 minutes.
2. Add the spinach, stir, and allow to cook until the spinach begins to wilt, about 1 minute; mix in the salt, pepper to taste, and 1 tablespoon of the chives. Turn off the heat, stir, and divide the mixture among four 8-ounce ramekins, tamping the mixture down into the bottom of each ramekin. Wash the inner pot.
3. Crack the eggs and add one to each of the ramekins, being careful not to break the yolks.
4. Add ½ cup water to the Foodi's inner pot, insert the reversible rack in the low position, and carefully set the ramekins on the rack. Lock on the Pressure Lid, making sure the valve is set to Seal, and set to Pressure on Low for 3 minutes. When the timer reaches 0, quick-release the pressure and carefully remove the lid. Lay 1 slice of cheese on top of each egg.
5. Spray the baguette slices on both sides with cooking spray and arrange on top of the cheese in each ramekin. Drop the Crisping Lid and set to Broil for 5 minutes, or until the cheese is melted.
6. Combine the lemon zest with the remaining teaspoon of chives. Lift the lid and carefully remove the rack and ramekins. Sprinkle with the zest and chives. Serve warm.

Giant Omelet

Prep time: 5 minutes | Cook time: 5 minutes | Serves 2

1 tablespoon unsalted butter
6 large eggs
½ teaspoon kosher salt
½ cup Chives, for garnish (optional)
Freshly ground black pepper, to taste

1. Add the butter to the Foodi's inner pot and set the Foodi to Sear/Saute on Medium. Use a silicone spatula to "paint" the bottom of the pot with the butter as it melts.
2. In a medium bowl, whisk together the eggs and salt until well combined and uniform in texture. Once the butter has completely melted, add the egg mixture to the inner pot and cook without stirring until just set, about 2 minutes.
3. After 2 minutes, stir the omelet once clockwise to create folds, then drop the Crisping Lid and set the Foodi to Air Crisp at 390ºF (199ºC) for 3 minutes, or until the omelet is just set.
4. Turn off the Foodi and allow the omelet to rest for 2 minutes. At this point, sprinkle any fillings you like over the omelet (the omelet is still hot enough to melt grated cheese, for example).
5. Lift the lid and remove the inner pot from the Foodi. Run a silicone spatula around the edge of the pot and shake the pot gently to slide the omelet out onto a plate. Fold the omelet over, garnish with chives, if desired, sprinkle with pepper, and enjoy.

Bacon and Gruyère Cheese Quiche

Prep time: 5 minutes | Cook time: 40 minutes | Makes 1 quiche

1 (9-inch) frozen piecrust (the kind that comes fitted into a tin pan)
6 large eggs
½ cup heavy cream
Kosher salt, to taste
Freshly ground black pepper to taste
8 ounces (227 g) Gruyère cheese, grated (about 1 cup)
1 cup cooked and crumbled bacon

1. Let the piecrust thaw for 15 minutes at room temperature. Prick the piecrust all over with the tines of a fork. Place the crust on the Foodi's reversible rack in the low position, then set the rack into the inner pot, drop the Crisping Lid, and set to Bake/Roast at 375ºF (190ºC) for 10 minutes, or until golden brown. Lift the lid and carefully remove the rack and piecrust from the Foodi; the crust won't be cooked all the way through—just slightly browned.
2. In a large bowl, whisk together the eggs and cream. Add a few pinches of salt and pepper, the grated cheese, and the bacon, and stir to combine.
3. Place the parbaked crust on the rack as before, place the rack in the Foodi's inner pot, and then carefully pour the egg filling into the crust. Drop the Crisping Lid and set the Foodi to Bake/Roast at 325ºF (163ºC) for 30 minutes, or until the center is set and the top is golden brown.
4. Lift the lid and carefully remove the rack and quiche, then set aside to cool. Serve warm or at room temperature. (The quiche can be refrigerated for up to 3 days and rewarmed before serving.)

Puffy Dutch Baby

Prep time: 10 minutes | Cook time: 16 minutes | Serves 4

¾ cup whole milk
3 large eggs
1 teaspoon vanilla extract
4 tablespoons unsalted butter, melted
½ cup all-purpose flour
2 tablespoons cornstarch
1 tablespoon granulated sugar
Whipped cream, for garnish
Assorted berries, for garnish
Confectioners' sugar, for garnish

1. In a medium bowl, vigorously whisk together the milk and eggs until frothy, about 1 minute. Add the vanilla and 2 tablespoons of the butter, whisk, then add the flour, cornstarch, and granulated sugar, whisking until well combined, about 1 minute more.
2. Set the Foodi to Sear/Saute on High and preheat the Foodi for 5 minutes. Add the remaining 2 tablespoons butter and stir it constantly, until browned, about 6 minutes. Add the batter—it should puff immediately—and cook until it begins to set, about 5 minutes. Drop the Crisping Lid and set to Bake/Roast at 375ºF (190ºC) for 5 minutes. At this point, the pancake will be set.
3. Lift the lid and carefully remove the inner pot from the Foodi. Run a silicone spatula around the edges of the pancake. Slide the Dutch Baby onto a plate and serve warm, topped with whipped cream, berries, and confectioners' sugar.

Japanese Pancake

Prep time: 10 minutes | Cook time: 22 minutes | Serves 4

2 cups all-purpose flour
3 tablespoons granulated sugar
2 teaspoons baking powder
½ teaspoon baking soda
½ teaspoon kosher salt
1½ cups whole milk
1 large egg
1 tablespoon fresh lemon juice
4 tablespoons unsalted butter, melted, plus extra for serving
Cooking spray
Confectioners' sugar or cocoa powder, for garnish
Warm maple syrup, for garnish

1. In a medium bowl, whisk together the flour, granulated sugar, baking powder, baking soda, and salt. In another medium bowl, whisk together the milk, egg, and lemon juice, and then whisk the melted butter into the milk mixture. Pour the wet ingredients into the dry ingredients, and whisk until completely combined and there aren't any flour streaks remaining in the batter (be cautious not to overmix or you'll end up with a less fluffy pancake).
2. Thoroughly spray the Foodi's inner pot with cooking spray. Add the batter. Lock on the Pressure Lid, making sure the valve is set to Seal, and set to Pressure on Low for 7 minutes. When the timer reaches 0, quick-release the pressure (if any) and carefully remove the lid.
3. Drop the Crisping Lid and set the Foodi to Air Crisp at 390°F (199°C) for 15 minutes, or until the pancake is golden brown and a toothpick inserted into the center comes out clean. While it cooks, open the lid and spray the top with cooking spray every 5 minutes. Use a silicone spatula to remove the pancake from the pot and place it on a platter. Dust with confectioners' sugar and serve in wedges like a pie, with butter and warm maple syrup.

Asparagus with Soft Boiled Eggs

Prep time: 5 minutes | Cook time: 4 minutes | Serves 6

1 pound (454 g) thick asparagus, ends trimmed
6 large eggs
Kosher salt, to taste
Freshly ground black pepper, to taste

1. Place the asparagus on the rack in the low position and set the whole, uncracked eggs directly on top of the asparagus. Add ½ cup water to the pot.
2. Lock on the Pressure Lid, making sure the valve is set to Seal, and set to Pressure on Low for 2 minutes. Fill a medium bowl with cold water and set aside.
3. When the timer reaches 0, quick-release the pressure and keep the lid on. Set the Foodi to Keep Warm for 2 minutes before removing the eggs.
4. Use tongs to transfer the eggs to the cold water and set aside until the eggs are cool enough to handle, about 3 minutes.
5. When the eggs are cool enough to handle and just before peeling them, divide the asparagus among the plates and season with salt and pepper. Lightly tap an egg against a flat work surface and peel away the shell. Repeat with the remaining eggs. Set 1 egg on top of each portion of asparagus, sprinkle with salt and pepper, and serve.

Scramble Tofu with Turmeric

Prep time: 15 minutes | Cook time: 8 minutes | Serves 4

3 tablespoons peanut oil or vegetable oil
½ medium yellow onion, diced
1 garlic clove, minced
8 ounces(227 g) sliced button or cremini mushrooms
1 cup finely chopped cauliflower
2 teaspoons ground cumin
2 teaspoons ground turmeric
1 cup drained canned diced fire-roasted tomatoes
1 (14- to 16-ounce / 397- to 454-g) block firm tofu, drained
1 cup baby spinach leaves
1 cup drained canned chickpeas
2 teaspoons kosher salt

1. Pour the oil into the Foodi's inner pot and set the Foodi to Sear/Saute on High to preheat for 4 minutes. Drop a piece of onion, when it sizzles in the oil, add all the onion and the garlic and cook until they begin to soften, about 3 minutes, stirring occasionally.
2. Add the mushrooms and cook until they begin to soften, about 3 more minutes, stirring occasionally.
3. Mix in the cauliflower, cumin, and turmeric and cook until aromatic, about 2 minutes, stirring occasionally.
4. Add the tomatoes and crumble the tofu into the pot. Lock on the Pressure Lid, making sure the valve is set to Seal, and set to Pressure on High for 0 minutes. When the timer reaches 0, turn off the Foodi and quick-release the pressure. Carefully remove the lid.
5. Stir in the spinach leaves and the chickpeas, vigorously mixing to break up the tofu even more. Add the salt and pepper to taste. Use a silicone slotted spoon to serve.

Freshly ground black pepper, to taste

Chinese Ginger Chicken Congee

Prep time: 5 minutes | Cook time: 15 minutes | Serves 8

2 cups medium-grain white rice
2 pounds (907 g) boneless, skinless chicken thighs
1 (2-inch) piece fresh ginger, peeled and minced
2 tablespoons kosher salt
Sliced scallions, for garnish (optional)
Soy sauce, for serving (optional)
Hot sauce or Chile oil, for serving (optional)
Cooked vegetables (optional)
Chopped fresh cilantro, for garnish (optional)
Soft-boiled egg, for serving (optional)

1. Place the rice, chicken, and ginger in the Foodi's inner pot and add enough water to come up to the fill line. Lock on the Pressure Lid, making sure the valve is set to Seal, and set the Foodi to Pressure on High for 15 minutes.
2. When the timer reaches 0, let the pressure release naturally for 40 minutes, then quick-release any remaining pressure. Carefully remove the lid and stir in the salt. Allow the congee to cool and thicken in the pot, stirring often, for about 10 minutes. Ladle into bowls and serve warm with your chosen garnishes.

Hanging Bacon

Prep time: 5 minutes | Cook time: 12 minutes | Makes 24 half-strips

1 pound (454 g) bacon strips
Cooking spray

1. Cut the bacon in half crosswise to make shorter strips. Coat the reversible rack with cooking spray and fold the bacon strips over every other rung of the rack.
2. Add ½ cup water to the Foodi's inner pot, then set the rack in the inner pot in the high position. Lock on the Pressure Lid, making sure the valve is set to Seal, and set to Pressure on High for 2 minutes. When timer reaches 0, quick-release the pressure and carefully remove the lid.
3. Drop the Crisping Lid and set the Foodi to Air Crisp at 390°F (199°C) for 10 to 15 minutes, depending on your preferred crispness. The bacon is actually fully cooked at this point—all you are doing now is crisping it up; I like my bacon crisp with a little chew here and there, so 13 minutes is my sweet spot.

Gooey Candied Bacon

Prep time: 5 minutes | Cook time: 22 minutes | Serves 6

1 pound (454 g) bacon strips
1 cup packed light brown sugar
1 teaspoon freshly ground black pepper

1. Place all the bacon in the Foodi's inner pot along with 1 cup water. Lock on the Pressure Lid, making sure the valve is set to Seal, and set to Pressure on High for 2 minutes. When the timer reaches 0, quick-release the pressure and carefully remove the lid.
2. Add the brown sugar and the pepper and stir to dissolve the brown sugar.
3. Drop the Crisping Lid and set the Foodi to Air Crisp at 390°F (199°C) for 20 minutes, lifting the lid every 5 minutes to stir the bacon, until it is crisp and sticky.
4. Lift the lid and use tongs to remove the bacon. Separate it into strips on a rack and allow the bacon to cool to room temperature, about 10 minutes to achieve maximum stickiness.

Pork Sausage Patties

Prep time: 5 minutes | Cook time: 20 minutes | Makes 6 patties

1 pound (454 g) ground pork
2 garlic cloves, minced
2 teaspoons finely minced fresh sage leaves
1 teaspoon maple syrup
1 teaspoon red pepper flakes
1 teaspoon kosher salt
¼ teaspoon freshly ground black pepper
Cooking spray

1. Add the pork, garlic, sage, maple syrup, red pepper flakes, salt, and pepper to a medium bowl and mix with your hands until all the ingredients are uniformly combined and sticking together. Lightly wet your hands (that helps the mixture from sticking to your hands) and form the mixture into 6 ½-inch-thick equal patties.
2. Insert the crisping basket into the Foodi's inner pot and generously spray it with cooking spray. Arrange the patties vertically, so that they lean against the walls of the crisping basket.
3. Drop the Crisping Lid and set the Foodi to Air Crisp at 390°F (199°C) for 15 minutes. Halfway through cooking, lift the lid and lay the patties down flat in a ring, slightly overlapping, drop the Crisping Lid again, and continue to cook for the remaining time, until the sausage patties begin to brown. Again, lift the lid and flip the patties, then drop the lid again and set the Foodi to Broil for 5 minutes, or until they are crisp. Use tongs to remove the patties and serve hot.

Spicy Red Shakshuka

Prep time: 10 minutes | Cook time: 18 minutes | Serves 6

2 red bell peppers, seeded, ribbed, and diced
½ medium yellow onion, diced
2 garlic cloves, minced
1 tablespoon tomato paste
1 (28-ounce / 794-g) can crushed tomatoes
2 tablespoons harissa
2 teaspoons ground cumin
¼ cup olive oil
½ teaspoon kosher salt
6 large eggs
Pita or good-quality bread, for serving

1. Place the bell peppers, onion, garlic, tomato paste, crushed tomatoes, harissa, cumin, olive oil, and ½ cup water in the Foodi's inner pot, stirring to combine. Lock on the Pressure Lid, making sure the valve is set to Seal, and set to Pressure on High for 5 minutes. When the timer reaches 0, quick-release the pressure and carefully remove the lid.
2. Set the Foodi to Sear/Saute on High, and cook until the vegetables have broken down and are kind of saucy, about 5 minutes. Turn off the Foodi and stir in the salt.
3. Crack 1 egg into a measuring cup, being careful not to break the yolk. Carefully pour the egg on top of the shakshuka. Repeat with the remaining eggs, spacing them evenly around the top.
4. Drop the Crisping Lid and set to Broil for 8 minutes, or until the whites are set. Serve immediately with pita or bread.

Green Veggies Shakshuka

Prep time: 15 minutes | Cook time: 27 minutes | Serves 6

3 tablespoons peanut oil or vegetable oil
1 medium yellow onion, diced
4 garlic cloves, minced
1 green bell pepper, ribbed, seeded, and diced
2 serrano chiles, ribbed, seeded, and diced
1 jalapeño, ribbed, seeded, and diced
1 tablespoon ground cumin
1 tablespoon ground coriander
8 ounces (227 g) kale, tough stems and ribs removed, leaves finely chopped
1 teaspoon kosher salt
Juice of ½ lemon
1 bunch cilantro leaves, stems removed and leaves finely chopped
6 large eggs
Crumbled feta cheese, for serving
Finely chopped fresh dill, for garnish
Pita or good-quality bread, for serving

1. Pour the oil into the Foodi's inner pot and set to Sear/Saute on High for 5 minutes to heat. Add the onion, garlic, bell pepper, chiles, and jalapeño and cook until they begin to soften, about 6 minutes more, stirring often.
2. Stir in the cumin and coriander and continue to cook until aromatic, about 3 minutes.
3. Add the kale to the inner pot. Lock on the Pressure Lid, making sure the valve is set to Seal, and set the Foodi to Pressure on High for 5 minutes. When the timer reaches 0, quick-release the pressure and carefully remove the lid. Stir in the salt and lemon juice, then add the cilantro.
4. Crack 1 egg into a measuring cup, being careful not to break the yolk. Carefully pour the egg on top of the shakshuka. Repeat with the remaining eggs, spacing them evenly around the top.
5. Drop the Crisping Lid and set to Air Crisp at 390°F (199°C) for 8 minutes, or until the whites are set. Sprinkle with feta and dill and serve hot with pita or bread.

Hash Browns

Prep time: 5 minutes | Cook time: 30 minutes | Serves 10 hash brown patties

4 medium russet potatoes, peeled and then grated on the medium holes of a box grater
2 tablespoons unsalted butter
¼ cup instant flour
1 tablespoon kosher salt
Freshly ground black pepper, to taste
Cooking spray

1. Place the grated potatoes in a large bowl and cover with water. Set aside for 1 hour.
2. Drain off the water and then, using cheesecloth, a clean towel, or a nut milk bag, squeeze the excess moisture from the potatoes.
3. Set the Foodi to Sear/Saute on High. Add the potatoes and the butter, and cook, stirring often, until potatoes are softened, about 10 minutes. Turn off the Foodi and add the instant flour, salt, and pepper, stirring until combined.
4. Line a sheet pan with parchment paper. Scoop about 1 cup of the potato mixture onto a piece of plastic wrap and use another piece of plastic wrap to press and shape the potato mixture into a somewhat rectangular patty that is a little larger than a credit card. Transfer the patty to the baking sheet and repeat with the remaining potato mixture; you should have about 10 patties. Freeze for at least 3 hours and up to 8 hours.
5. When you are ready to eat the hash browns, unwrap them, place them in the crisping basket (in a single layer so they cook evenly or vertically), and set the basket in the Foodi's inner pot. Spray all sides of the hash browns with cooking spray. Drop the Crisping Lid and set the Foodi to Air Crisp at 390ºF (199ºC) for 20 minutes, or until the hash browns are browned and crisp. Serve hot.

Tex-Mex Red Potatoes

Prep time: 5 minutes | Cook time: 29 minutes | Serves 6

3 pounds (1.4kg) baby red potatoes
1 tablespoon plus 1 teaspoon kosher salt
Cooking spray
1 tablespoon sweet paprika
Freshly ground black pepper

1. Place the potatoes into the crisping basket and set the basket into the Foodi's inner pot. Add 1 tablespoon of the salt and 1 cup water to the pot. Lock on the Pressure Lid, making sure the valve is set to Seal, and set to Pressure on High for 4 minutes. When the timer reaches 0, quick-release the pressure and carefully remove the lid.
2. Remove the crisping basket and remove the inner pot from the Foodi. Discard the water remaining in the inner pot. Return the crisping basket to the inner pot and place the pot in the Foodi. Spray the potatoes heavily with cooking spray, gently tossing to make sure they are thoroughly coated. Season the potatoes with the remaining teaspoon salt, the paprika, and the pepper.
3. Drop the Crisping Lid and set the Foodi to Air Crisp at 390ºF (199ºC) for 25 minutes. Lift the lid and stir potatoes every 5 minutes with a silicone spoon or spatula, breaking them open slightly; spray them with more cooking spray so the interiors are also well coated. Cook until the potato skins are crisp and browned. Serve hot.

Cheddar Shrimp and Grits

Prep time: 10 minutes | Cook time: 22 minutes | Serves 4

3 tablespoons unsalted butter
1 cup Quaker Oats Quick 5-Minute Grits
2 garlic cloves, minced
1 teaspoon kosher salt, plus more as needed
Freshly ground black pepper, to taste
2 cups whole milk
½ cup shredded cheddar cheese
2 tablespoons minced pickled jalapeño
12 ounces (340 g) frozen, peeled, and deveined raw extra jumbo shrimp (16–20 count)
Cooking spray
Chopped fresh chives, for garnish

1. Set the Foodi to Sear/Saute on High. Add the butter to the inner pot and cook until melted, stirring the butter occasionally with a silicone spatula, about 4 minutes.
2. Add the grits, garlic, 1 teaspoon salt, and the pepper and allow to cook until the garlic begins to soften, about 3 minutes, stirring occasionally. Add 2 cups water and stir the grits once. Lock on the Pressure Lid, making sure the valve is set to Seal, and set to Pressure on High for 0 minutes. When the timer reaches 0, quick-release the pressure and carefully remove the lid.
3. Stir in the milk, cheese, and jalapeño. Insert the reversible rack in the high position.
4. In a bowl, spray both sides of the shrimp with cooking spray. Season with salt and pepper, then place the shrimp on the rack. Drop the Crisping Lid and set the Foodi to Broil for 10 minutes. After 5 minutes, lift the lid and flip the shrimp. Drop the lid and continue to cook until the shrimp are pink, about another 5 minutes. Set the shrimp aside.
5. Stir the grits and divide among 4 bowls. Top each bowl with a few shrimp, then sprinkle with chives and serve immediately.

Korean Casserole with Chile Sauce

Prep time: 20 minutes | Cook time: 45 minutes | Serves 4

For the Chile Sauce:
½ cup gochujang paste
¼ cup hard apple cider (not cider vinegar)
1 tablespoon maple syrup
2 teaspoons apple cider vinegar
1 teaspoon toasted sesame oil
½ teaspoon ground cinnamon

For the Casserole:
6 tablespoons peanut oil or vegetable oil
4 large eggs
1 teaspoon toasted sesame seeds
5 ounces (142 g) fresh shiitake mushrooms, stems removed and caps sliced
1 tablespoon apple cider vinegar
2 cups diced butternut squash
2 cups fresh baby spinach leaves
4 ounces (113 g) snow peas, ends trimmed
Cooking spray
1 (20-ounce / 567-g) bag frozen sweet potato fries
Kosher salt, to taste
1 teaspoon toasted sesame oil

1. Make the chile sauce: In a small bowl, combine the gochujang, cider, maple syrup, vinegar, sesame oil, and cinnamon. Set aside.
2. Make the casserole: Add 3 tablespoons of the oil to the Foodi's inner pot. Set the Foodi to Sear/Saute on High, and heat the oil for 4 minutes. (We are adding a fair amount of liquid to the pot, so I like to let the oil heat up a little extra.)
3. Crack the eggs into a medium bowl, being careful not to break the yolks. Carefully pour the eggs into the inner pot and sprinkle with the sesame seeds. Cook until the bottoms of the whites are set, about 2 minutes. Drop the Crisping Lid, and set the Foodi to Broil for 1 minute, or until the top of the whites are set.
4. Lift the lid and use a silicone spatula to carefully loosen the eggs from the Foodi pot. Remove the inner pot and slide the eggs out onto a sheet pan.
5. Put the inner pot back in the Foodi and set to Sear/Saute on High for 3 minutes. Add the mushrooms and cook, stirring once, until they are softened, about 4 minutes. Add the vinegar, stir, and continue to cook until most of the vinegar is absorbed, about 1 more minute. Transfer the mushrooms to the sheet pan with the eggs, placing them in a separate area.
6. Add the remaining 3 tablespoons oil to the inner pot and set the Foodi to Sear/Saute for 1 minute. Add the butternut squash and cook until it begins to soften, about 3 minutes, stirring every minute or so.
7. Push the butternut squash to one side of the pot and add the spinach to the open space. Clear some room on the bottom of the inner pot and insert the reversible rack in the high position. Add the snow peas to the rack in a single layer, then spray the snow peas generously with cooking spray. Drop the Crisping Lid and set the Foodi to Air Crisp at 390ºF (199ºC) for 6 minutes. The snow peas will be crisp yet blistered.
8. Lift the lid and carefully remove the rack. Transfer the snow peas to the sheet pan with the eggs and mushrooms and then spoon the spinach and butternut squash onto it, as well.
9. Insert the crisping basket into the inner pot again and spray it liberally with cooking spray. Add the sweet potato fries, spraying them with more cooking spray. Drop the lid and set the Foodi to Air Crisp at 390ºF (199ºC) for 20 minutes, or until the potatoes are crisp, shaking the basket halfway through the cooking.
10. Lift the lid and remove the crisping basket. Pour the frozen fries directly into the inner pot and season with salt to taste. Carefully arrange the other veggies on top of the sweet potato fries. Drizzle the sesame oil over the veggies and fries, then carefully place the eggs on top.
11. Drop the Crisping Lid and set the Foodi to Air Crisp at 390ºF (199ºC) for 2 minutes, or until the eggs and veggies are reheated. Lift the lid and drizzle with the chile sauce to taste. Mix lightly, scoop out, and serve.

Chapter 2: Poultry

Roasted Whole Chicken

Prep time: 10 minutes | Cook time: 40 minutes | Serves 4

1 (4½- to 5-pound / 2.0- to 2.3-kg) whole
    chicken
1 head garlic
2 fresh whole sprigs rosemary
2 fresh whole sprigs parsley
1 lemon, halved
¼ cup hot water
¼ cup white wine
Juice of 2 lemons
¼ cup unsalted butter, melted
3 tablespoons extra-virgin olive oil
5 garlic cloves, minced
2 teaspoons minced fresh parsley
2 teaspoons minced fresh rosemary
½ teaspoon sea salt
¼ teaspoon freshly ground black pepper

1. Discard the neck from inside the chicken cavity and remove any excess fat and leftover feathers. Rinse the chicken inside and out under running cold water. Stuff the garlic head into the chicken cavity along with the rosemary and parsley sprigs and lemon halves. Tie the legs together with cooking twine.
2. Add the water, wine, and lemon juice. Place the chicken into the Cook & Crisp Basket and insert the basket in the pot. Assemble pressure lid, making sure the pressure release valve is in the SEAL position.
3. Select PRESSURE and set to HI. Set time to 15 minutes. Select START/STOP to begin.
4. When pressure cooking is complete, quick release the pressure by moving the pressure release valve to the VENT position. Carefully remove lid when the unit has finished releasing pressure.
5. In a small bowl, combine the butter, olive oil, minced garlic, minced parsley, minced rosemary, salt, and pepper. Brush the mixture over the chicken. Close crisping lid.
6. Select AIR CRISP, set temperature to 400ºF (204ºC), and set time to 20 minutes. Select START/STOP to begin.
7. Cooking is complete when the internal temperature of the chicken reaches 165ºF (74ºC) on a meat thermometer inserted into the thickest part of the meat (it should not touch the bone). Carefully remove the chicken from the basket using 2 large serving forks.
8. Let the chicken rest for 10 minutes before carving and serving.

Chinese Flavor Spicy Chicken with Cashew

Prep time:10 minutes | Cook time: 13 minutes | Serves 4

1 pound (454 g) chicken breast, cut into
    ½-inch pieces
4 tablespoons stir-fry sauce, divided
3 tablespoons canola oil
12 arbol chiles
1 teaspoon Sichuan peppercorns
2 teaspoons grated fresh ginger
2 garlic cloves, minced
¾ cup cashews
6 scallions, cut into 1-inch pieces
2 teaspoons dark soy sauce
½ teaspoon sesame oil

1. Place the chicken in a zip-top bag and add 2 tablespoons of stir-fry sauce. Let marinate for 4 hours, or overnight.
2. Select SEAR/SAUTÉ and set to HI. Select START/STOP to begin. Let preheat for 5 minutes.
3. Add the oil, chiles, peppercorns, ginger, and garlic and cook for 1 minute.
4. Add half the chicken and cook for 2 minutes, stirring occasionally. Transfer the chicken to a plate and set aside. Add the remaining chicken and cook for 2 minutes, stirring occasionally. Return the first batch of chicken to the pot and add the cashews. Cook for 2 minutes, stirring occasionally.
5. Add the scallions, soy sauce, sesame oil, and remaining 2 tablespoons of stir-fry sauce to pot and cook for 1 minute, stirring frequently.
6. When cooking is complete, serve immediately over steamed rice, if desired.

Stir-Fried Chicken and Broccoli Rice Bowl

Prep time: 5 minutes | Cook time: 20 minutes | Serves 4

1 cup long-grain white rice
1 cup chicken stock
2 tablespoons canola oil
3 boneless, skinless chicken breasts, cut into 1-inch cubes
1 medium head broccoli, cut into 1-inch florets
2 teaspoons kosher salt
½ teaspoon freshly ground black pepper
1 tablespoon ground ginger
¼ cup teriyaki sauce
Sesame seeds, for garnish

1. Place the rice and chicken stock into the pot. Assemble pressure lid, making sure the pressure release valve is in the SEAL position.
2. Select PRESSURE and set to HI. Set time to 2 minutes. Select START/STOP to begin.
3. When pressure cooking is complete, allow pressure to naturally release for 10 minutes. After 10 minutes, quick release remaining pressure by turning the pressure release valve to the VENT position. Carefully remove lid when unit has finished releasing pressure.
4. Transfer the rice to a bowl and cover to keep warm. Clean the cooking pot and return to unit.
5. Select SEAR/SAUTÉ and set to HI. Select START/STOP to begin. Let preheat for 5 minutes.
6. Add the oil and heat for 1 minute. Add the chicken and cook, stirring frequently, for about 6 minutes.
7. Stir in the broccoli, salt, pepper, and ginger. Cook for 5 minutes, stirring frequently. Stir in the teriyaki sauce and cook, stirring frequently, until the chicken has reached internal temperature of 165ºF (74ºC) on a food thermometer.
8. Serve the chicken and broccoli mixture over the rice. Garnish with sesame seeds if desired.

Chicken and Bean Burrito Rice Bowl

Prep time: 5 minutes | Cook time: 10 minutes | Serves 4

1 pound (454 g) boneless, skinless chicken breasts, cut into 1-inch chunks
1 tablespoon chili powder
1½ teaspoons cumin
1 teaspoon sea salt
1 teaspoon freshly ground black pepper
½ teaspoon paprika
¼ teaspoon garlic powder
¼ teaspoon onion powder
¼ teaspoon cayenne pepper
¼ teaspoon dried oregano
1 cup chicken stock
¼ cup water
1¼ cups of your favorite salsa
1 (15-ounce / 425-g) can corn kernels, drained
1 (15-ounce / 425-g) can black beans, rinsed and drained
1 cup rice
¾ cup shredded Cheddar cheese

1. Add the chicken, chili powder, cumin, salt, black pepper, paprika, garlic powder, onion powder, cayenne pepper, oregano, chicken stock, water, salsa, corn, and beans and stir well.
2. Add the rice to the top of the ingredients in the pot. Assemble pressure lid, making sure the pressure release valve is in the SEAL position.
3. Select PRESSURE and set to HI. Set time to 10 minutes. Select START/STOP to begin.
4. When pressure cooking is complete, quick release the pressure by moving the pressure release valve to the VENT position. Carefully remove lid when the unit has finished releasing pressure.
5. Add the cheese and stir. Serve immediately.

Chicken Rice Pilaf

Prep time: 5 minutes | Cook time: 14 minutes | Serves 4

1 (6-ounce / 170-g) box rice pilaf
1¾ cups water
1 tablespoon unsalted butter
4 boneless, skin-on chicken thighs
1 tablespoon extra-virgin olive oil
1 teaspoon kosher salt
1 teaspoon garlic powder

1. Place the rice pilaf, water, and butter in the pot and stir.
2. Place Reversible Rack in pot, making sure it is in the higher position. Place the chicken thighs on the rack. Assemble pressure lid, making sure the pressure release valve is in the SEAL position.
3. Select PRESSURE and set to HI. Set time to 4 minutes. Select START/STOP to begin.
4. Stir together the olive oil, salt, and garlic powder in a small bowl.
5. When pressure cooking is complete, quick release the pressure by moving the pressure release valve to the VENT position. Carefully remove lid when unit has finished releasing pressure.
6. Brush the chicken with the olive oil mixture. Close crisping lid.
7. Select BROIL and set time to 10 minutes. Select START/STOP to begin.
8. When cooking is complete, serve the chicken with the rice.

Jerk Chicken with Sweet Mash

Prep time: 10 minutes | Cook time: 20 minutes | Serves 6

4 boneless, skin-on chicken thighs
½ cup spicy jerk marinade
3 large sweet potatoes, peeled and cut into 1-inch cubes
½ cup unsweetened full-fat coconut milk
Kosher salt
Freshly ground black pepper
2 bananas, peeled and quartered
2 tablespoons agave nectar

1. Place the chicken thighs and jerk marinade in a container, rubbing the marinade all over the chicken. Cover the container with plastic wrap and marinate 15 minutes.
2. Place the sweet potatoes, coconut milk, salt, and pepper in the pot. Place Reversible Rack in pot, making sure it is in the higher position. Place the chicken skin-side up on the rack, leaving space between the pieces. Assemble pressure lid, making sure the pressure release valve is in the SEAL position.
3. Select PRESSURE and set to HI. Set time to 4 minutes. Select START/STOP to begin.
4. When pressure cooking is complete, quick release the pressure by turning the pressure release valve to the VENT position. Carefully remove lid when unit has finished releasing pressure.
5. Place the bananas in the spaces between chicken thighs. Close crisping lid.
6. Select BROIL and set time to 15 minutes. Select START/STOP to begin.
7. After 10 minutes, remove the bananas and set aside. Turn over the chicken thighs. Close lid and continue cooking.
8. When cooking is complete, remove rack and chicken and let rest 5 to 10 minutes. Add the roasted bananas and agave nectar and mash them along with the sweet potatoes. Once rested, serve the chicken and sweet potato and banana mash.

Parmesan and Mozzarella Chicken Cutlets

Prep time: 5 minutes | Cook time: 20 minutes | Serves 4

1 cup all-purpose flour
1 teaspoon sea salt
2 eggs, beaten
2 tablespoons water
1 cup seasoned bread crumbs
½ cup grated Parmesan cheese
4 (6-ounce / 170-g) chicken cutlets
2 tablespoons extra-virgin olive oil
¼ cup marinara sauce
1 cup shredded Mozzarella cheese

1. Place the flour and salt in a shallow bowl and stir. In another shallow bowl, add the eggs and water, whisking to combine. Place the bread crumbs and Parmesan cheese in a third shallow bowl.
2. Dredge each piece of chicken in the flour. Tap off any excess, then coat the chicken in the egg wash. Transfer the chicken to the breadcrumb mixture and evenly coat. Repeat until all the chicken is coated.
3. Place Reversible Rack in pot, making sure it is in the higher position. Place the chicken on the rack and brush lightly with the oil. Close crisping lid.
4. Select AIR CRISP, set temperature to 325°F (163°C), and set time to 15 minutes. Select START/STOP to begin.
5. After 15 minutes, open lid and spread the marinara sauce on top of the chicken. Top with the Mozzarella. Close crisping lid.
6. Select BROIL and set time to 5 minutes. Select START/STOP to begin.
7. When the cheese is fully melted, cooking is complete. Serve.

Bacon and Chicken Penne

Prep time: 5 minutes | Cook time: 10 minutes | Serves 4

3 strips bacon, chopped
½ pound (227 g) boneless, skinless chicken breast, cut into ½-pieces
1 teaspoon dried basil
1 teaspoon dried oregano
¼ teaspoon sea salt
1 tablespoon unsalted butter
3 garlic cloves, minced
1 cup chicken stock
1½ cups water
8 ounces (227 g) dry penne pasta
½ cup half-and-half
½ cup grated Parmesan cheese, plus more for serving

1. Select SEAR/SAUTÉ and set to HI. Select START/STOP to begin. Let preheat for 5 minutes.
2. Add the bacon and cook, stirring frequently, for about 5 minutes or until crispy. Using a slotted spoon, transfer the bacon to a paper towel-lined plate to drain.
3. Season the chicken with the basil, oregano, and salt, coating all the pieces.
4. Add the butter, chicken, and garlic and sauté for 2 minutes, until the chicken begins to brown and the garlic is fragrant.
5. Add the chicken stock, water, and penne pasta. Assemble pressure lid, making sure the pressure release valve is in the SEAL position.
6. Select PRESSURE and set to HI. Set time to 3 minutes. Select START/STOP to begin.
7. When pressure cooking is complete, allow pressure to naturally release for 2 minutes. After 2 minutes, quick release remaining pressure by moving the pressure release valve to the VENT position. Carefully remove lid when unit has finished releasing pressure.
8. Add the half-and-half, cheese, and bacon, and stir constantly to thicken the sauce and melt the cheese. Serve immediately, with additional Parmesan cheese to garnish.

Chicken Spaghetti Carbonara

Prep time: 5 minutes | Cook time: 15 minutes | Serves 4

4 strips bacon, chopped

1 medium onion, diced

1½ pounds (680 g) chicken breast, cut into ¾ inch-cubes

6 garlic cloves, minced

2 cups chicken stock

8 ounces (227 g) dry spaghetti, with noodles broken in half

2 cups freshly grated Parmesan cheese, plus more for serving

2 eggs

Sea salt

Freshly ground black pepper

1. Select SEAR/SAUTÉ and set to HI. Select START/STOP to begin. Let preheat for 5 minutes.
2. Add the bacon and cook, stirring frequently, for about 6 minutes, or until crispy. Using a slotted spoon, transfer the bacon to a paper towel-lined plate to drain. Leave any bacon fat in the pot.
3. Add the onion, chicken, and garlic and sauté for 2 minutes, until the onions start to become translucent and the garlic is fragrant.
4. Add the chicken stock and spaghetti noodles. Assemble pressure lid, making sure the pressure release valve is in the SEAL position.
5. Select PRESSURE and set to HI. Set time to 6 minutes. Select START/STOP to begin.
6. When pressure cooking is complete, allow pressure to naturally release for 5 minutes. After 5 minutes, quick release remaining pressure by moving the pressure release valve to the VENT position. Carefully remove lid when unit has finished releasing pressure.
7. Add the cheese and stir to fully combine. Close the crisping lid, leaving the unit off, to keep the heat inside and allow the cheese to melt.
8. Whisk the eggs until full beaten.
9. Open lid, select SEAR/SAUTÉ, and set to LO. Select START/STOP to begin. Add the eggs and stir gently to incorporate, taking care to ensure the eggs are not scrambling while you work toward your desired sauce consistency. If your pot gets too warm, turn unit off.
10. Add the bacon back to the pot and season with salt and pepper. Stir to combine. Serve, adding more cheese as desired.

Baked Ranch Chicken and Bacon

Prep time: 10 minutes | Cook time: 30 minutes | Serves 6

1 pound (454 g) chicken breast, cut in 1-inch cubes

2 tablespoons extra-virgin olive oil

3 tablespoons ranch seasoning mix, divided

4 strips bacon, chopped

1 small onion, chopped

2 garlic cloves, minced

1 cup long-grain white rice

2 cups chicken broth

½ cup half-and-half

2 cups shredded Cheddar cheese, divided

2 tablespoons chopped fresh parsley

1. Select SEAR/SAUTÉ and set to HI. Select START/STOP to begin. Let preheat for 5 minutes.
2. In a large bowl, toss the chicken with the olive oil and 2 tablespoons of ranch seasoning mix.
3. Add the bacon to the pot and cook, stirring frequently, for about 6 minutes, or until crispy. Using a slotted spoon, transfer the bacon to a paper towel-lined plate to drain.
4. Add the onion and cook for about 5 minutes. Add the garlic and cook for 1 minute more. Add the chicken and stir, cooking until chicken is cooked through, about 3 minutes.
5. Add the rice, chicken broth, and remaining ranch mix. Assemble pressure lid, making sure the pressure release valve is in the SEAL position.
6. Select PRESSURE and set to HI. Set time to 7 minutes. Select START/STOP to begin.
7. When complete, quick release the pressure by turning the valve to the VENT position. Carefully remove lid when unit has finished releasing pressure.
8. Stir in half-and-half and 1 cup of Cheddar cheese. Top with the remaining 1 cup of cheese. Close crisping lid.
9. Select BROIL and set time to 8 minutes. Select START/STOP to begin. When cooking is complete, serve garnished with fresh parsley.

Tuscan Chicken and Spinach Penne

Prep time: 10 minutes | Cook time: 6 minutes | Serves 8

2 pounds (907 g) chicken stock
1 (7-ounce / 198-g) jar oil-packed sun-dried tomatoes, drained
2 teaspoons Italian seasoning
3 garlic cloves, minced
1 pound (454 g) chicken breast, cubed
1 (16-ounce / 454-g) box penne pasta
4 cups spinach
1 (8-ounce / 227-g) package cream cheese, cubed
1 cup shredded Parmesan cheese
Kosher salt
Freshly ground black pepper

1. Place the chicken stock, sun-dried tomatoes, Italian seasoning, garlic, chicken breast, and pasta and stir. Assemble pressure lid, making sure the pressure release valve is in the SEAL position.
2. Select PRESSURE and set to HI. Set time to 6 minutes. Select START/STOP to begin.
3. When pressure cooking is complete, quick release the pressure by turning the pressure release valve to the VENT position. Carefully remove lid when unit has finished releasing pressure.
4. Add the spinach and stir, allowing it to wilt with the residual heat. Add the cream cheese, Parmesan cheese, salt and pepper and stir until melted. Serve.

Slow Cooked Garlic Chicken Thighs

Prep time: 5 minutes | Cook time: 4 hours | Serves 6

6 (4- to 6-ounce / 113- to 170-g) bone-in, skin-on, chicken thighs
10 garlic cloves, peeled
6 cups chicken broth
1 cup dry white wine
2 teaspoons dried oregano
2 teaspoons kosher salt
1 teaspoon freshly ground black pepper
¼ cup capers, drained
1 tablespoon chopped fresh parsley

1. Place the chicken, garlic cloves, chicken broth, wine, oregano, salt, and pepper in the cooking pot.
2. Assemble pressure lid, making sure the pressure release valve is in the VENT position. Select SLOW COOK and set to HI. Set time to 4 hours. Select START/STOP to begin.
3. When cooking is complete, carefully remove the lid. Stir in the capers.
4. Serve garnished with fresh parsley.

Buttermilk-Breaded Crispy Chicken

Prep time: 15 minutes | Cook time: 30 minutes | Serves 4

1½ pounds (680 g) boneless, skinless chicken breasts
1 to 2 cups buttermilk
2 large eggs
¾ cup all-purpose flour
¾ cup potato starch
½ teaspoon granulated garlic, divided
1 teaspoon salt, divided
2 teaspoons freshly ground black pepper, divided
1 cup bread crumbs
½ cup panko bread crumbs
Olive oil or cooking spray

1. In a large bowl, combine the chicken breasts and buttermilk, turning the chicken to coat. Cover the bowl with plastic wrap and refrigerate the chicken to soak at least 4 hours or overnight.
2. In a medium shallow bowl, whisk the eggs. In a second shallow bowl, stir together the flour, potato starch, ¼ teaspoon of granulated garlic, ½ teaspoon of salt, and 1 teaspoon of pepper. In a third shallow bowl, stir together the bread crumbs, panko, remaining ¼ teaspoon of granulated garlic, remaining ½ teaspoon of salt, and remaining 1 teaspoon of pepper.
3. Working one piece at a time, remove the chicken from the buttermilk, letting the excess drip into the bowl. Dredge the chicken in the flour mixture, coating well on both sides. Then dip the chicken in the eggs, coating both sides. Finally, dip the chicken in the bread crumb mixture, coating both sides and pressing the crumbs onto the chicken. Spritz both sides of the coated chicken pieces with olive oil.
4. Place the Cook & Crisp Basket into the unit.
5. Select AIR CRISP, set the temperature to 400ºF (204ºC), and set the time to 30 minutes. Select START/STOP to begin and allow to preheat for 5 minutes.
6. Spritz both sides of the coated chicken pieces with olive oil. Working in batches as needed, place the chicken breasts in the Cook & Crisp Basket, ensuring the chicken pieces do not touch each other.
7. After 12 minutes, turn the chicken with a spatula so you don't tear the breading. Close the crisping lid and continue to cook, checking the chicken for an internal temperature of 165ºF (74ºC).
8. When cooking is complete, transfer the chicken to a wire rack to cool.

Broccoli and Chicken Casserole

Prep time: 10 minutes | Cook time: 30 minutes | Serves 6

4 (8-ounce / 227-g) boneless, skinless chicken breasts
2 cups chicken stock
1 cup whole milk
1 (10½-ounce / 298-g) cans condensed Cheddar cheese soup
1 teaspoon paprika
2 cups shredded Cheddar cheese
Kosher salt
Freshly ground black pepper
2 cups crushed buttered crackers

1. Place the chicken and stock in the pot. Assemble pressure lid, making sure the pressure release valve is in the SEAL position.
2. Select PRESSURE and set to HI. Set timer to 20 minutes. Select START/STOP to begin.
3. When pressure cooking is complete, quick release the pressure by turning the pressure release valve to the VENT position. Carefully remove lid when unit has finished releasing pressure.
4. Using silicone-tipped utensils, shred the chicken inside the pot.
5. Add the milk, condensed soup, paprika, and cheese. Stir to combine with the chicken. Season with salt and pepper. Top with the crushed crackers. Close crisping lid.
6. Select AIR CRISP, set temperature to 360ºF (182ºC), and set time to 10 minutes. Select START/STOP to begin.
7. When cooking is complete, open lid and let cool before serving.

Marinara Chicken and Mozzarella Stick Casserole

Prep time: 5 minutes | Cook time: 35 minutes | Serves 6

2 (11-ounce / 312-g) boxes frozen breaded Mozzarella sticks
4 (6-ounce / 170-g) frozen boneless, skinless chicken breasts
½ cup water
1 (23-ounce / 652-g) jar marinara sauce

1. Remove the Mozzarella sticks from freezer and let sit at room temperature for 15 to 20 minutes to assure easy chopping.
2. Place the chicken and water in the pot. Assemble pressure lid, making sure the pressure release valve is in the SEAL position.
3. Select PRESSURE and set to HI. Set time to 20 minutes. Select START/STOP to begin.
4. Chop up the Mozzarella sticks.
5. When pressure cooking is complete, quick release the pressure by moving the pressure release valve to the VENT position. Carefully remove lid when unit has finished releasing pressure.
6. Using a silicone-tipped utensil, shred the chicken inside the pot. Stir in the marinara sauce. Evenly sprinkle the top of chicken with the pieces of Mozzarella sticks. Close crisping lid.
7. Select BAKE/ROAST, set temperature to 390ºF (199ºC), and set time to 15 minutes. Select START/STOP to begin.
8. After 10 minutes, open lid and check the Mozzarella sticks for desired crispiness and doneness. If necessary, cook for up to 5 minutes more.
9. When cooking is complete, open lid and serve.

Mushroom And Chicken Bowl

Prepping time: 10 minutes| Cooking time: 25 minutes |For 4 servings

1 and ½ cups unsweetened coconut milk
1 pound chicken thigh, skinless
3-4 garlic cloves, crushed
½ an onion, finely diced
2-inch knob ginger, minced
1 cup mushrooms, sliced
4 ounces baby spinach
½ teaspoon of cayenne pepper
½ teaspoon turmeric
1 teaspoon salt
1 teaspoon Garam Masala
¼ cup cilantro, chopped

1. Add the listed   to your Ninja Foodi
2. Lock lid and cook on HIGH pressure for 15 minutes
3. Release pressure naturally over 10 minutes
4. Remove chicken and roughly puree the veggies using an immersion blender
5. Shred chicken and add it back to the pot. Add cream and stir. Serve and enjoy!

Chicken And Broccoli Platter

Prepping time: 10 minutes| Cooking time: 15 minutes |For 4 servings

1 tablespoon olive oil
1 tablespoon butter
2 large chicken breasts, boneless
½ cup onion, chopped
14 ounces chicken broth
½ teaspoon salt
½ teaspoon pepper
1/8 teaspoon red pepper flakes
1 tablespoon parsley
1 tablespoon arrowroot
2 tablespoons water
4 ounces light cream cheese, cubed
1 cup cheddar cheese, shredded
3 cups steamed broccoli, chopped

1. Season the chicken breast with pepper and salt
2. Set your Ninja Foodi to Saute mode and add butter and vegetable oil
3. Allow it to melt and transfer the seasoned chicken to the pot. Allow it to brown
4. Remove the chicken and add the onions to the pot, Saute them for 5 minutes
5. Add chicken broth, pepper, red pepper and salt, parsley. Add the browned breast
6. Lock up the lid and cook for about 5 minutes at high pressure
7. Once done, quick release the pressure. Remove the chicken and shred it up into small portions
8. Take a bowl and add 2 tablespoons of water and dissolve cornstarch |
9. Select the simmer mode and add the mixture to the Ninja Foodi
10. Toss in the cubed and shredded cheese. Stir completely until everything is melted
11. Toss in the diced chicken again and the steamed broccoli and cook for 5 minutes
12. Once done, sever with white rice and shredded cheese as garnish

Complex Garlic And Lemon Chicken

Prepping time: 10 minutes| Cooking time: 30 minutes |For 6 servings

1-2 pounds chicken breast
1 teaspoon salt
1 onion, diced
1 tablespoon ghee
5 garlic cloves, minced
½ cup organic chicken broth
1 teaspoon dried parsley
1 large lemon juice
3-4 teaspoon arrowroot flour

1. Set your Ninja Foodi to Saute mode. Add diced up onion and cooking fat
2. Allow the onions to cook for 5 -10 minutes
3. Add the rest of the   except arrowroot flour
4. Lock up the lid and set the pot to poultry mode. Cook until the timer runs out
5. Allow the pressure to release naturally
6. Once done, remove ¼ cup of the sauce from the pot and add arrowroot to make a slurry
7. Add the slurry to the pot to make the gravy thick. Keep stirring well. Serve!

Chicken Puttanesca

Prepping time: 10 minutes| Cooking time: 50 minutes |For 6 servings

6 chicken thigh, skin on
2 tablespoons extra virgin olive oil
2 garlic cloves, crushed
Salt and pepper to taste
½ teaspoon red chili flakes
14 and ½ ounces tomatoes, chopped
6 ounces black olives, pitted
1 tablespoon capers
1 tablespoon fresh basil, chopped
¾ cup of water

1. Set your Ninja Foodi to Saute mode and add oil, allow the oil to heat up
2. Add chicken pieces and Saute for 5 minutes until browned, transfer the browned chicken to a platter
3. Add chopped tomatoes, olives, water, capers, garlic, chopped basil, salt, pepper, red chili flakes and stir well, bring the mix to a simmer. Add the chicken pieces to your pot
4. Lock up the lid and cook on HIGH pressure for 12 minutes
5. Release the pressure naturally. Serve with a side of veggies if wanted, enjoy!

Awesome Ligurian Chicken

Prepping time: 10 minutes| Cooking time: 15 minutes |For 4 servings

2 garlic cloves, chopped
3 sprigs fresh rosemary
2 sprigs fresh sage
½ bunch parsley
3 lemon, juiced
4 tablespoons extra virgin olive oil
1 teaspoon salt
¼ teaspoon pepper
1 and ½ cup of water
1 whole chicken, cut into parts
3 and ½ ounces black gourmet salt-cured olives
1 fresh lemon

1. Take a bowl and add chopped up garlic, parsley, sage, and rosemary
2. Pour lemon juice, olive oil to a bowl and season with salt and pepper
3. Remove the chicken skin and from the chicken pieces and carefully transfer them to a dish
4. Pour the marinade on top of the chicken pieces and allow them to chill for 2-4 hours
5. Set your Ninja Foodi to Saute mode and add olive oil, allow it to heat up. Add chicken and browned on all sides
6. Measure out the marinade and add to the pot (it should cover the chicken, add a bit of water if needed). Lock up the lid and cook on HIGH pressure for 10 minutes
7. Release the pressure naturally. The chicken out and transfer to a platter
8. Cover with a foil and allow them to coolSet your pot in Saute mode and reduce the liquid to ¼
9. Add the chicken pieces again to the pot and allow them to warm
10. Sprinkle a bit of olive, lemon slices, and rosemary. Enjoy!

Garlic And Lemon Chicken Dish

Prepping time: 10 minutes| Cooking time: 30 minutes |For 4 servings

2-3 pounds chicken breast
1 teaspoon salt
1 onion, diced
1 tablespoon ghee
5 garlic cloves, minced
½ cup organic chicken broth
1 teaspoon dried parsley
1 large lemon, juiced
3-4 teaspoon arrowroot flour

1. Set your pot to Saute mode. Add diced up onion and cooking fat
2. Allow the onions to cook for 5 -10 minutes
3. Add the rest of the   except arrowroot flour
4. Lock up the lid and set the pot to poultry mode. Cook until the timer runs out
5. Allow the pressure to release naturally
6. Once done, remove ¼ cup of the sauce from the pot and add arrowroot to make a slurry
7. Add the slurry to the pot to make the gravy thick. Keep stirring well. Serve!

The Hungarian Chicken Meal

Prepping time: 10 minutes| Cooking time: 8 hours |For 6 servings

1 tablespoon extra-virgin olive oil
2 pounds boneless chicken thigh
½ cup chicken broth
Juice and zest of 1 lemon
2 teaspoon garlic, minced
2 teaspoon paprika
½ teaspoon salt
1 cup cashew cream
1 tablespoon parsley, chopped

1. Lightly grease the inner pot of your Ninja Foodi with olive oil. Add chicken thigh to Ninja Foodi
2. Take a bowl and add broth, lemon juice, garlic, paprika, zest, and salt
3. Mix and pour the mixture over chicken. Cook on LOW for 7-8 hours
4. Remove heat and stir in cashew cream. Serve with a topping of parsley. Enjoy!

Lime And Cilantro Chicken Meal

Prepping time: 10 minutes| Cooking time: 2 hours 45 minutes |For 4 servings

2 small limes
¼ cup cilantro, chopped
½ tablespoon fresh garlic, minced
1 teaspoon salt
½ teaspoon pepper
4 pounds chicken drumsticks

1. Juice the lime and add them to your Ninja Foodi
2. Add ¼ cup of chopped cilantro, 1 teaspoon of salt, ½ a tablespoon of freshly minced garlic
3. Add the chicken drumsticks to the Ninja Foodi and coat them well
4. Cover and cook on SLOW COOK MODE (HIGH) for 2 and a ½ hour
5. Pre-heat your oven to a temperature of 500 degrees F. Line up a cookie sheet with foil
6. Transfer the cooker drumstick from the cooker to the foil using tongs
7. Bake for 10 minutes until they are nicely browned, making sure to turn them halfway through
8. Serve with the cooking juices. Enjoy!

The Original Mexican Chicken Cacciatore

Prepping time: 10 minutes| Cooking time: 33 minutes |For 4 servings

Extra virgin olive oil'
3 shallots, chopped
4 garlic cloves, crushed
1 green bell pepper, sliced
½ cup organic chicken broth
10 ounces mushrooms, sliced
5-6 skinless chicken breasts
2 cans (14.5 ounces organic crushed tomatoes
2 tablespoons organic tomato paste
1 can (14.5 ounces black olives, pitted
Fresh parsley
Salt and pepper to taste

1. Add oil to your pot and set the Ninja Foodi to Saute mode
2. Add shallots, bell pepper and cook for 2 minutes
3. Add broth and bring to a boil for 23 minutes. Add garlic and mushrooms
4. Gently place the chicken on the top of the whole mixture
5. Cover the chicken with tomato paste and crushed tomatoes
6. Lock up the lid and cook on HIGH pressure for 8 minutes
7. Release the pressure naturally over 10 minutes and stir in parsley, olive oil, pepper, salt, and red pepper flakes. Serve!

Magnificent Chicken Curry Soup

Prepping time: 10 minutes| Cooking time: 30 minutes |For 4 servings

1 and ½ cups unsweetened coconut milk
1 pound chicken thigh, skinless
3-4 garlic cloves, crushed
½ an onion, finely diced
2-inch knob ginger, minced
1 cup mushrooms, sliced
4 ounces baby spinach
½ teaspoon of cayenne pepper
½ teaspoon turmeric
1 teaspoon salt
1 teaspoon Garam Masala
¼ cup cilantro, chopped

1. Add the listed   to Ninja Foodi
2. Lock lid and cook on HIGH pressure for 10 minutes. Naturally, release pressure over 10 minutes
3. Remove meat and shred it, return the shredded meat to the pot
4. Set your pot to Saute mode and stir for a minute
5. Serve and enjoy!. Enjoy!

Summer Time Chicken Salad

Prepping time: 10 minutes| Cooking time: 10 minutes |For 4 servings

8 boneless chicken thighs
Kosher salt
1 tablespoon of ghee
1 small onion, chopped
2 medium carrots, chopped
½ a pound of cremini mushrooms
3 garlic cloves, peeled and crushed
2 cups of 14-ounce cherry tomatoes
½ a cup of 2 ounces of pitted green olives
¼ teaspoon of freshly cracked black pepper
½ a cup of thinly sliced basil leaves
¼ a cup of coarsely chopped Italian parsley

1. Season the chicken thigh with ¾ teaspoon of kosher salt and keep it in your fridge for about 2 days
2. Set your Ninja Foodi to Saute mode and add ghee and allow it to melt
3. Once the Ghee is simmering, add carrots, onions, mushrooms and ½ a teaspoon of salt
4. Saute the veggies until they are tender (should be around 3-5 minutes
5. Drop the tomato paste and garlic to your pot and cook for 30 seconds
6. Add seasoned chicken to the pot alongside olives and cherry tomatoes
7. Give everything a stir
8. Lock up the lid and cook for 7-10 minutes at HIGH pressure
9. Once done, allow the pressure to quick release
10. Stir in fresh herbs and enjoy!

Ham And Stuffed Turkey Rolls

Prepping time: 10 minutes| Cooking time: 20 minutes |For 4 servings

4 tablespoons fresh sage leaves
8 ham slices
8 (6 ounces turkey cutlets
Salt and pepper to taste
2 tablespoons butter, melted

1. Season turkey cutlets with salt and pepper
2. Roll turkey cutlets and wrap each of them with ham slices tightly
3. Coat each roll with butter and gently place sage leaves evenly over each cutlet
4. Transfer to Ninja Foodi
5. Lock lid and select Bake/Roast mode and bake for 10 minutes at 360 degrees F
6. Open lid and flip, lock lid and bake for 10 minutes more. Enjoy!

High-Quality Belizean Chicken Stew

Prepping time: 10 minutes| Cooking time: 20 minutes |For 4 servings

4 whole chicken
1 tablespoon coconut oil
2 tablespoons achiote seasoning
2 tablespoons white vinegar
3 tablespoons Worcestershire sauce
1 cup yellow onion, sliced
3 garlic cloves, sliced
1 teaspoon ground cumin
1 teaspoon dried oregano
½ teaspoon black pepper
2 cups chicken stock

1. Take a large sized bowl and add achiote paste, vinegar, Worcestershire sauce, oregano, cumin and pepper. Mix well and add chicken pieces and rub the marinade all over them
2. Allow the chicken to sit overnight. Set your pot to Saute mode and add coconut oil
3. Once the oil is hot, add the chicken pieces to the pot and brown them in batches (each batch for 2 minutes. Remove the seared chicken and transfer them to a plate
4. Add onions, garlic to the pot and Saute for 2-3 minutes . Add chicken pieces back to the pot
5. Pour chicken broth to the bowl with marinade and stir well. Add the mixture to the pot
6. Seal up the lid and cook for about 20 minutes at high pressure
7. Once done, release the pressure naturally . Season with a bit of salt and serve!

The Great Poblano Chicken Curry

Prepping time: 10 minutes| Cooking time: 15 minutes |For 4 servings

1 cup onion, diced
3 poblano peppers, chopped
5 garlic cloves,1 cup cauliflower, diced
1 and ½ pounds large chicken breast chunks
¼ cup cilantro, chopped
1 teaspoon ground coriander
1 teaspoon ground cumin
1-2 teaspoons salt
2 and ½ cups of water
2 ounces cream cheese

1. Add everything to your Ninja Foodi except cheese and lock up the lid
2. Cook on HIGH pressure for 15 minutes. Release the pressure naturally over 10 minutes
3. Remove the chicken with tongs and place it on the side
4. Use an immersion blender to blend the soup and veggies. Set your pot to Saute mode
5. Once the broth is hot add cream cheese (Cut in chunks. Whisk well
6. Shred the chicken and transfer it back to the pot. Serve and enjoy!

Hearty Chicken Yum

Prepping time: 30 minutes| Cooking time: 40 minutes |For 4 servings

2 tablespoons fresh boneless chicken thigh
3 tablespoons homemade ketchup
1 and ½ teaspoon salt
2 teaspoons garlic powder
¼ cup ghee
½ teaspoon ground black pepper
3 tablespoons organic tamari
¼ cup stevia

1. Add the listed   to your Ninja Foodi and give it a nice stir
2. Lock up the lid and cook for about 18 minutes under HIGH pressure
3. Quick release the pressure. Open the lid and transfer the chicken to a bowl
4. Shred it u using a fork
5. Set your pot to Saute mode and allow the liquid to be reduced for 5 minutes
6. Pour the sauce over your chicken Yum and serve with vegetables. Enjoy!

The Turkey Pizza Casserole

Prepping time: 10 minutes| Cooking time: 10 minutes |For 4 servings

2 cups tomatoes, crushed
1 pound ground turkey
1 pack pepperoni
½ cup mozzarella cheese
½ cup oregano cheese
½ teaspoon salt
2 garlic cloves, minced
½ teaspoon pepper
½ teaspoon onion powder

1. Take a medium sized bowl and add crushed tomatoes, seasoning
2. Pour ¼ of crushed tomatoes to your Ninja Foodi
3. Layer ¼ of ground turkey, pepperoni and cheese on top
4. Keep repeating until the   are used up
5. Lock up the lid and cook on HIGH pressure for 6 minutes
6. Remove and allow it to cool for about 15 minutes. Cut it up and serve. Enjoy!

Heartfelt Chicken Curry Soup

Prepping time: 10 minutes| Cooking time: 10 minutes |For 4 servings

1 teaspoon Garam Masala
½ teaspoon cayenne
½ teaspoon ground turmeric
1 teaspoon salt
4 ounces baby spinach
1 cup mushrooms, sliced
1 (2-inch piece) ginger, finely chopped
3-4 garlic cloves, crushed
½ onion, diced
1 and ½ cups unsweetened coconut milk
1 pound boneless, skinless chicken thighs
¼ cup chopped fresh cilantro

1. Add chicken, coconut milk, onion, garlic, ginger, mushrooms, spinach, salt, turmeric, cayenne, garam masala and cilantro to the inner pot of your Ninja Foodi
2. Lock lid and cook on HIGH pressure for 10 minutes
3. Release pressure naturally over 10 minutes. Use tongs to transfer chicken to a plate, shred it
4. Stir chicken back to the soup and stir. Enjoy!

Your's Truly Lime Chicken Chili

Prepping time: 10 minutes| Cooking time: 23 minutes |For 6 servings

¼ cup cooking wine (Keto-Friendly)
½ cup organic chicken broth
1 onion, diced
1 teaspoon salt
½ teaspoon paprika
5 garlic cloves, minced
1 tablespoon lime juice
¼ cup butter
2 pounds chicken thighs
1 teaspoon dried parsley
3 green chilies, chopped

1. Set your Ninja-Foodi to Sauté mode and add onion and garlic
2. Sauté for 3 minutes, add remaining
3. Lock lid and cook on Medium-HIGH pressure for 20 minutes
4. Release pressure naturally over 10 minutes. Serve and enjoy!

Hungry Man's Indian Chicken Keema

Prepping time: 10 minutes| Cooking time: 10 minutes |For 6 servings

1 tablespoon coconut oil
1 teaspoon cumin seeds
½ teaspoon turmeric
1 tablespoon garlic, grated
1 tablespoon ginger, grated
1 large onion, diced
2 tomatoes, diced
2 teaspoons mild red chili powder
1 teaspoon Garam masala
1 teaspoon salt
2 tablespoons coriander powder
1 pound ground chicken
½ cup cilantro

1. Set your Ninja Foodi to Saute mode and add cumin seeds
2. Toast for 30 seconds. Add turmeric powder and give it a nice mix
3. Add garlic, ginger and mix well again. Add onion and Saute for 2 minutes
4. Add tomatoes, Garam Masala, red chili powder, coriander, salt and mix well
5. Add ground chicken and keep Sautéing it while breaking it up with a spatula
6. Add ½ a cup of water . Lock up the lid and cook on HIGH pressure for 4 minutes
7. Release the pressure naturally over 10 minutes
8. Garnish with a bit of cilantro and serve . Enjoy!

The Borderline Crack Chicken

Prepping time: 10 minutes| Cooking time: 25 minutes |For 4 servings

4 ounces cheddar cheese
3 tablespoons arrowroot
1 cup of water
8 ounces cream cheese
1 pack ranch seasoning
2 pounds boneless chicken breast
6-8 cooked bacon

1. Add chicken to your Ninja Foodi. Add cream cheese
2. Sprinkle ranch seasoning over chicken add water
3. Lock lid and cook for 25 minutes on HIGH pressure. Quick release pressure
4. Take the chicken out and shred into pieces
5. Set your pot to SAUTE mode and add a mixture of arrowroot and water
6. Add cheese and shredded chicken. Stir and bacon. Enjoy!

The Decisive Red Curry Chicken

Prepping time: 10 minutes| Cooking time: 10 minutes |For 6 servings

1 tablespoon of olive oil
2-4 tablespoon of red curry paste
1 and a ½ pound of thin chicken breast
1-2 tablespoon of fish sauce
1 tablespoon of stevia
1 jalapeno chili
1 cup yellow onion, sliced
1 cup red pepper, sliced
1 cup yellow pepper, sliced
1 cup orange pepper, sliced
A handful of Thai basil leaves

1. Set your Ninja Foodi to Saute mode and add oil, allow the oil to heat up
2. Add 2 tablespoon of red curry paste. Saute for 30 seconds
3. Add chicken and mix it well with the curry paste. Add coconut milk
4. Lock up the lid and cook on HIGH pressure for 2 minutes
5. Release the pressure naturally over 10 minutes. Open and stir in fish sauce and stevia
6. Add onion, red, yellow, orange peppers and stir well
7. Set your Ninja Foodi to Saute mode and bring the curry to a gentle boil. Serve and enjoy!

Spinach And Chicken Curry

Prepping time: 10 minutes| Cooking time: 12 minutes |For 4 servings

10 ounce of Spinach
1 pound of chicken thigh cut up into 2-3 pieces
1 tablespoon of oil
½ a teaspoon of cumin seeds
1-inch ginger chopped up
6 pieces of cloves
2 medium onions cut up into pieces

Spices

¼ teaspoon of turmeric
½ a teaspoon of red chili powder
2 teaspoon of coriander
1 teaspoon of salt

1. Set your Ninja Foodi to Saute mode and add oil, allow the oil to heat up
2. Add cumin seeds, garlic, and ginger and cook for 30 seconds
3. Stir in garlic and the cut onions and Saute them for 1 minute more
4. Add spices and give it a nice stir. Add spinach with the chicken pieces on top of the spinach
5. Lock up the lid and allow them to cook at HIGH pressure for 8 minutes
6. Once done, do a quick release and open up the lid. Remove the chicken pieces from the pot and keep them on the side
7. Take an immersion blender and blend the whole mixture until you have a creamy texture
8. Cut up your chicken in small portions and add them back to the curry
9. Set the pot to Saute mode once more and give the whole curry a quick boil (without lid).Enjoy!

Cheese Dredged Lemon Chicken

Prepping time: 10 minutes| Cooking time: 8 minutes |For 4 servings

1 tablespoon olive oil
3 chicken breast, boneless and skinless
1 cup spicy salsa
½ cup feta cheese, crumbled
½ teaspoon ground cumin
½ teaspoon red chili powder
¼ cup fresh lime juice

1. Add olive oil to Instant Pot and set your pot to Saute mode
2. Add chicken breast to the pot and brown both sides. Transfer chicken to a plate
3. Add cumin, chili powder, lime juice, salsa to pot. Stir and return chicken
4. Lock lid and cook on HIGH pressure for 8 minutes. Quick release pressure
5. Transfer chicken breast and sauté to plate. Sprinkle crumbled cheese. Serve and enjoy!

Best Chicken Wings

Prepping time: 10 minutes| Cooking time: 25 minutes |For 4 servings

24 chicken wing segments
2 tablespoons toasted sesame oil
2 tablespoons Asian-Chile-Garlic sauce
2 tablespoons stevia
2 garlic cloves, minced
1 tablespoon toasted sesame seeds

1. Add 1 cup water to Foodie's inner pot, place reversible rack in the pot in lower portions, place chicken wings in the rack. Place lid into place and seal the valve
2. Select pressure mode to HIGH and cook for 10 minutes
3. Make the glaze by taking a large bowl and whisking in sesame oil, Chile-Garlic sauce, honey and garlic
4. Once the chicken is cooked, quick release the pressure and remove pressure lid
5. Remove rack from the pot and empty remaining water. Return inner pot to the base
6. Cover with crisping lid and select Air Crisp mode, adjust the temperature to 375 degrees F, pre-heat for 3 minutes
7. While the Foodi pre-heats, add wings to the sauce and toss well to coat it
8. Transfer wings to the basket, leaving any excess sauce in the bowl
9. Place the basket in Foodi and close with Crisping mode, select Air Crisp mode and let it cook for 8 minutes, gently toss the wings and let it cook for 8 minutes more
10. Once done, drizzle any sauce and sprinkle sesame seeds. Enjoy!

Simple And Juicy Chicken Stock

Prepping time: 10 minutes| Cooking time: 2hours |For 4 servings

2 pounds meaty chicken bones
¼ teaspoon salt
3 and ½ cups of water

1. Place chicken parts in Foodi and season with salt
2. Add water, place the pressure cooker lid and seal the valve, cook on HIGH pressure for 90 minutes. Release the pressure naturally over 10 minutes
3. Line a colander with cheesecloth and place it over a large bowl, pour chicken parts and stock into the colander and strain out the chicken and bones
4. Let the stock cool and let it peel off any layer of fat that might accumulate on the surface
5. Use as needed!

Keto-Friendly Chicken Tortilla

Prepping time: 15 minutes| Cooking time: 15 minutes |For 4 servings

1 tablespoon avocado oil
1 pound pastured organic boneless chicken breasts
½ cup of orange juice
2 teaspoons gluten-free Worcestershire sauce
1 teaspoon garlic powder
1 teaspoon salt
½ teaspoon chili powder
½ teaspoon paprika

1. Set your Ninja Foodi to Sauté mode and add oil, let the oil heat up
2. Add chicken on top, take a bowl and add remaining   mix well
3. Pour the mixture over chicken. Lock lid and cook on HIGH pressure for 15 minutes
4. Release pressure naturally over 10 minutes
5. Shred the chicken and serve over salad green shells such as cabbage or lettuce. Enjoy!

Chapter 3: Beef, Pork and Lamb

Pork and Orecchiette Ragu

Prep time: 10 minutes | Cook time: 25 minutes | Serves 6

3 tablespoons extra-virgin olive oil, divided
1 pound (454 g) pork shoulder, cut into large
    pieces
1 small onion, diced
1 carrot, diced
1 celery stalk, diced
1 garlic clove, minced
1 (28-ounce / 794-g) can crushed tomatoes
1 (28-ounce / 794-g) can tomato purée
1 cup red wine
2 cups beef stock
1 (16-ounce / 454-g) box orecchiette pasta
1 teaspoon sea salt
1 teaspoon Italian seasoning
1 bunch Tuscan kale, ribs and stems
    removed, torn
¼ cup unsalted butter, cubed
½ cup grated Parmesan cheese

1. Select SEAR/SAUTÉ and set to HI. Select START/STOP to begin. Let preheat for 5 minutes.
2. Place 2 tablespoons of oil in the pot. Once hot, add the pork pieces and sear on all sides, turning until brown, about 10 minutes in total. Transfer the pork to a large plate and set aside.
3. Add onion, carrot, and celery and cook for about 5 minutes. Add the garlic and cook for 1 minute.
4. Add the crushed tomatoes, tomato purée, red wine, beef stock, pasta, salt, and Italian seasoning. Place the pork back in the pot. Assemble pressure lid, making sure the pressure release valve is in the SEAL position.
5. Select PRESSURE and set to LO. Set time to 0 minutes. Select START/STOP to begin.
6. When pressure cooking is complete, allow pressure to naturally release for 10 minutes. After 10 minutes, quick release remaining pressure by moving the pressure release valve to the VENT position. Carefully remove lid when unit has finished releasing pressure.
7. Pull the pork pieces apart using two forks. Add the remaining 1 tablespoon of olive oil, kale, butter, and Parmesan cheese and stir until the butter melts and the kale is wilted. Serve.

Dogs in Blankets

Prep time: 15 minutes | Cook time: 15 minutes | Serves 4

4 beef hot dogs
4 bacon strips
Cooking spray
4 bakery hot dog buns, split and toasted
½ red onion, chopped
1 cup sauerkraut, rinsed and drained

1. Place Cook & Crisp Basket in pot. Close crisping lid. Select AIR CRISP, set temperature to 360ºF (182ºC), and set time to 5 minutes. Select START/STOP to begin preheating.
2. Wrap each hot dog with 1 strip of bacon, securing it with toothpicks as needed.
3. Once unit has preheated, open lid and coat the basket with cooking spray. Place the hot dogs in the basket in a single layer. Close crisping lid.
4. Select AIR CRISP, set temperature to 360ºF (182ºC), and set time to 15 minutes. Select START/STOP to begin.
5. After 10 minutes, open lid and check doneness. If needed, continue cooking until it reaches your desired doneness.
6. When cooking is complete, place the hot dog in the buns with the onion and sauerkraut. Top, if desired, with condiments of your choice, such as yellow mustard, ketchup, or mayonnaise.

Pork and Peanut Lettuce Wraps

Prep time: 10 minutes | Cook time: 30 minutes | Serves 6

3 pounds (1.4 kg) boneless pork shoulder, cut into 1- to 2-inch cubes
2 cups light beer
1 cup brown sugar
1 teaspoon chipotle chiles in adobo sauce
1 cup barbecue sauce
1 head iceberg lettuce, quartered and leaves separated
1 cup roasted peanuts, chopped or ground
Cilantro leaves

1. Place the pork, beer, brown sugar, chipotle, and barbecue sauce in the pot. Assemble pressure lid, making sure the pressure release valve is in the SEAL position.
2. Select PRESSURE and set to HI. Set the timer to 30 minutes. Select START/STOP to begin.
3. When pressure cooking is complete, quick release the pressure by turning the pressure release valve to the VENT position. Carefully remove lid when unit has finished releasing pressure.
4. Using a silicone-tipped utensil, shred the pork in the pot. Stir to mix the meat in with the sauce.
5. Place a small amount of pork in a piece of lettuce. Top with peanuts and cilantro to serve.

Baked Taco Elbow Pasta

Prep time: 10 minutes | Cook time: 20 minutes | Serves 6

1 tablespoon extra-virgin olive oil
1 small onion, diced
1 pound (454 g) ground beef
1 packet taco seasoning
1 (14½-ounce / 411-g) can diced tomatoes
1 (4-ounce / 113-g) can diced green chiles
1 (16-ounce / 454-g) box dry elbow pasta
4 cups beef broth
2 ounces (57 g) cream cheese, cut into pieces
3 cups shredded Mexican blend cheese, divided
Optional toppings:
Sour cream, for garnish
Red onion, for garnish
Chopped cilantro, for garnish

1. Select SEAR/SAUTÉ and set to MD:HI. Select START/STOP to begin. Let preheat for 5 minutes.
2. Place the oil, onion, and beef in the pot and cook for about 5 minutes, using a wooden spoon to break apart the beef as it cooks. Add the taco seasoning and mix until the beef is coated.
3. Add the tomatoes, green chiles, pasta, and beef broth. Assemble pressure lid, making sure the pressure release valve is in the SEAL position.
4. Select PRESSURE and set to LO. Set time to 0 minutes. Select START/STOP to begin.
5. When pressure cooking is complete, allow pressure to naturally release for 10 minutes. After 10 minutes, quick release remaining pressure by moving the pressure release valve to the VENT position. Carefully remove lid when unit has finished releasing pressure.
6. Add the cream cheese and 2 cups of cheese. Stir well to melt cheese and ensure all ingredients are combined. Cover the pasta evenly with the remaining 1 cup of cheese. Close crisping lid.
7. Select BROIL and set time to 5 minutes. Select START/STOP to begin.
8. When cooking is complete, serve immediately.

Kielbasa Sausage with Cabbage

Prep time: 10 minutes | Cook time: 1 hour | Serves 6

1½ pounds (680 g) fresh kielbasa sausage links
½ stick (¼ cup) unsalted butter
½ medium onion, thinly sliced
2 garlic cloves, minced
1 large head red cabbage, cut into ¼-inch slices
¼ cup granulated sugar
⅓ cup apple cider vinegar
½ cup water

1. Insert Cook & Crisp Basket into pot and close crisping lid. Select AIR CRISP, set temperature to 390ºF (199ºC), and set time to 15 minutes. Select START/STOP to begin. Let preheat for 5 minutes.
2. Add the sausage to the basket. Close lid and cook for 10 minutes.
3. When cooking is complete, open lid and remove basket and sausage. Set aside.
4. Select SEAR/SAUTÉ and set to HI. Select START/STOP to begin.
5. Add the butter and let it heat for 5 minutes. Add the onion and garlic and cook for 3 minutes.
6. Add the cabbage, sugar, vinegar, water, and caraway seeds, and season with salt and pepper. Assemble pressure lid, making sure the pressure release valve is in the SEAL position.

2 teaspoons caraway seeds
Kosher salt
Freshly ground black pepper

7. Select PRESSURE and set to HI. Set time to 10 minutes. Select START/STOP to begin.
8. When pressure cooking is complete, quick release the pressure by moving the pressure release valve to the VENT position.
9. Select SEAR/SAUTÉ and set to HI. Set time to 10 minutes. Select START/STOP to begin.
10. After 5 minutes, open lid and add the sausage to the top of cabbage. Close lid and continue cooking.
11. When cooking is complete, open lid and serve.

Mac and Cheese with Bacon

Prep time: 10 minutes | Cook time: 30 minutes | Serves 6

4 strips bacon, chopped
5 cups water
1 (16-ounce / 454-g) box elbow pasta
2 tablespoons unsalted butter
1 tablespoon ground mustard
1 (5-ounce / 142-g) can evaporated milk
8 ounces (227 g) Cheddar cheese, shredded
8 ounces (227 g) Gouda, shredded
Sea salt
Freshly ground black pepper
2 cups panko or Italian bread crumbs
1 stick (½ cup) butter, melted

1. Select SEAR/SAUTÉ and set temperature to HI. Select START/STOP to begin. Let preheat for 5 minutes.
2. Add the bacon and cook, stirring frequently, for about 6 minutes or until crispy. Using a slotted spoon, transfer the bacon to a paper towel-lined plate to drain.
3. Add the water, pasta, 2 tablespoons of butter, and mustard. Assemble pressure lid, making sure the pressure release valve is in the SEAL position.
4. Select PRESSURE and set to LO. Set time to 0 minutes. Select START/STOP to begin.
5. When pressure cooking is complete, allow pressure to naturally release for 10 minutes. After 10 minutes, quick release remaining pressure by moving the pressure release valve to the VENT position. Carefully remove lid when unit has finished releasing pressure.
6. Add the evaporated milk, Cheddar cheese, Gouda cheese and the bacon. Season with salt and pepper. Stir well to melt the cheeses and ensure all ingredients are combined.
7. In a medium bowl, stir together the bread crumbs and melted butter. Cover the pasta evenly with the mixture. Close crisping lid.
8. Select AIR CRISP, set temperature to 360ºF (182ºC), and set time to 7 minutes. Select START/STOP to begin.
9. When cooking is complete, serve immediately.

Italian Rigatoni, Sausage, and Meatball Potpie

Prep time: 20 minutes | Cook time: 55 minutes | Serves 8

5 cups, plus 1 teaspoon water, divided
1 (16-ounce / 454-g) box rigatoni pasta
4 (4-ounce / 113-g) fresh Italian sausage links
1 (12-ounce / 340-g) bag frozen cooked meatballs
16 ounces (454 g) whole milk Ricotta cheese
1 (25½-ounce / 723-g) jar marinara sauce
2 cups shredded Mozzarella cheese
1 refrigerated store-bought pie crust, room temperature
1 large egg

1. Pour 5 cups of water and the rigatoni in the pot. Assemble pressure lid, making sure the pressure release valve is in the SEAL position.
2. Select PRESSURE and set to LO. Set time to 0 minutes. Select START/STOP to begin.
3. When pressure cooking is complete, quick release the pressure by turning the pressure release valve to the VENT position. Carefully remove lid when unit has finished releasing pressure.
4. Drain the pasta and set it aside, keeping warm. Wipe out pot and return it to base. Insert Cook & Crisp Basket into pot. Close crisping lid.
5. Select AIR CRISP, set temperature to 390ºF (199ºC), and set time to 15 minutes. Select START/STOP to begin. Let preheat for 5 minutes.
6. Open lid and place the sausages in the basket. Close lid and cook for 10 minutes.
7. When cooking is complete, remove sausages to a cutting board. Add the meatballs to the basket. Close crisping lid.
8. Select AIR CRISP, set temperature to 390ºF (199ºC), and set time to 10 minutes. Select START/STOP to begin.
9. Slice sausages into very thin rounds.
10. When cooking is complete, transfer the meatballs to the cutting board and slice them in half.
11. In the pot, in this order, add a layer of Ricotta, marinara sauce, sausage, Mozzarella cheese, pasta, marinara sauce, meatballs, Mozzarella cheese, pasta, Ricotta, and marinara sauce. Place the pie crust on top of the filling.
12. In a small bowl, whisk together the egg and remaining 1 teaspoon of water. Brush this on top of the pie crust. With a knife, slice a couple of small holes in the middle of crust to vent it. Close crisping lid.
13. Select BAKE/ROAST, set temperature to 350ºF (177ºC), and set time to 30 minutes. Select START/STOP to begin.
14. When cooking is complete, open lid. Let sit for 10 minutes before serving.

BBQ Burnt Ends

Prep time: 5 minutes | Cook time: 1 hour 50 minutes | Serves 6

3 pounds (1.4 kg) beef brisket, some (but not all) fat trimmed
¼ cup barbecue spice rub
1 cup water
2 cups barbecue sauce

1. Season the brisket liberally and evenly with the barbecue spice rub.
2. Add the water, then place the brisket in the pot. Assemble pressure lid, making sure the pressure release valve is in the SEAL position.
3. Select PRESSURE and set to HI. Set time to 1 hour, 30 minutes. Select START/STOP to begin.
4. When pressure cooking is complete, quick release the pressure by moving the pressure release valve to the VENT position. Carefully remove lid when unit has finished releasing pressure.
5. Carefully remove the brisket from the pot and place on a cutting board. Let cool at room temperature for 10 minutes, or until brisket can be easily handled.
6. Cut the brisket into 2-inch chunks. Drain the cooking liquid from the pot. Place the brisket chunks in the pot. Add the barbecue sauce and stir gently so the brisket chunks are coated. Close crisping lid.
7. Select AIR CRISP, set temperature to 360°F (182°C), and set time to 20 minutes (for more charred-like results, set time to 23 minutes). Select START/STOP to begin.
8. When cooking is complete, open lid and serve.

Super Cheesy Pepperoni Calzones

Prep time: 10 minutes | Cook time: 18 minutes | Serves 4

All-purpose flour, for dusting
16 ounces (454 g) store-bought pizza dough
1 egg, beaten
2 cups shredded Mozzarella cheese
1 cup Ricotta cheese
½ cup grated Parmesan cheese
½ cup sliced pepperoni
Cooking spray
Pizza sauce, for dipping

1. Dust a clean work surface with the flour. Divide the pizza dough into four equal pieces. Place the dough on the floured surface and roll each piece into an 8-inch round of even thickness. Dust your rolling pin and work surface with additional flour, as needed, to ensure the dough does not stick. Brush egg wash around the edges of each round.
2. Place Cook & Crisp Basket in pot. Close crisping lid. Select AIR CRISP, set temperature to 390°F (199°C), and set time to 5 minutes. Select START/STOP to begin preheating.
3. In a medium bowl, combine the Mozzarella, Ricotta, and Parmesan cheese. Fold in the pepperoni.
4. Spoon one-quarter of the cheese mixture onto one side of each dough round. Fold the other half over the filling and press firmly to seal the edges together. Brush each calzone all over with the egg wash.
5. Once unit is preheated, open lid and coat the basket with cooking spray. Place two calzones in the basket in a single layer. Close crisping lid.
6. Select AIR CRISP, set temperature to 390°F (199°C), and set time to 9 minutes. Select START/STOP to begin.
7. After 7 minutes, open lid to check for doneness. If desired, cook for up to 2 minutes more, until golden brown.
8. When cooking is complete, remove calzone from basket. Repeat steps 5 and 6 with the remaining calzones. Serve warm.

Lime Steak Tacos

Prep time: 5 minutes | Cook time: 16 minutes | Serves 4

2 pounds (907 g) flank steak, cut into ¼-inch strips
¼ cup freshly squeezed lime juice
3 tablespoons grated garlic
3 tablespoons extra-virgin olive oil
2 teaspoons kosher salt
2 teaspoons freshly ground black pepper
2 tablespoons canola oil
12 (8-inch) flour tortillas

1. Place the steak, lime juice, garlic, olive oil, salt, and pepper in a large resealable plastic bag. Refrigerate and marinate for a minimum of 30 minutes or up to 3 hours.
2. Select SEAR/SAUTÉ and set to MD:HI. Select START/STOP to begin. Let preheat for 5 minutes.
3. Add the canola oil and heat for 1 minute. Working in batches, place the steak in the pot and cook, stirring frequently, until the steak is browned, about 8 minutes per batch.
4. Divide the steak slices evenly between the tortillas. Add desired toppings, such as guacamole or sliced avocado, sour cream, pineapple chunks, salsa, and cilantro, and serve immediately.

Thai Beef Rice Bowl

Prep time: 10 minutes | Cook time: 20 minutes | Serves 8

2 pounds (907 g) ground beef
2 tablespoons sriracha
4 tablespoons fish sauce
3 tablespoons soy sauce
Zest of 2 limes
Juice of 2 limes
3 tablespoons brown sugar
2 shallots, diced
2 tablespoons minced garlic
1 red bell pepper, diced
1 bunch Thai basil leaves
6 scallions, sliced
Basmati rice, for serving

1. Select SEAR/SAUTÉ and set temperature to HI. Select START/STOP to begin. Let preheat for 5 minutes.
2. Add the ground beef. Cook, stirring occasionally, until the beef is fully cooked, 3 to 5 minutes.
3. In a small bowl, whisk together the sriracha, fish sauce, soy sauce, lime zest and juice, and brown sugar.
4. Once the beef is cooked, add the shallot and garlic and cook until soft, about 2 minutes.
5. Add sauce mixture and stir. Let boil until reduced slightly, about 5 minutes.
6. Add the bell pepper and basil. Cook just until the basil wilts, about 1 minute.
7. When cooking is complete, garnish with the scallions and serve over rice.

Brisket with Onion

Prep time: 5 minutes | Cook time: 1 hour 10 minutes | Serves 4

3 pounds (1.4 kg) beef brisket, quartered
1 onion, cut into quarters
2 cups beef broth
Splash Worcestershire sauce
1 teaspoon kosher salt

1. Select SEAR/SAUTÉ and set temperature to MD:HI. Select START/STOP to begin and allow to preheat for 5 minutes.
2. Add the brisket (fat side down) into the cooking pot and sear for 5 minutes. Using tongs, carefully flip the brisket over and sear on the other side for an additional 5 minutes.
3. In the cooking pot, combine the onion, beef broth, Worcestershire sauce, and salt.
4. Assemble the pressure lid, making sure the pressure release valve is in the SEAL position.
5. Select PRESSURE and set to HI. Set the time to 60 minutes. Select START/STOP to begin.
6. When pressure cooking is complete, allow the pressure to naturally release for 20 minutes. After 20 minutes, quick release any remaining pressure by moving the pressure release valve to the VENT position. Carefully remove lid when unit has finished releasing pressure.
7. Shred or slice the meat, as desired for serving.

Pork Chop Quinoa Bowl

Prep time: 5 minutes | Cook time: 17 minutes | Serves 4

¼ cup smoked paprika
2 tablespoons ground cumin
½ teaspoon cayenne pepper
2 tablespoons dark brown sugar
3 tablespoons kosher salt, divided
2 teaspoons freshly ground black pepper
2 (6-ounce / 170-g) boneless pork chops
2 cups quinoa
3 cups chicken stock

1. In a small bowl, mix together the paprika, cumin, cayenne pepper, sugar, salt, and pepper.
2. Pat the pork chops dry with a paper towel, then rub the spice mixture over the meat ensuring that it's fully covered.
3. Place the quinoa, chicken stock, and salt into the pot. Assemble pressure lid, making sure the pressure release valve is in the SEAL position.
4. Select PRESSURE and set to HI. Set time to 2 minutes. Select START/STOP to begin.
5. When pressure cooking is complete, allow pressure to naturally release for 10 minutes. After 10 minutes, quick release remaining pressure by turning the pressure release valve to the VENT position. Carefully remove lid when unit has finished releasing pressure.
6. Place Reversible Rack in pot in the higher position. Place the pork on the rack. Close crisping lid.
7. Select AIR CRISP, set temperature to 375°F (191°C), and set time to 15 minutes. Select START/STOP to begin.
8. After 8 minutes, open lid, and using tongs, flip the pork chops. Close lid and continue cooking until the pork chops have reached an internal temperature of 165°F (74°C).
9. When cooking is complete, remove the pork and rice from the pot. Slice the pork and serve in bowls over the rice with desired toppings, such as mint, avocado, mango, blueberries, sprouts, or grape tomatoes.

Pineapple Rack Ribs

Prep time: 10 minutes | Cook time: 29 minutes | Serves 4

1 (3-pound / 1.4-kg) rack St. Louis ribs, cut in thirds
1 teaspoon sea salt
½ teaspoon freshly ground black pepper
½ cup water
¼ cup apple cider vinegar
½ cup tomato ketchup
1 (8-ounce / 227-g) can crushed pineapple
3 tablespoons brown sugar
2 tablespoons cornstarch
1 tablespoon soy sauce

1. Season the ribs with salt and pepper.
2. Pour the water into the pot. Place the ribs in the Cook & Crisp Basket and insert basket in pot. Assemble pressure lid, making sure the pressure release valve is in the SEAL position.
3. Select PRESSURE and set to HI. Set time to 19 minutes. Select START/STOP to begin.
4. Add the vinegar, ketchup, pineapple, brown sugar, cornstarch, and soy sauce to a blender and blend under high speed until well combined.
5. When pressure cooking is complete, quick release the pressure by turning the pressure release valve to the VENT position. Carefully remove pressure lid when unit has finished releasing pressure.
6. Liberally brush the ribs with the sauce. Close crisping lid.
7. Select AIR CRISP, set temperature to 400ºF (204ºC), and set time to 20 minutes. Select START/STOP to begin.
8. After 10 minutes, open lid and liberally brush ribs with additional sauce. Flip the ribs and brush the other side. Close lid and continue cooking. Add additional time and basting as desired for crispier results.
9. When cooking is complete, the internal temperature of the meat should read at least 185ºF (85ºC) on a meat thermometer. Remove basket and ribs and serve.

Garlic-Hosin Pork Shoulder and Broccoli

Prep time: 5 minutes | Cook time: 1 hour 5 minutes | Serves 4

1 boneless pork shoulder, between 2½ (1.1 kg) and 3 pounds (1.4 kg)
2½ cups garlic-hoisin sauce, divided, plus additional for glazing
¾ cups water
1 head broccoli, cut into 2-inch florets
1 tablespoon canola oil
Kosher salt
Freshly ground black pepper

1. Place the pork shoulder and 1½ cups of hoisin sauce in large, resealable plastic bag. Move contents to ensure that all pork has been coated with the sauce and seal bag. Refrigerate and let marinate for at least 10 minutes and up to 4 hours.
2. Place Cook & Crisp Basket in pot. Place the water in the pot. Place the pork in the basket. Assemble pressure lid, making sure the pressure release valve is in the SEAL position.
3. Select PRESSURE and set to HI. Set time to 45 minutes. Select START/STOP to begin.
4. Combine the broccoli, oil, ½ cup of hoisin sauce, and salt and pepper in a large bowl. Mix well to coat broccoli with sauce and seasonings.
5. When pressure cooking is complete, quick release the pressure by moving the pressure release valve to the VENT position. Carefully remove lid when unit has finished releasing pressure.
6. Move the pork to one side of the basket and place broccoli in the other side. Brush the remaining ½ cup of hoisin sauce over the pork. Close crisping lid.
7. Select AIR CRISP, set temperature to 390ºF (199ºC), and set time to 20 minutes. Select START/STOP to begin.
8. Every 5 minutes or so, open lid and glaze pork with additional hoisin sauce. Close lid and continue cooking. Begin checking pork for desired crispiness after 15 minutes, cooking for up to an additional 5 minutes if desired.
9. When cooking is complete, remove pork and broccoli and serve in a family-style dish. If desired, pour some of the cooking liquid over the top of pork and broccoli for even more flavor.

Korean Honey Back Ribs

Prep time: 10 minutes | Cook time: 25 minutes | Serves 4

½ cup soy sauce
2 tablespoons rice vinegar
2 tablespoons sesame oil
1 tablespoon cayenne pepper
8 garlic cloves, minced
1 tablespoon grated fresh ginger
1 small onion, minced
1 (3-pound / 1.4-kg) rack baby back ribs, cut into quarters
½ cup water
¼ cup honey
Sesame seeds, for garnish

1. In a mixing bowl, combine the soy sauce, rice vinegar, sesame oil, cayenne pepper, garlic, ginger, and onion. Pour the mixture over the ribs, cover, and let marinate in the refrigerator for 30 minutes.
2. Place the ribs in the Cook & Crisp Basket, reserving the remaining marinade. Pour the water in the pot and place basket in pot. Assemble pressure lid, making sure the pressure release valve is in the SEAL position.
3. Select PRESURE and set to HI. Set time to 10 minutes. Select START/STOP to begin.
4. When pressure cooking is complete, quick release the pressure by turning the pressure release valve to the VENT position. Carefully remove lid when pressure has finished releasing.
5. Pour the remaining marinade over the ribs. Close lid.
6. Select AIR CRISP, set temperature to 400°F (204°C), and set time to 15 minutes. Select START/STOP to begin.
7. After 10 minutes, open lid and liberally brush the ribs with the honey. Close lid and continue cooking.
8. When cooking is complete, open lid and remove the ribs. Cut them into individual ribs. Sprinkle with the sesame seeds and serve.

Green Bean Pork with Scalloped Potatoes

Prep time: 15 minutes | Cook time: 45 minutes | Serves 2

1½ cups chicken broth
2 cups half-and-half
¼ cup cornstarch
2 teaspoons garlic powder
Kosher salt
Freshly ground black pepper
4 Russet potatoes, sliced ¼-inch thick
4 cups shredded Cheddar cheese, divided
2 bone-in pork chops
½ pound (227 g) green beans, ends trimmed
1 teaspoon minced garlic
1 teaspoon extra-virgin olive oil

1. In a medium bowl, whisk together the chicken broth, half-and-half, cornstarch, garlic powder, salt, and pepper. Pour just enough broth mixture to cover the bottom of the pot.
2. Layer half of the sliced potatoes in the bottom of the pot. Cover the potatoes with 1 cup of cheese, then layer the remaining potatoes over the cheese. Cover the second layer of potatoes with 1 cup of cheese, then pour in the remaining broth mixture to cover potatoes. Assemble pressure lid, making sure the pressure release valve is in the SEAL position.
3. Select PRESSURE and set to HI. Set time to 25 minutes. Select START/STOP to begin.
4. When pressure cooking is complete, allow pressure to release naturally for 25 minutes. After 25 minutes, quick release remaining pressure by moving the pressure release valve to the VENT position. Carefully remove lid when unit has finished releasing pressure.
5. Cover the potatoes with remaining 2 cups of cheese. Place the Reversible Rack in the broil position in the pot. Close crisping lid.
6. Select BROIL and set time to 20 minutes. Select START/STOP to begin.
7. Season the pork chops with salt and pepper.
8. After 4 minutes, open lid. Place the pork chops on the rack. Close the lid and continue cooking for another 12 minutes.
9. In a large bowl, toss the green beans with the garlic and oil, and season with salt and pepper.
10. After 12 minutes, open lid and add the green beans to the rack with the pork chops. Close lid and continue cooking for the remaining 4 minutes.
11. When cooking is complete, open lid and serve.

Herbed Pork with Chutney

Prep time: 10 minutes | Cook time: 23 minutes | Serves 4

1 pound (454 g) pork tenderloin
2½ tablespoons minced rosemary, divided
2½ tablespoons minced thyme, divided
Kosher salt
Freshly ground black pepper
2 tablespoons extra-virgin olive oil
1 small white onion
1 tablespoon minced garlic
¾ cup apple juice
2 apples, cut into ½-inch cubes
2½ tablespoons balsamic vinegar
1 tablespoon honey
2½ teaspoons cornstarch
3 tablespoons unsalted butter, cubed

1. Select SEAR/SAUTÉ and set to HI. Select START/STOP to begin. Let preheat for 5 minutes.
2. Season the pork with 1 tablespoon of rosemary, 1 tablespoon of thyme, salt, and pepper.
3. Once unit is preheated, add the olive oil. Once hot, add the pork and sear for 3 minutes on each side. Once seared, place the pork on a plate and set aside.
4. Add the onion, garlic, and apple juice. Stir, scraping the bottom of the pot to remove any brown bits. Add apples and vinegar and stir. Return the pork to the pot, nestling it in the apple mixture. Assemble pressure lid, making sure the pressure release valve is in the SEAL position.
5. Select PRESSURE and set to HI. Set time to 7 minutes. Select START/STOP to begin.
6. When pressure cooking is complete, allow pressure to naturally release for 14 minutes. After 14 minutes, quick release the pressure by turning the pressure release valve to the VENT position. Carefully remove lid when unit has finished releasing pressure.
7. Remove the pork from the pot, place it on a plate, and cover with aluminum foil.
8. Slightly mash the apples with a potato masher. Stir the honey into the mixture.
9. Remove ¼ cup of cooking liquid from the pot and mix it with the cornstarch until smooth. Pour this mixture into the pot and stir until thickened. Add the butter, 1 tablespoon of rosemary, and 1 tablespoon of thyme and stir until the butter is melted.
10. Slice the pork and serve it with the chutney. Garnish with the remaining ½ tablespoon of rosemary and ½ tablespoon of thyme.

Asian Beef Meatballs in Lettuce

Prep time: 10 minutes | Cook time: 20 minutes | Serves 8

1 pound (454 g) frozen beef meatballs
1¼ cups garlic-hoisin sauce
¼ cup soy sauce
½ cup rice vinegar
2 tablespoons brown sugar
½ tablespoon sriracha
2 tablespoons freshly squeezed lime juice
2 tablespoons cornstarch
2 tablespoons water
1 head butter lettuce

1. Place the meatballs, hoisin sauce, soy sauce, rice vinegar, brown sugar, sriracha, and lime juice in the pot and stir. Assemble pressure lid, making sure the pressure release valve is in the SEAL position.
2. Select PRESSURE and set to HI. Set the time to 20 minutes. Select START/STOP to begin.
3. When pressure cooking is complete, quick release the pressure by turning the pressure release valve to the VENT position. Carefully remove the lid when the unit has finished releasing pressure.
4. Transfer the meatballs to a serving bowl.
5. In a small bowl, mix together the cornstarch and water until smooth. Pour this mixture into the pot, whisking it into the sauce. Once sauce has thickened, pour it over the meatballs.
6. Serve the meatballs in lettuce cups with the toppings of your choice, such as sesame seeds, sliced scallions, chopped peanuts, and julienned cucumber.

Hearty Korean Meatloaf

Prep time: 15 minutes | Cook time: 30 minutes | Serves 4

1 pound (454 g) beef, pork, and veal meatloaf mix
1 large egg
1 cup panko bread crumbs
½ cup whole milk
⅓ cup minced onion
¼ cup chopped cilantro
1 garlic clove, grated
1 tablespoon grated fresh ginger
½ tablespoon fish sauce
1½ teaspoons sesame oil
1 tablespoon, plus 1 teaspoon soy sauce
¼ cup, plus 1 tablespoon gochujang
1 cup water
1 tablespoon honey

1. In a large bowl, stir together the beef, egg, bread crumbs, milk, onion, cilantro, garlic, ginger, fish sauce, sesame oil, 1 teaspoon of soy sauce, and 1 tablespoon of gochujang.
2. Place the meat mixture in the Ninja Loaf Pan or an 8½-inch loaf pan and cover tightly with aluminum foil.
3. Pour the water into the pot. Place the loaf pan on the Reversible Rack, making sure the rack is in the lower position. Place the rack with pan in the pot. Assemble pressure lid, making sure the pressure release valve is in the SEAL position.
4. Select PRESSURE and set to HI. Set time to 15 minutes. Select START/STOP to begin.
5. When pressure cooking is complete, quick release the pressure by moving the pressure release valve to the VENT position. Carefully remove lid when unit has finished releasing pressure.
6. Carefully remove the foil from the pan. Close crisping lid.
7. Select BAKE/ROAST, set temperature to 360°F (182°C), and set time to 15 minutes. Select START/STOP to begin.
8. In a small bowl stir together the remaining ¼ cup of gochujang, 1 tablespoon of soy sauce, and honey.
9. After 7 minutes, open lid and top the meatloaf with the gochujang barbecue mixture. Close lid and continue cooking.
10. When cooking is complete, open lid and remove meatloaf from the pot. Let cool for 10 minutes before serving.

Ricotta Pork Meatballs with Grits

Prep time: 15 minutes | Cook time: 26 minutes | Serves 8 to 10

2 pounds (907 g) ground pork
1 cup whole milk Ricotta cheese
2 eggs
1 cup panko bread crumbs
4 garlic cloves, minced
¼ cup parsley, minced, plus more for garnishing
1½ cups grated Parmesan cheese, divided
2 tablespoons kosher salt, divided
1 teaspoon freshly ground black pepper
2 tablespoons canola oil
4 cups whole milk
1 cup coarse ground grits

1. In a large bowl, combine the pork, Ricotta, eggs, bread crumbs, garlic, parsley, ½ cup of Parmesan, 1 tablespoon of salt, and pepper. Use your hands or a sturdy spatula to mix well.
2. Use a 3-ounce (85-g) ice cream scoop to portion the mixture into individual meatballs. Use your hands to gently form them into balls.
3. Select SEAR/SAUTÉ and set to HI. Select START/STOP to begin. Let preheat for 5 minutes.
4. Add the oil. Add half the meatballs and sear for 6 minutes, flipping them after 3 minutes. Remove from the pot and repeat with the remaining meatballs. Remove the second batch of meatballs from the pot.
5. Add the milk, grits, and remaining 1 tablespoon of salt and stir. Gently place meatballs back in the pot. They will sink slightly when placed in the milk. Assemble pressure lid, making sure pressure release valve is in the SEAL position.
6. Select PRESSURE and set to HI. Set time to 6 minutes. Select START/STOP to begin.
7. When pressure cooking is complete, quick release the pressure by moving the pressure release valve to the VENT position. Carefully remove lid when unit has finished releasing pressure.
8. Sprinkle the remaining 1 cup of Parmesan cheese over the top of the grits and meatballs. Close crisping lid.
9. Select BROIL and set time to 8 minutes. Select START/STOP to begin.
10. When cooking is complete, serve immediately.

Brisket Green Chili Verde

Prep time: 10 minutes | Cook time: 19 minutes | Serves 4

1 tablespoon vegetable oil
½ white onion, diced
1 jalapeño pepper, diced
1 teaspoon garlic, minced
1 pound (454 g) brisket, cooked
1 (19-ounce / 539-g) can green chile
    enchilada sauce
1 (4-ounce / 113-g) can fire-roasted
    diced green chiles
Juice of 1 lime
1 teaspoon seasoning salt
½ teaspoon ground chipotle pepper

1. Select SEAR/SAUTÉ and set temperature to HI. Select START/STOP to begin and allow to preheat for 5 minutes.
2. Add oil to the pot and allow to heat for 1 minute. Add the onion, jalapeño, and garlic. Sauté for 3 minutes or until onion is translucent.
3. Add the brisket, enchilada sauce, green chiles, lime juice, salt, and chipotle powder. Mix well.
4. Assemble the pressure lid, making sure the pressure release valve is in the SEAL position.
5. Select PRESSURE and set to HI. Set the time to 15 minutes. Select START/STOP to begin.
6. When cooking is complete, quick release the pressure by turning the pressure release valve to the VENT position. Carefully remove the lid when the unit has finished releasing pressure.

Pork, Bean, and Chile Pie

Prep time: 10 minutes | Cook time: 45 minutes | Serves 8

2 tablespoons extra-virgin olive oil
1 pound (454 g) ground pork
1 yellow onion, diced
1 (12-ounce / 340-g) can black beans, drained
1 cup frozen corn kernels
1 (4-ounce / 113-g) can green chiles
2 tablespoons chili powder
1 box cornbread mix
1½ cups milk
1 cup shredded Cheddar cheese

1. Select SEAR/SAUTÉ and set temperature to MED. Select START/STOP to begin. Let preheat for 3 minutes.
2. Add the olive oil, pork, and onion. Brown the pork, stirring frequently to break the meat into smaller pieces, until cooked through, about 5 minutes.
3. Add the beans, corn, chiles, and chili powder and stir. Simmer, stirring frequently, about 10 minutes.
4. In a medium bowl, combine the cornbread mix, milk, and cheese. Pour it over simmering mixture in an even layer. Close crisping lid.
5. Select BAKE/ROAST, set temperature to 360ºF (182ºC), and set time for 25 minutes. Select START/STOP to begin.
6. After 20 minutes, use wooden toothpick to check if cornbread is done. If the toothpick inserted into the cornbread does not come out clean, close lid and cook for the remaining 5 minutes.
7. When cooking is complete, open lid. Let cool for 10 minutes before slicing and serving.

Chunk and Bell Pepper Ropa Vieja

Prep time: 15 minutes | Cook time: 1 hour 25 minutes | Serves 6

2 tablespoons canola oil, divided
1 red bell pepper, thinly sliced
1 yellow bell pepper, thinly sliced
1 green bell pepper, thinly sliced
1 large onion, thinly sliced
4 garlic cloves, minced
Kosher salt
Freshly ground black pepper
2½ pounds (1.1 kg) chuck roast, cut in half
1 cup beef stock
2 bay leaves

½ cup dry white wine
1 tablespoon white vinegar
1 (16-ounce / 454-g) can crushed tomatoes
1 (8-ounce / 227-g) can tomato paste
2 teaspoons dried oregano
1½ teaspoons ground cumin
1 teaspoon paprika
⅛ teaspoon ground allspice
1 cup green olives with pimentos
Cilantro, for garnish
Lime wedges, for garnish

1. Select SEAR/SAUTÉ and set to HI. Select START/STOP to begin. Let preheat for 5 minutes.
2. Add 1 tablespoon of oil, the bell peppers, onions, and garlic, and season with salt and pepper. Cook, stirring occasionally, for about 5 minutes, or until vegetables have softened and are fragrant.
3. Liberally season the chuck with salt and pepper.
4. When the vegetables are cooked, remove and set aside.
5. Add the remaining 1 tablespoon of oil and meat. Sear the roast on both sides so that a dark crust forms, about 5 minutes per side.
6. Add the beef stock and bay leaves. Scrape the bottom of the pot with a rubber or wooden spoon to release any browned bits stuck to it. Assemble pressure lid, making sure the pressure release valve is in the SEAL position.
7. Select PRESSURE and set to HI. Set time to 40 minutes. Select START/STOP to begin.
8. When pressure cooking is complete, quick release the pressure by turning the pressure release valve to the VENT position. Carefully remove lid when unit has finished releasing pressure.
9. Carefully shred the beef in the pot using two forks.
10. Select SEAR/SAUTÉ and set to MED. Select START/STOP to begin. Add the vegetables, wine, vinegar, crushed tomatoes, tomato paste, oregano, cumin, paprika, and allspice and stir with a rubber or wooden spoon, being sure to scrape the bottom of the pot. Simmer, stirring occasionally, for about 25 minutes or until sauce has reduced and thickened.
11. Add the olives and continue cooking for 2 minutes. Serve, garnished with cilantro and lime wedges.

Advanced Smothered Pork Chops

Prepping time: 5 minutes| Cooking time: 28 minutes |For 6 servings

6 ounce of boneless pork loin chops
1 tablespoon of paprika
1 teaspoon of garlic powder
1 teaspoon of onion powder
1 teaspoon of black pepper
1 teaspoon of salt
¼ teaspoon of cayenne pepper
2 tablespoon of coconut oil
½ of a sliced medium onion
6-ounce baby Bella mushrooms, sliced
1 tablespoon of butter
½ a cup of whip cream
¼ teaspoon of xanthan gum
1 tablespoon parsley, chopped

1. Take a small bowl and add garlic powder, paprika, onion powder, black pepper, salt, and cayenne pepper. Rinse the pork chops and pat them dry
2. Sprinkle both sides with 1 teaspoon of the mixture making sure to rub the seasoning all over the meat. Reserve the remaining spice
3. Set your Ninja Foodi to Saute mode and add coconut oil, allow the oil to heat up
4. Brown the chops 3 minutes per sides. Remove and cancel the Saute mode
5. Add sliced onion to the base of your pot alongside mushrooms
6. Top with the browned pork chops. Lock up the lid and cook on HIGH pressure for 25 minutes
7. Release the pressure naturally over 10 minutes, remove the pork chops and keep them on a plate. Set your pot to Saute mode and whisk in remaining spices mix, heavy cream, and butter
8. Sprinkle ¼ teaspoon of xanthan gum and stir. Simmer for 3-5 minutes and remove the heat
9. Add a bit more xanthan gum if you require a heavier gravy
10. Top the pork chops with the gravy and sprinkle parsley. Serve!

The Big Deal Bone-y Pork Chops

Prepping time: 10 minutes| Cooking time: 13 minutes |For 4 servings

4 and ¾ thick bone-in pork chops
Salt and pepper as needed
1 cup baby carrots
1 onion, chopped
1 cup of mixed vegetables
3 tablespoons Worcestershire sauce

1. Take a bowl and add pork chops, season with pepper and salt
2. Take a skillet and place it over medium heat, add 2 teaspoons of butter and melt it
3. Toss the pork chops and brown them. Each side should take about 3-5 minutes
4. Set your Ninja Foodi to Saute mode and add 2 tablespoons of butter, add carrots and Saute them. Pour broth and Worcestershire
5. Add pork chops and lock up the lid. Cook on HIGH pressure for 13 minutes
6. Release the pressure naturally over 10 minutes. Enjoy!

Coconut And Ginger Pork Dish

Prepping time: 5 minutes| Cooking time: 45 minutes |For 6 servings

1 tablespoon avocado oil
¾ pound pork butt
1 teaspoon ground coriander
1 teaspoon ground cumin
1 teaspoon salt
1 teaspoon pepper
2-inch piece ginger, peeled and chopped
1 onion, peeled and cut
½ a can coconut milk
Lime wedges, garnish

1. Take a bowl and add coriander, salt, pepper, and cumin
2. Use your finger to rub the seasoning all over the roast
3. Coat the bottom of your Ninja Foodi with 1 tablespoon of avocado oil
4. Add the meat to the pot. Surround it with onions, ginger, garlic and a half can of coconut milk
5. Lock up the lid and cook on HIGH pressure for 45 minutes. Serve in bowls and garnish with lime
6. Enjoy!

Bacon Kale And Winning Delight

Prepping time: 5 minutes| Cooking time: 6 hours |For 6 servings

2 tablespoons bacon fat
2 pounds kale, rinsed and chopped
2 bacon slices, cooked and chopped
2 teaspoons garlic, minced
2 cups vegetable broth
Salt and pepper to taste

1. Grease inner pot of your Ninja Foodi with bacon fat
2. Add kale, garlic, bacon, and broth to insert and toss to coat
3. Cover and cook on SLOW COOK Mode (LOW for 6 hours
4. Season with salt and pepper. Serve and enjoy!

Rosemary Pork Roast

Prepping time: 5 minutes| Cooking time: 8 hours |For 6 servings

3 pounds pork shoulder roast
1 cup bone broth
6 sprigs fresh rosemary
4 sprigs basil leaves
1 tablespoon chives, chopped
¼ teaspoon ground black pepper

1. Add listed   to Ninja Foodi
2. Lock lid and cook on SLOW COOK Mode (LOW) for 8-10 hours. Serve and enjoy!

Apple And Sauerkraut Loin

Prepping time: 5 minutes| Cooking time: 50 minutes |For 6 servings

2-3 pounds pork loin roast
½ teaspoon salt
½ teaspoon fresh ground pepper
2 large onion, chopped
3 garlic cloves, chopped
2-3 cups chicken bone broth
4-6 cups sauerkraut, rinsed and drained
3 apples, peeled and cored

1. Season the roast with pepper and salt. Set your pot to Saute mode and add ghee
2. Add roast and brown on all sides. Remove the roast and keep it on the side
3. Add garlic, onion, and broth and Scrap brown bits from the Ninja Foodi
4. Return the roast to your Ninja Foodi to lock up the lid. Cook on HIGH pressure for 45 minutes
5. Perform quick release. Add sauerkraut, apple to the cooker
6. Lock up the lid and cook on HIGH pressure for 5 minutes longer
7. Quick release the pressure. Slice the roast and serve with the sauce. Enjoy!

Bacon And Brussels Platter

Prepping time: 10 minutes| Cooking time: 5 minutes |For 4 servings

5 bacon slices, chopped
6 cups Brussels sprouts, chopped
¼ teaspoon salt
Pepper as needed
2 tablespoons water
2 tablespoons balsamic vinegar

1. Set your Ninja Foodi to Saute mode and add chopped bacon, Saute until crispy
2. Add chopped Brussels sprouts and stir well to coat it
3. Add water and sprinkle a bit of salt
4. Lock up the lid and cook on HIGH pressure for 4-6 minutes
5. Release the pressure naturally
6. Set your pot to Saute mode and Saute the Brussels for a while longer
7. Transfer to serving the dish
8. Drizzle balsamic vinegar on top and enjoy!

Lemon And Pork Chops Artichokes

Prepping time: 10 minutes| Cooking time: 24 minutes |For 4 servings

2 tablespoons clarified butter
2 pieces 2-inch thick bone-in pork chops
3 ounces pancetta, diced
2 teaspoons ground black pepper
1 medium shallot, minced
4 lemon zest strips, 2-inch size
1 teaspoon dried rosemary
2 teaspoons garlic, minced
1 box (9 ounces box frozen artichoke heart,
    quarters
¼ cup chicken broth

1. Set your pot to Saute mode and add pancetta, cook for 5 minutes
2. Transfer the browned pancetta to a plate and season your chops with pepper
3. Add the chops to your pot and cook for 4 minutes
4. Transfer the chops to a plate and keep repeating until they all of them are browned
5. Add shallots to the pot and cook for 1 minute
6. Add lemon zest, garlic, rosemary, and garlic, and stir until aromatic
7. After a while, stir in broth and artichokes. Return the pancetta back to the cooker
8. return the chops to your pot
9. Lock up the lid and let it cook for about 24 minutes at high pressure
10. Release pressure quickly. Unlock and transfer the chops to a carving board
11. Slice up the eye of your meat off the bone and slice the meat into strips
12. Divide in serving bowls and sauce ladled up

Simple Pressure Cooked Lamb Meat

Prepping time: 5 minutes |Cooking time: 55 minutes |For 4 servings

2 tablespoons butter
½ teaspoon turmeric powder
1 pound ground lamb meat
1 cup onions, chopped
1 teaspoon salt
1 tablespoon garlic, minced
½ teaspoon ground coriander
½ teaspoon cayenne pepper
1 tablespoon ginger, minced
½ teaspoon cumin powder

1. Set your Ninja Foodi to Saute mode and add garlic, ginger, and onions
2. Saute for 3 minutes and add ground meat, spices
3. Lock lid and cook on HIGH pressure for 20 minutes
4. Release pressure naturally over 10 minutes.Serve and enjoy!

Sassy Evergreen Pork Chops

Prepping time: 10 minutes| Cooking time: 4 hours |For 4 servings

6-8 boneless pork chops
¼ cup arrowroot flour
2 teaspoons dry mustard
1 teaspoon garlic powder
1 and ½ cups beef stock
Cooking fat
Salt and pepper to taste

1. Take a bowl and add flour, garlic powder, black pepper, dry mustard and salt
2. Coat the pork chop with the mixture and keep any extra flour on the side
3. Take a skillet and place it over medium-high heat. Add cooking fat and allow the fat to melt
4. Brown the chops for 1-2 minutes per side and transfer to your Ninja Foodi
5. Add beef stock to the flour mixture and mix well
6. Pour the beef stock mix to the chops and place lid
7. Cook on SLOW COOK MODE (HIGH) for 3 hours. Enjoy!

The Pork "Loin" With Pear

Prepping time: 5 minutes| Cooking time: 12 minutes |For 4 servings

2 tablespoons clarified butter
4 pieces ½ inch thick bone-in pork loin
½ teaspoon salt
½ teaspoon pepper
2 medium yellow onion, peeled and cut up into 8 wedges
2 large Bosc pears, peeled and cored, cut into 4 wedges
½ cup unsweetened pear, cider
½ teaspoon ground allspice
Dash of hot pepper

1. Set your Ninja Foodi to Saute mode and add 1 tablespoon of butter, allow the butter to melt
2. Add chops and Saute for 4 minutes
3. Transfer the chops to a plate and cook the remaining and brown them
4. Add onion and pears in the pot and allow them to Saute for 3 minutes more until the pears are slightly browned. Pour cider and stir in allspice, pepper sauce
5. Nestle the chops back. Lock up the lid and cook on HIGH pressure for 10 minutes
6. Perform quick release. Serve over rice!

Creative Garlic And Butter Pork

Prepping time: 5 minutes + marinate time |Cooking time: 40 minutes |For 4 servings

1 tablespoon coconut butter
1 tablespoon coconut oil
2 teaspoons garlic cloves, grated
2 teaspoons parsley
Salt and pepper to taste
4 pork chops, sliced into strips

1. Add listed   to Pork Strips and mix well
2. Marinate for 1 hour. Transfer pork to Ninja Foodi
3. Lock Crisping Lid and Air Crisp for 10 minutes at 400 degrees F. Serve and enjoy!

Elegant Lamb Spare Ribs

Prepping time: 4-5 hours|Cooking time: 20 minutes |For 4 servings

For the Lamb

2.5 pounds of pastured lamb spare ribs
2 teaspoons of kosher salt
1 tablespoon of curry powder

For the sauce

1 t tablespoon of coconut oil
1 large sized coarsely chopped onion
½ a pound of minced garlic
1 tablespoon of curry powder
1 tablespoon of kosher salt
Juice from about 1 lemon
1 and a 1/4th cup of divided cilantro
4 thinly sliced scallion

1. Take a bowl and add spare ribs
2. Season with 2 teaspoons of salt, 1 teaspoon of curry powder and mix well making sure that the ribs are coated fully. Cover it up and allow them to chill for 4 hours
3. Cover it up and let them freeze for at least 4 hours
4. Set your Ninja Foodi to Saute mode and add coconut oil and allow it to heat up
5. Add spare ribs and allow them to brown. Once done, transfer them to another plate
6. Take a blender and add tomatoes and onion and blend them well to a paste
7. Add the minced garlic to your Ninja Foodi (still in Saute mode)
8. Keep stirring the garlic while carefully pouring the prepared paste
9. Add curry powder, chopped up cilantro, salt, and lemon juice
10. Allow the whole mixture to come to a boil. Add spare ribs and stir until it is coated well
11. Lock up the lid and cook for 20 minutes at HIGH pressure
12. Allow the pressure to release naturally once done.Scoop out the grease and season with some salt. Enjoy!

Cool Lamb Tajine

Prepping time: 5 minutes| Cooking time: 50 minutes |For 6 servings

2 and a /13 pound of lamb shoulder
1 teaspoon of cinnamon powder
1 teaspoon of ginger powder
1 teaspoon of turmeric powder
2 cloves of crushed garlic
3 tablespoon of olive oil
10 ounce of prunes pitted and soaked
1 cup of vegetable stock
2 medium roughly sliced onion
1 piece of bay leaf
1 stick of cinnamon
1 teaspoon of pepper
1 and a ½ teaspoon of salt
3 and a ½ ounce of almonds
1 tablespoon of sesame seeds

1. Take a bowl and add ground cinnamon, ginger, turmeric, garlic and 2 spoons of olive oil
2. Make a paste. Cover the lamb with the paste
3. Take a bowl and add dried prunes with boiling water and cover, keep it on the side
4. Set your Ninja Foodi to Saute mode and add olive oil. Add onion and cook for 3 minutes
5. Transfer the onion to a bowl and keep it on the side
6. Add meat and brown all sides for about 10 minutes. Deglaze using vegetable stock
7. Add onions, cinnamon stick, bay leaf.Lock up the lid and cook on HIGH pressure for 35 minutes
8. Release the pressure naturally. Add rinsed and drained prunes and set the pot to Saute mode
9. Reduce the liquid by simmer for 5 minutes
10. Discard the bay leaf and sprinkle toasted almonds alongside sesame seeds. Enjoy

Pork And Cauliflower Dish

Prepping time: 10 minutes| Cooking time: 65 minutes |For 4 servings

1 onion, chopped
4 cloves garlic, crushed and minced
4 cups cauliflower, chopped
2 ribs celery
Salt and pepper to taste
3-pound pork roast
8 ounces mushrooms, sliced
2 tablespoons coconut oil
2 tablespoons ghee

1. Add onion, garlic, cauliflower, celery to Ninja Foodi
2. Put pork roast on top. Season with salt and pepper
3. Add 2 cups of water. Lock lid and cook on HIGH pressure 60 minutes
4. Quick release pressure. Transfer roast to baking pan
5. Add pan to oven and bake for 5 minutes at 400 degrees F
6. Prepare gravy by transfer the remaining contents from the pot to a blender
7. Blend until smooth. Set your pot to Saute mode and add coconut oil and ghee
8. Add mushrooms and blended mixture. Cook for 5 minutes
9. Serve pot roast with mushroom gravy and enjoy!

Lime And Ginger Low Carb Pork

Prepping time: 10 minutes| Cooking time:4-7 hours |For 4 servings

1 tablespoon avocado oil
2 and ½ pounds pork loin
Salt and pepper to taste
1 teaspoon stevia drops
¼ cup tamari
1 tablespoon Worcestershire sauce
Juice of 1 lime
2 garlic cloves, minced
1 tablespoon fresh ginger
Fresh cilantro

1. Set your Ninja Foodi to Saute mode and add oil, let the oil heat up
2. Season pork with salt and pepper and add to the pot
3. Take a bowl and whisk in remaining   except for cilantro and pour it over pork
4. Lock lid and cook on SLOW COOK mode. Cook for 4-7 hours on HIGH pressure
5. Naturally, release pressure over 10 minutes. Garnish with cilantro. Serve and enjoy!

Generous Indian Lamb Shanks

Prepping time: 5 minutes| Cooking time: 45 minutes |For 5 servings

3 pounds lamb shanks
Salt as needed
Fresh ground pepper as needed
2 tablespoons ghee
2 onion, chopped
2 celery, chopped
1 large onion, chopped
1 tablespoon tomato paste
3 garlic cloves, peeled and mashed
1 cup bone broth
1 teaspoon red boat fish sauce
1 tablespoon vinegar

1. Season the shanks with pepper and salt
2. Set your pot to Saute mode and add ghee, allow the ghee to melt and heat up
3. Add shanks and cook for 8-10 minutes until a nice brown texture appears
4. In the meantime, chop the vegetables
5. Once you have a nice brown texture on your lamb, remove it from the Instant Pot and keep it on the side. Add vegetables and season with salt and pepper
6. Add a tablespoon of ghee and mix
7. Add vegetables, garlic clove, tomato paste and give it a nice stir
8. Add shanks and pour broth, vinegar, fish sauce. Sprinkle a bit of pepper and lock up the lid
9. Cook on HIGH pressure for 45 minutes. Release the pressure naturally over 10 minutes
10. Serve the shanks and enjoy!

Greek Lamb Gyros

Prepping time: 5 minutes |Cooking time: 25 minutes |For 4 servings

8 garlic cloves
1 and ½ teaspoon salt
2 teaspoons dried oregano
1 and ½ cups of water
2 pounds lamb meat, ground
2 teaspoons rosemary
½ teaspoon pepper
1 small onion, chopped
2 teaspoons ground marjoram

1. Add onion, garlic, marjoram, rosemary, salt and pepper to food processor and process
2. Add ground lamb meat and process again. Press meat mixture into pan
3. Transfer loaf to Ninja Foodi and "BAKE/ROAST" for 25 minutes at 375 degrees f
4. Serve and enjoy!

Pork Dish With Coconut Added In

Prepping time: 10 minutes| Cooking time: 4 hours |For 4 servings

2 tablespoons coconut oil
4 pounds boneless pork shoulder, cut into 2-inch pieces
Salt and pepper to taste
1 large onion, chopped
3 tablespoons garlic cloves, minced
3 tablespoons fresh ginger, minced
1 tablespoon curry powder
1 tablespoon ground cumin
½ teaspoon ground turmeric
1 cup unsweetened coconut milk
Chopped cilantro, green onions for garnish

1. Take a large sized skillet and add coconut oil
2. Allow it to heat up and add pork in batches, brown them and season with a bit of salt and pepper. Transfer to a Ninja Foodi
3. Making sure that there are 2 tablespoons of the worth of fat in the skillet, add onion, garlic, ginger, cumin, curry, turmeric and cook over low heat for 5 minutes
4. Add the mix to your Ninja Foodi and place the lid
5. Cook on SLOW COOK MODE (LOW) for 4 hours
6. Serve with a garnish of cilantro and scallions. Enjoy!

Tastiest Pork Cheek Stew

Prepping time: 10 minutes| Cooking time: 45 minutes |For 4 servings

4 pounds of pork cheeks
2 tablespoons avocado oil
1 and ½ cups of chicken broth
8 ounces cremini mushrooms
1 large leek, cut into ½ inch chunks
1 small onion, diced
6 garlic cloves, peeled
1 teaspoon salt
Juice of ½ lemon

1. Set your Ninja Foodi to Saute mode and add oil
2. Cut up the cheeks into 2 x 3 inch even pieces and add them to the Pot
3. Sear them until nicely browned
4. Pour broth over the browned cheeks alongside mushroom, onion, leek, garlic, sea salt
5. Lock up the lid and cook on HIGH pressure for 45 minutes
6. Release the pressure naturally and shred the meat. Stir the meat well with the sauce and serve!

Veal And Rosemary Stew

Prepping time: 10 minutes| Cooking time: 20 minutes |For 4 servings

2 sprigs rosemary
1 tablespoon olive oil
1 tablespoon butter
8 ounces shallots
2 carrots, chopped
2 stalks celery, chopped
2 tablespoons almond flour
3 pounds veal
Water as needed
2 teaspoon salt

1. Set the Ninja Foodi to Saute mode and add olive oil, allow the oil to heat up
2. Add butter and chopped rosemary and stir. Add celery, shallots, carrots and Saute for a while
3. Shove the veggies on the side and add the meat cubes, brown them slightly and pour just enough stock to gently cover them
4. Lock up the lid and cook on 20 minutes on HIGH pressure
5. Release the pressure naturally over 10 minutes
6. Open and set the pot to Saute mode, allow it to simmer. Enjoy!

Keto – Suitable Steamed Pork

Prepping time: 5 minutes| Cooking time: 45 minutes |For 4 servings

2 boneless pork chops
2 tablespoons fresh orange juice
2 cups of water
¼ teaspoon ground cloves
¼ teaspoon ground coriander
¼ teaspoon cinnamon, ground
1 pinch cayenne pepper

1. Add listed   to Ziploc bag and let them marinate for 2 hours
2. Place a reversible rack inside the pot and attach Crisping Lid
3. Pour water into a pot and place marinated meat on the rack
4. Lock lid and STEAM for 45 minutes
5. Serve and enjoy!

Refined Carrot And Bacon Soup

Prepping time: 10 minutes| Cooking time: 4 minutes |For 4 servings

2 pounds carrots, peeled
4 cups broth
½ cup yellow onion, chopped
½ pack bacon cut into ¼ inch pieces
½ cup apple cider vinegar
½ cup white vinegar

1. Set your Ninja Foodi to Saute mode and add butter, allow the butter to melt and add bacon and onion, Saute for a while. Slice 1 -2 heirloom carrots thinly and add them to a small bowl
2. Add vinegar to cover them, allow them to pickle
3. Chop the remaining carrots into inch long pieces
4. Add chopped carrots and broth to your Instant Pot
5. Lock up the lid and cook on HIGH pressure for 4 minutes. Perform a natural release
6. Use an immersion blender break down the carrots until you have a smooth mix
7. Stir in onions and bacon, salt and apple cider vinegar. Serve and enjoy!

Lovely Pulled Pork Ragu

Prepping time: 10 minutes| Cooking time: 45 minutes |For 4 servings

18 ounce of pork tenderloin
1 teaspoon of kosher salt
Black pepper as needed
1 teaspoon of olive oil
5 cloves of garlic
1 can of 28-ounce tomatoes, crushed
1 small sized jar of roasted red peppers
2 sprigs of thyme
2 pieces of bay leaves
1 tablespoon fresh parsley, chopped

1. Set your Ninja Foodi to Saute mode. Season the pork with pepper and salt
2. Add oil to your pot and allow the oil to heat up. Add garlic and Saute for 1 and a ½ minute
3. Remove with a slotted spoon. Add pork and brown for 2 minutes on both sides
4. Add the remaining   and garlic (make sure to reserve half of the kale for later use)
5. Lock up the lid and cook on HIGH pressure for 45 minutes
6. Naturally, release the pressure over 10 minutes and discard the bay leaves
7. Shred the pork using a fork and garnish with parsley. Enjoy!

The Calabacita Squash meal

Prepping time: 10 minutes| Cooking time: 90 minutes |For 4 servings

1 pork tenderloin
1 tablespoon of chili powder
1 tablespoon of ground cumin
1 tablespoon of garlic powder
1 and a ½ teaspoon of salt
1 tablespoon of butter/ghee
14 ounce of tomatoes, diced
6 Calabacita squash, deseeded

For the chipotle cream sauce

1/3 cup of canola-oil free mayo
3 tablespoon of fresh lime juice
1 and a ½ a teaspoon of chipotle/ chili powder

1. Prepare the tenderloin by dusting it with half of the chili powder, garlic, cumin and salt
2. Set your Ninja Foodi to Saute mode and add butter, allow the butter to melt
3. Add seasoned pork and sear all sides for 3-4 minutes until browned
4. Add 4-6 cups of water and lock up the lid
5. Cook on MEAT mode at default settings and release the pressure naturally over 10 minutes
6. Transfer the pork to a large mixing bowl and shred it into small pieces
7. Add canned tomatoes and remaining spice to the bowl. Stir well
8. Spread the deseeded squash into a large rimmed baking sheet with the cut side facing up
9. Stuff the squash with the pork mixture and bake for 45 minutes at 350 degrees Fahrenheit
10. Prepare the sauce by mixing the sauce
11. Pour the sauce on top of the pork and garnish with cilantro. Serve and enjoy!

Beef And Broccoli Platter

Prepping time: 10 minutes| Cooking time: 20 minutes |For 4 servings

3 pounds beef chuck roast, cut into thin strips
1 tablespoon olive oil
1 yellow onion, peeled and chopped
½ cup beef stock
1 pound broccoli florets
2 teaspoons toasted sesame oil
2 tablespoons arrowroot

For Marinade
1 cup coconut aminos
1 tablespoon sesame oil
2 tablespoons fish sauce
5 garlic cloves, peeled and minced
3 red peppers, dried and crushed
½ teaspoon Chinese five spice powder
Toasted sesame seeds, for serving

1. Take a bowl and mix in coconut aminos, fish sauce, 1 tablespoon sesame oil, garlic, five spice powder, crushed red pepper and stir
2. Add beef strips to the bowl and toss to coat. Keep it on the side for 10 minutes
3. Set your Ninja Foodi to "Saute" mode and add oil, let it heat up, add onion and stir cook for 4 minutes. Add beef and marinade, stir cook for 2 minutes. Add stock and stir
4. Lock the pressure lid of Ninja Foodi and cook on HIGH pressure for 5 minutes
5. Release pressure naturally over 10 minutes
6. Mix arrowroot with ¼ cup liquid from the pot and gently pour the mixture back to the pot and stir
7. Place a steamer basket in the pot and add broccoli to the steamer rack, lock lid and cook on HIGH pressure for 3 minutes more, quick release pressure
8. Divide the dish between plates and serve with broccoli, toasted sesame seeds and enjoy!

Alternative Corned Cabbage And Beef

Prepping time: 10 minutes| Cooking time: 100 minutes |For 4 servings

1 corned beef brisket
4 cups of water
1 small onion, peeled and quartered
3 garlic cloves, smashed and peeled
2 bay leaves
3 whole black peppercorns
½ teaspoon allspice berries
1 teaspoon dried thyme
5 medium carrots
1 cabbage, cut into wedges

1. Add corned beef, onion, garlic cloves, water, allspice, peppercorn, thymes to the Ninja Foodi
2. Lock up the lid and cook for about 90 minutes at HIGH pressure
3. Allow the pressure to release naturally once done . Open up and transfer the meat to your serving plate. Cover it with tin foil and allow it to cool for 15 minutes
4. Add carrots and cabbage to the lid and let them cook for 10 minutes at HIGH pressure
5. Once done, do a quick release . Take out the prepped veggies and serve with your corned beef

Marked Beef Goulash

Prepping time: 10 minutes| Cooking time: 15-20 minutes |For 4 servings

1-2 pounds extra lean beef, ground
2 teaspoons olive oil + 11 teaspoons extra
1 large red bell pepper, stemmed and seeded
1 large onion, cut into short strips
1 tablespoon garlic, minced
2 tablespoons sweet paprika
½ teaspoon hot paprika
4 cups beef stock
2 cans tomatoes, diced and petite

1. Set your Ninja Foodi to Saute mode and add 2 teaspoons of olive oil
2. Add ground beef to the pot and cook, making sure to stir it until it breaks apart
3. Once the beef is browned, transfer it to a bowl. Cut the steam off the pepper and deseed them and cut into strips. Cut the onion into short strips as well
4. Add a teaspoon of olive oil to the pot alongside pepper and onion
5. Saute for 3-4 minutes.Add minced garlic, sweet paprika, hot paprika and cook for 2-3 minutes
6. Add beef stock alongside the tomatoes. Add ground beef
7. Allow it to cook for about 15 minutes on Soup mode over the low pressure
8. Once done, quick release the pressure and have fun!

Lemon Delicious Pork Chop

Prepping time: 10 minutes| Cooking time: 5 minutes |For 4 servings

½ cup hot sauce
½ cup of water
2 tablespoons butter
1/3 cup lemon juice
1 pound pork cutlets
½ teaspoon paprika

1. Add listed   to your Ninja Foodi cook and crisp basket, place the basket inside
2. Lock lid and cook on HIGH pressure for 5 minutes, release pressure naturally over 10 minutes
3. Gently stir and serve, enjoy!

Meat Dredged Loaf

Prepping time: 10 minutes| Cooking time: 1 hour 10 minutes |For 6 servings

½ cup onion, chopped
2 garlic cloves, minced
¼ cup sugar-free ketchup
1 pound grass fed lean ground beef
½ cup green bell pepper, seeded and chopped
1 cup cheddar cheese, grated
2 organic eggs, beaten
1 teaspoon dried thyme, crushed
3 cups fresh spinach, chopped
6 cups mozzarella cheese, freshly grated
Black pepper to taste

1. Take a bowl and add all of the listed   except cheese and spinach
2. Place a wax paper on a smooth surface and arrange the meat over it
3. Top with spinach, cheese and roll the paper around the paper to form a nice meatloaf
4. Remove wax paper and transfer loaf to your Ninja Foodi
5. Lock lid and select "Bake/Roast" mode, setting the timer to 70 minutes and temperature to 380 degrees F. Let it bake and take the dish out once done. Serve and enjoy!

The Chipotle Copycat Dish

Prepping time: 5 minutes| Cooking time: 90 minutes |For 6 servings

3 pounds grass-fed chuck roast, large chunks
1 large onion, peeled and sliced
6 garlic cloves
2 cans (14.5 ounces green chilies
1 tablespoon oregano
1 teaspoon salt and pepper
3 dried chipotle pepper, stems removed, broken into small pieces
Juice of 3 limes
3 tablespoons coconut vinegar
1 tablespoon cumin
½ cup of water

1. Add the listed   to your Ninja Foodi
2. Stir and lock up the lid, cook on HIGH pressure for 60 minutes
3. Release the pressure naturally over 10 minutes . Remove the lid and shred using a fork
4. Set your pot to Saute mode and reduce for 30 minutes . Enjoy once ready!

All-Buttered Up Beef

Prepping time: 5 minutes| Cooking time: 60 minutes |For 6 servings

3 pounds beef roast
1 tablespoon olive oil
2 tablespoons Keto-Friendly ranch dressing
1 jar pepper rings, with juices
8 tablespoons butter
1 cup of water

1. Set your Ninja Foodi to Saute mode and add 1 tablespoon of oil
2. Once the oil is hot, add roast and sear both sides
3. Set the Saute off and add water, seasoning mix, reserved juice, and pepper rings on top of your beef. Lock up the lid and cook on HIGH pressure for 60 minutes
4. Release the pressure naturally over 10 minutes. Cut the beef with salad sheers and serve with pureed cauliflower. Enjoy!

Beef And Broccoli Delight

Prepping time: 5 minutes| Cooking time:6-8 hours |For 6 servings

1 and ½ pounds beef round steak, cut into 2 inches by 1/8 inch strips
1 cup broccoli, diced
½ teaspoon red pepper flakes
2 teaspoon garlic, minced
2 teaspoons olive oil
2 tablespoons apple cider vinegar
2 tablespoons coconut aminos
2 tablespoons white wine vinegar
1 tablespoons arrowroot
¼ cup beef broth

1. Take a large sized bowl and make the sauce by mixing in red pepper flakes, olive oil, coconut aminos, garlic, white wine vinegar, apple cider vinegar, broth and arrowroot
2. Mix well. Add the mix to your Ninja Foodi. Add beef and place a lid
3. Cook on SLOW COOK MODE (LOW) for 6-8 hours
4. Uncover just 30 minutes before end time and add broccoli, lock lid again and let it finish
5. Serve and enjoy!

Rich Beef Rendang

Prepping time: 5 minutes| Cooking time: 25 minutes |For 6 servings

1 cup onion, chopped
1 tablespoon ginger, chopped
1 tablespoon garlic, minced
1 small jalapeno pepper
2 tablespoons olive oil
1 pack rendang curry paste
1 pound skirt steak, cut into 2 inch chunks
½ cup of water
1 cup coconut milk (full fat)
2 tablespoons coconut, shredded

1. Mince the onion, garlic, and ginger. Set your Ninja Foodi to Saute mode and add oil
2. Allow the oil to heat up and add veggies and stir them well. Add rending paste and stir for 3-4 minutes. Add skirt steak and stir to coat with the spices for about 2 minutes
3. Pour ¼ cup of water and deglazed. Lock up the lid and cook on HIGH pressure for 25 minutes
4. Release the pressure naturally over 10 minutes . Add ½ a cup of coconut milk and stir
5. Garnish with shredded coconut and serve!

Spiritual Indian Beef Dish

Prepping time: 15 minutes| Cooking time: 20 minutes |For 4 servings

½ yellow onion, chopped
1 tablespoon olive oil
2 garlic cloves, minced
1 jalapeno pepper, chopped
1 cup cherry tomatoes, quartered
1 teaspoon fresh lemon juice
1-2 pounds grass-fed ground beef
1-2 pounds fresh collard greens, trimmed and chopped

Spices

1 teaspoon cumin, ground
½ teaspoon ginger, ground
1 teaspoon coriander, ground
½ teaspoon fennel seeds, ground
½ teaspoon cinnamon, ground
Salt and pepper to taste
½ teaspoon turmeric, ground

1. Set your Ninja Foodi to sauté mode and add garlic, onions
2. sauté for 3 minutes. Add jalapeno pepper, beef, and spices
3. Lock lid and cook on Medium-HIGH pressure for 15 minutes
4. Release pressure naturally over 10 minutes, open lid
5. Add tomatoes, collard greens and sauté for 3 minutes
6. Stir in lemon juice, salt, and pepper. Stir well
7. Once the dish is ready, transfer the dish to your serving bowl and enjoy!

Premium Mexican Beef Dish

Prepping time: 5 minutes| Cooking time: 12 minutes |For 4 servings

2 and ½ pounds boneless beef short ribs
1 tablespoon chili powder
1 and ½ teaspoons salt
1 tablespoon fat
1 medium onion, thinly sliced
1 tablespoon tomato sauce
6 garlic cloves, peeled and smashed
½ cup roasted tomato salsa
½ cup bone broth
Fresh ground black pepper
½ cup cilantro, minced
2 radishes, sliced

1. Take a large sized bowl and add the cubed beef, salt, and chili powder, give it a nice mix
2. Set your Ninja Foodi to Saute mode and add butter, allow it to melt
3. Add garlic and tomato paste and Saute for 30 seconds. Add seasoned beef, stock and fish sauce
4. Lock up the lid and cook on HIGH pressure for 35 minutes on MEAT/STEW mode
5. Release the pressure naturally over 10 minutes . Season with some salt and pepper and enjoy!

All-Tim Favorite Beef Chili

Prepping time: 10 minutes| Cooking time: 40 minutes |For 4 servings

1 and ½ pounds ground beef
1 sweet onion, peeled and chopped
Salt and pepper to taste
28 ounces canned tomatoes, diced
17 ounces beef stock
6 garlic clove, peeled and chopped
7 jalapeno peppers, diced
2 tablespoons olive oil
4 carrots, peeled and chopped
3 tablespoons chili powder
1 bay leaf
1 teaspoon chili powder

1. Set your Ninja Foodi to "Saute" mode and add half of the oil, let it heat up
2. Add beef and stir brown for 8 minutes, transfer to a bowl
3. Add remaining oil to the pot and let it heat up, add carrots, onion, jalapenos, garlic and stir Saute for 4 minutes. Add tomatoes and stir
4. Add bay leaf, stock, chili powder, chili powder, salt, pepper, and beef, stir and lock lid
5. Cook on HIGH pressure for 25 minutes . Release pressure naturally over 10 minutes
6. Stir the chili and serve. Enjoy!

Ingenious Bo Kho

Prepping time: 5 minutes| Cooking time: 45 minutes |For 6 servings

½ teaspoon ghee
2 and ½ pounds grass-fed beef brisket
1 yellow onion, peeled and diced
1 and ½ teaspoon curry powder
2 and ½ tablespoons fresh ginger, peeled
2 cups tomatoes, drained and crushed
3 tablespoons red boat fish sauce
1 large stalk lemongrass
2 whole star anise
1 bay leaf
1 cup bone broth

1. Set your Ninja Foodi to Saute mode and add ghee
2. Allow it to melt. Add briskets. Keep frying them until they have a nice brown texture
3. Remove the brisket and add onion and Saute them
4. Add curry powder, ginger, seared beef, fish sauce, star anise, diced tomatoes
5. Stir well and add bay leaf and lemongrass. Pour broth and lock up the lid
6. Cook for 35 minutes at HIGH pressure. Allow the pressure to release naturally
7. Add carrots . Cook for another 7 minutes at HIGH pressure
8. Release the pressure naturally. Serve hot!

Sesame Beef Ribs

Prepping time: 10 minutes| Cooking time: 60 minutes |For 6 servings

1 tablespoon sesame oil
2 garlic cloves, peeled and smashed
Knob fresh ginger, peeled and finely chopped
1 pinch red pepper flakes
¼ cup white wine vinegar
2/3 cup coconut aminos
2/3 cup beef stock
4 pounds beef ribs, chopped in half
2 tablespoons arrowroot
1-2 tablespoons water

1. Set your Ninja Foodi to Saute mode and add sesame oil, garlic, ginger, red pepper flakes and Saute for 1 minute. Deglaze pot with vinegar and mix in coconut aminos and beef stock
2. Add ribs to the pot and coat them well. Lock lid and cook on HIGH pressure for 60 minutes
3. Release pressure naturally over 10 minutes . Remove the ribs and keep them on the side
4. Take a small bowl and mix in arrowroot and water, stir and mix in the liquid into the pot, set the pot to Saute mode and cook until the liquid reaches your desired consistency
5. Put the ribs under a broiler to brown them slightly (also possible to do this in the Ninja Foodi using the Air Crisping lid) . Serve ribs with the cooking liquid. Enjoy!

Balsamic Pot Roast Of Beef

Prepping time: 10 minutes| Cooking time: 55 minutes |For 4 servings

1 teaspoon of each pepper and garlic powder
1 tablespoon kosher salt
1 (3 pounds boneless chuck roast
¼ cup balsamic vinegar
½ cup onion, chopped
2 cups of water
¼ teaspoon xanthan game
For garnish, chopped parsley

1. Slice roast in half and season with garlic powder, salt, and pepper
2. Set your Ninja Foodi to Saute mode and add meat, brown the meat
3. Add onion and pour water and vinegar. Lock lid and cook on HIGH pressure for 35 minutes
4. Release pressure naturally over 10 minutes. Transfer meat to a container and break it apart, discard fat. Set your pot to Saute mode and simmer the cooking liquid
5. Whisk in xanthan gum to the Pot and transfer back the chicken. Stir
6. Cancel Saute mode. Garnish and enjoy!

Extremely Satisfying Beef Curry

Prepping time: 10 minutes| Cooking time: 20 minutes |For 4 servings

2 pounds beef steak, cubed
2 tablespoons extra virgin olive oil
1 tablespoon Dijon mustard
2 and ½ tablespoons curry powder
2 yellow onions, peeled and chopped
2 garlic cloves, peeled and minced
10 ounces canned coconut milk
2 tablespoons tomato sauce
Salt and pepper to taste

1. Set your Ninja Foodi to "Saute" mode and add oil, let it heat up
2. Add onions, garlic, stir cook for 4 minutes. Add mustard, stir and cook for 1 minute
3. Add beef and stir until all sides are browned
4. Add curry powder, salt, and pepper, stir cook for 2 minutes
5. Add coconut milk and tomato sauce, stir, and cove
6. Lock lid and cook on HIGH pressure for 10 minutes
7. Release pressure naturally over 10 minutes. Serve and enjoy!

Braised Up Bone Short Ribs

Prepping time: 10 minutes| Cooking time: 35 minutes |For 4 servings

4 pounds beef short ribs
A generous amount of kosher salt
1 tablespoon beef fat
1 onion, skin on, quartered
3 garlic cloves
Water as needed

1. Season the ribs generously with salt
2. Take a skillet and heat up the beef oil over medium-high. Toss in the ribs and gently cook them until browned. Once browned, toss in the garlic, onion and about 2 inches of water.
3. Once mixed, transfer the mixture to the instant pot
4. Lock lid and cook on HIGH pressure for 35 minutes . Release pressure naturally over 10 minutes
5. Once the ribs complete, serve the dish with the dish on the bone
6. Alternatively, you can also pull the meat from the bones and braise the liquid and skim the fat. Store them in a jar and serve the ribs with the broth making sure to season them well.

The Authentic Beef Casserole

Prepping time: 10 minutes| Cooking time: 8 hours |For 4 servings

½ cabbage, roughly sliced
1 onion, diced
3 cloves garlic, chopped
1 and ½ pounds ground beef
2 cups cauliflower rice
4 tablespoons Ghee
1 heaping tablespoon Italian seasoning
½ teaspoon crushed red pepper
Salt and pepper to taste
½ cup fresh parsley, chopped

1. Add the listed   to your Ninja Foodi (except parsley) and give it a nice stir
2. Place lid and cook on SLOW COOK MODE (LOW) for 7-8 hours until the beef is cooked
3. Stir in parsley and serve. Enjoy!

The Great Pepper Steak

Prepping time: 5 minutes| Cooking time: 20 minutes |For 6 servings

1 pound boneless Beef Eye, Round Steak
80 ounces mushrooms, sliced
1 red pepper, sliced
1 tablespoon garlic, minced
1 pack onion soup mix
1 tablespoon sesame oil
1 cup of water

1. Add the listed   to your Ninja Foodi
2. Lock up the lid and cook on HIGH pressure for 20 minutes
3. Release the pressure naturally over 10 minutes
4. Serve the pepper steak and enjoy!

The Ground Beef Root Chili

Prepping time: 5 minutes| Cooking time: 10 minutes |For 6 servings

10 ounce of sliced beets
1 cup of cooked ground beef
1 and a 1/3 cup of diced carrot
1 and 1/3 cups of peeled and diced sweet potato
10 and a 2/3 ounce of pumpkin
1 teaspoon of dried rosemary
1 teaspoon of sea salt
2 teaspoon of dried basil
2/3 teaspoon of cinnamon
13 and a 1/3 of beef bone broth
1 and a 1/3 tablespoon of Apple Cider Vinegar

1. Add beets to a food processor and puree. Transfer the beets to your Ninja Foodi
2. Add the rest of the   . Lock up the lid and cook on HIGH pressure for 10 minutes
3. Release the pressure naturally over 10 minutes. Enjoy!

Ground Beef With Green Beans

Prepping time: 5 minutes| Cooking time: 30 minutes |For 6 servings

1 teaspoon olive oil
1 pound lean ground beef
1 medium onion, chopped
1 tablespoon garlic, minced
1 teaspoon thyme
1 teaspoon oregano
½ pound green beans, ends
    trimmed and cut into 1-inch pieces
2 cans (14.5 ounces diced tomatoes, with juice
Salt and pepper to taste
Fresh parmesan for serving

1. Set your Ninja Foodi to Saute mode and add oil, allow the oil to heat up
2. Add ground beef and stir well as it cooks
3. Once the beef is browned up, add chopped onion, dried thyme, minced garlic, dried oregano and cook for 3 minutes. Add petite-dice tomatoes alongside the juice and beef broth
4. Allow them to heat for a while. Trim the beans on both ends and cut into 1-inch pieces
5. Add beans to your pot. Lock up the lid and cook on SLOW COOK (LOW) mode for 30 minutes
6. Perform a quick release . Season with salt and pepper
7. Serve freshly with a grating of parmesan. Enjoy!

Delicious Tomatillo Beef And Pork Chili

Prepping time: 5 minutes| Cooking time: 35 minutes |For 6 servings

1 pound ground beef
1 pound ground pork
3 tomatillos, chopped
1 teaspoon garlic powder
1 jalapeno pepper
1 tablespoon ground cumin
1 tablespoon chili powder
Salt as needed

1. Set your Ninja Foodi to Saute mode and add beef and pork, brown them slightly
2. Add the rest of the   to the pot onion, tomatillo, garlic, tomato paste, jalapeno, cumin, water, chili powder . Mix well
3. Lock up the lid and cook on HIGH pressure for 35 minutes and release the pressure naturally
4. Serve and enjoy!

Quinoa, Nut, and Chickpea Stuffed Butternut Squash

Prep time: 10 minutes | Cook time: 13 minutes | Serves 4

2 tablespoons extra-virgin olive oil
1 tablespoon minced garlic
1 small shallot, minced
Kosher salt
Freshly ground black pepper
½ cup dried cranberries
1 cup tri-colored quinoa
2¾ cups water, divided
2 cups roughly chopped kale
1 small butternut squash, top trimmed, halved lengthwise
1 tablespoon freshly squeezed orange juice
Zest of 1 orange
1 (2-ounce / 57-g) jar pine nuts
1 (15-ounce / 425-g) can chickpeas, rinsed and drained

1. Select SEAR/SAUTÉ and set to HI. Select START/STOP to begin. Let preheat for 5 minutes.
2. Add the olive oil, garlic, shallot, salt, and pepper. Cook until garlic and shallot have softened and turned golden brown, about 2 minutes.
3. Stir in the cranberries, quinoa, and 1¼ cups of water. Assemble pressure lid, making sure the pressure release valve is in the SEAL position.
4. Select PRESSURE and set to HI. Set time to 2 minutes. Select START/STOP to begin.
5. When pressure cooking is complete, allow pressure to naturally release for 10 minutes. After 10 minutes, quick release remaining pressure by turning the pressure release valve to the VENT position. Carefully remove lid when the unit has finished releasing pressure.
6. Place the quinoa in a large bowl. Stir in the kale. Cover the bowl with aluminum foil and set aside.
7. Pour the remaining 1½ cups of water into the pot. Place the butternut squash cut-side up on the Reversible Rack, then lower it into the pot. Assemble pressure lid, making sure the pressure release valve is in the SEAL position.
8. Select PRESSURE and set to HI. Set the time to 8 minutes. Select START/STOP to begin.
9. Mix the orange juice, orange zest, pine nuts, and chickpeas into the quinoa mixture.
10. When pressure cooking is complete, quick release the pressure by turning the pressure release valve to the VENT position. Carefully remove lid when unit has finished releasing pressure.
11. Carefully remove rack from pot. Using a spoon slightly hollow out the squash. Spoon the quinoa mixture into the squash. Cut in half and serve.

Cauliflower and Chickpea Green Salad

Prep time: 10 minutes | Cook time: 15 minutes | Serves 6

1 head cauliflower, cut into florets
1 (14-ounce / 397-g) can chickpeas, rinsed and drained
3 tablespoons, plus ¼ cup extra-virgin olive oil
1 tablespoon chili powder
2 teaspoons paprika
3 garlic cloves, minced
4 cups mixed baby greens
1 cucumber, sliced
3 tablespoons chopped fresh parsley
Juice of 1 lemon
2 tablespoons honey
2 tablespoons Dijon mustard
2 tablespoons apple cider vinegar
⅓ cup crumbled feta cheese
Sea salt
Freshly ground black pepper

1. Insert Cook & Crisp Basket in pot. Close crisping lid. Select AIR CRISP, set temperature to 390ºF (199ºC), and set the time to 5 minutes. Select START/STOP to begin preheating.
2. In a large bowl combine the cauliflower florets, chickpeas, 3 tablespoons of olive oil, chili powder, paprika, and garlic.
3. Once unit has preheated, open lid and add the cauliflower and chickpeas to the basket. Close lid.
4. Select AIR CRISP, set temperature to 390ºF (199ºC), and set time to 15 minutes. Select START/STOP to begin.
5. In another large bowl, combine the mixed greens, cucumber, and parsley.
6. In a small bowl, whisk together the lemon juice, honey, mustard, and vinegar.
7. When cooking is complete, carefully remove basket with cauliflower and chickpeas. Add them to the bowl of greens and toss well to combine. Top with feta cheese and dressing, season with salt and pepper, and serve.

Mushroom and Cheddar Poutine

Prep time: 10 minutes | Cook time: 46 minutes | Serves 4

2 tablespoons unsalted butter
1 small yellow onion, diced
1 garlic clove, minced
8 ounces (227 g) cremini mushrooms, sliced
¼ cup red wine
3 cups vegetable stock
¼ cup all-purpose flour
Kosher salt
Freshly ground black pepper
1 pound (454 g) frozen French fries
8 ounces (227 g) Cheddar cheese, cubed

1. Select SEAR/SAUTÉ and set to MED. Select START/STOP to begin. Let preheat for 3 minutes.
2. Add the butter, onion, and garlic. Cook, stirring occasionally, for 5 minutes. Add the mushrooms and sauté for 5 minutes. Add the wine and let it simmer and reduce for 3 minutes.
3. In large bowl, slowly whisk together the stock and flour. Whisk this mixture into the vegetables in the pot. Cook the gravy for 10 minutes. Season with salt and pepper. Transfer the gravy to a medium bowl and set aside. Clean out the pot and return to unit.
4. Insert Cook & Crisp Basket and add the French fries. Close crisping lid.
5. Select AIR CRISP, set temperature to 360°F (182°C), and set time to 18 minutes. Select START/STOP to begin.
6. Every 5 minutes, open lid and remove and shake basket to ensure even cooking.
7. Once cooking is complete, remove fries from basket and place in the pot. Add the cheese and stir. Cover with the gravy. Close crisping lid.
8. Select AIR CRISP, set temperature to 375°F (191°C), and set time 5 minutes. Select START/STOP to begin.
9. When cooking is complete, serve immediately.

Wine-Glazed Roasted Cabbage

Prep time: 5 minutes | Cook time: 32 minutes | Serves 8

1 head green cabbage
½ cup, plus 1 tablespoon water
1 tablespoon extra-virgin olive oil
Kosher salt
Freshly ground black pepper
2 cups white wine
¼ cup minced red onion
1 cup heavy (whipping) cream
¼ cup minced fresh dill
¼ cup minced fresh parsley
2 tablespoons whole-grain mustard
1 tablespoon cornstarch

1. Place the cabbage and ½ cup of water, stem-side down, in the pot.
2. With a knife cut an X into the top of the cabbage cutting all the way through to the bottom through the core. Assemble pressure lid, making sure the pressure release valve is in the SEAL position.
3. Select PRESSURE and set temperature to HI. Set time to 15 minutes. Select START/STOP to begin.
4. When pressure cooking is complete, quick release the pressure by turning the pressure release valve to the VENT position. Carefully remove lid when unit has finished releasing pressure.
5. Brush the cabbage with the olive oil and season with salt and pepper. Close crisping lid.
6. Select AIR CRISP, set temperature to 390°F (199°C), and set time to 12 minutes. Select START/STOP to begin.
7. Once cooking is complete, open lid, lift out the cabbage, wrap with foil, and set aside. Leave any remaining water in the pot.
8. Select SEAR/SAUTÉ. Set temperature to HI. Select START/STOP to begin.
9. Add the white wine and onion and stir, scraping any brown bits off the bottom of the pot. Stir in the cream, dill, parsley, and mustard. Let simmer for 5 minutes.
10. In a small bowl, whisk together the cornstarch and the remaining 1 tablespoon of water until smooth. Stir it into the mixture in the pot. Cook until the sauce has thickened and coats the back of a spoon, about 2 minutes.
11. Pour half of the sauce over the cabbage. Cut the cabbage into 8 pieces and serve with remaining sauce.

Lentils and Paneer Curry

Prep time: 15 minutes | Cook time: 35 minutes | Serves 8

1 tablespoon vegetable oil
1 small onion, diced
1 small bell pepper, diced
1 large potato, cut into 1-inch cubes
1 teaspoon ground turmeric
1 teaspoon cumin seeds
1 teaspoon ground cumin
1 teaspoon garam masala (optional)
1 teaspoon curry powder
1 (15-ounce / 425-g) jar curry sauce, plus 1 jar water
1 (14-ounce / 397-g) can diced tomatoes
1 cup dried red lentils
8 ounces (227 g) paneer, cubed (optional)
1 cup fresh cilantro, roughly chopped (optional)
Salt
Freshly ground black pepper

1. Select SEAR/SAUTÉ and set temperature to HI. Select START/STOP to begin and allow to preheat for 5 minutes.
2. Add the oil to the pot and allow to heat for 1 minute. Add the onion and bell pepper and sauté for 3 to 4 minutes.
3. Add the potato, turmeric, cumin seeds, cumin, garam masala, and curry powder. Stir and cook for 5 minutes.
4. Stir in the curry sauce, water, tomatoes, and lentils.
5. Assemble the pressure lid, making sure the pressure release valve is in the SEAL position.
6. Select PRESSURE and set to HI. Set the time to 15 minutes. Select START/STOP to begin.
7. When pressure cooking is complete, allow the pressure to naturally release for 10 minutes. After 10 minutes, quick release any remaining pressure by moving the pressure release valve to the VENT position. Carefully remove the lid when the unit has finished releasing pressure.
8. Stir in the paneer (if using) and cilantro. Taste and season with salt and pepper, as needed.

Harissa Broccoli and Bean Roast

Prep time: 10 minutes | Cook time: 30 minutes | Serves 4

2 cups water
2 small heads broccoli, cut in half
2 tablespoons unsalted butter
½ white onion, minced
2 garlic cloves, minced
1 (15½-ounce / 439-g) can cannellini beans, rinsed and drained
1 (10-ounce / 283-g) can fire-roasted tomatoes and peppers
1 tablespoon spicy harissa
Sea salt
Freshly ground black pepper
¼ cup tahini
¼ cup walnuts, toasted and chopped
Zest of 1 lemon
Juice of 1 lemon

1. Place Reversible Rack in pot, making sure it is in the lowest position. Pour the water into the pot and place the broccoli on the rack. Assemble the pressure lid, making sure the pressure release valve is in the SEAL position.
2. Select STEAM. Set time to 8 minutes. Select START/STOP to begin.
3. When steaming is complete, quick release the pressure by turning the pressure release valve to the VENT position. Carefully remove lid when unit has finished releasing pressure.
4. Remove rack and broccoli and set aside. Drain the remaining water from the pot and reinsert it in base.
5. Select SEAR/SAUTÉ and set to HI. Select START/STOP to begin. Let preheat for 5 minutes.
6. Add the butter to pot. Once melted, add the onions and garlic and cook for 3 minutes. Add the beans, tomatoes, harissa, and season with salt and pepper. Cook for 4 minutes.
7. Reinsert rack and broccoli. Close crisping lid.
8. Select AIR CRISP, set temperature to 390°F (199°C), and set time to 15 minutes. Select START/STOP to begin.
9. After 10 minutes, open lid and flip the broccoli. Close lid and continue cooking.
10. When cooking is complete, remove rack with broccoli from pot. Place the beans in serving dishes and top with the broccoli. Drizzle tahini over the broccoli and sprinkle with walnuts. Garnish with the lemon zest and juice and serve.

Tempeh Hash in Kale with Avocado

Prep time: 20 minutes | Cook time: 20 minutes | Serves 6

2 pounds (907 g) Red Bliss potatoes, diced
½ cup water
2 tablespoons coconut oil
8 ounces (227 g) tempeh, diced
1 yellow onion, diced
3 garlic cloves, minced
3 Roma tomatoes, diced
Kosher salt
Freshly ground black pepper
2 tablespoons soy sauce
1 tablespoon maple syrup
2 cups baby kale
1 ripe avocado, diced

1. Place the potatoes in the Cook & Crisp Basket. Add the water to the pot and insert basket into unit. Assemble pressure lid, making sure the pressure release valve is in the SEAL position.
2. Select PRESSURE and set to HI. Set time to 2 minutes. Select START/STOP to begin.
3. Once pressure cooking is complete, quick release the pressure by turning the pressure release valve to the VENT position. Carefully remove lid when unit has finished releasing pressure.
4. Remove basket. Drain any remaining water from the pot and reinsert it into base.
5. Select SEAR/SAUTÉ and set to MD:HI. Select START/STOP to begin. Let preheat for 3 minutes.
6. Add the coconut oil and tempeh. Crisp the tempeh for 5 minutes, stirring occasionally.
7. Transfer the tempeh to a plate and add the onion, garlic, and tomatoes. Season with salt and pepper. Stir to incorporate, then add the potatoes.
8. Press START/STOP to pause. Stir in the tempeh, soy sauce, and maple syrup. Fold in the kale. Close crisping lid.
9. Select AIR CRISP, set temperature to 375ºF (191ºC), and set time to 10 minutes. Select START/STOP to begin.
10. When cooking is complete, top with diced avocados and serve.

Tofu and Kimchi Fried Rice

Prep time: 10 minutes | Cook time: 30 minutes | Serves 6

1 cup Texmati brown rice
1¼ cups water
2 tablespoons canola oil
2 garlic cloves, minced
1 tablespoon minced fresh ginger
8 ounces (227 g) extra-firm tofu, cut into ½-inch squares
½ cup frozen peas and carrots
1 large egg, beaten
½ cup kimchi, chopped
2 scallions, sliced thin
¼ cup basil, coarsely chopped
1 tablespoon soy sauce
Kosher salt
Freshly ground black pepper

1. Rinse the rice under cold running water in a fine-mesh strainer.
2. Place the rice and water in the pot. Assemble pressure lid, making sure the pressure release valve is in the SEAL position.
3. Select PRESSURE and set to HI. Set time to 2 minutes. Select START/STOP to begin.
4. When pressure cooking is complete, allow pressure to naturally release for 10 minutes. After 10 minutes, quick release remaining pressure by moving the pressure release valve to the VENT position. Carefully remove lid when unit has finished releasing pressure.
5. Evenly layer the rice on a sheet pan and refrigerate until cool, preferably overnight.
6. Select SEAR/SAUTÉ and set to HI. Select START/STOP to begin. Add the canola oil and let heat for 5 minutes.
7. Add the garlic and ginger and cook for 1 minute. Add the tofu, rice, and peas and carrots, and cook for 5 minutes, stirring occasionally.
8. Move the rice to one side and add the egg to empty side of pot. Cook 30 seconds, stirring occasionally to scramble it. Add the kimchi, scallions, basil, and soy sauce, and stir. Cook for 5 minutes, stirring frequently.
9. Season with salt, pepper, and more soy sauce, if needed. Serve.

Avocado and Spinach Pasta

Prep time: 15 minutes | Cook time: 2 minutes | Serves 8

1 (16-ounce / 454-g) box dry pasta, such as rigatoni or penne
4 cups water
2 tablespoons extra-virgin olive oil, divided
2 teaspoons kosher salt, divided
3 avocados
Juice of 2 limes
2 tablespoons minced cilantro
1 red onion, chopped
1 cup cherry tomatoes, halved
4 heaping cups spinach, half an 11-ounce (312-g) container
¼ cup shredded Parmesan cheese, divided
Freshly ground black pepper, for serving

1. Place the pasta, water, 1 tablespoon of olive oil, and 1 teaspoon of salt in the pot. Stir to incorporate. Assemble pressure lid, making sure the pressure release valve is in the SEAL position.
2. Select PRESSURE and set to LO. Set time to 2 minutes. Select START/STOP to begin.
3. While pasta is cooking, place the avocados in a medium-sized mixing bowl and mash well with a wooden spatula until a thick paste forms. Add all remaining ingredients to the bowl and mix well to combine.
4. When pressure cooking is complete, allow pressure to naturally release for 10 minutes. After 10 minutes, quick release remaining pressure by moving the pressure release valve to the VENT position. Carefully remove lid when unit has finished releasing pressure.
5. If necessary, strain pasta to remove any residual water and return pasta to pot. Add avocado mixture to pot and stir.
6. Garnish pasta with Parmesan cheese and black pepper, as desired, then serve.

Cauliflower and Tomato Enchiladas

Prep time: 15 minutes | Cook time: 25 minutes | Serves 5

2 tablespoons canola oil
1 large head cauliflower, cut into 1-inch florets
2 teaspoons ground cumin
1 teaspoon ground chili pepper
2 teaspoons kosher salt
½ teaspoon freshly ground black pepper
1 (14½-ounce / 411-g) can diced tomatoes, drained
5 (6-inch) flour tortillas
1 (10-ounce / 283-g) can red enchilada sauce
1½ cups shredded Mexican blend cheese
½ cup chopped cilantro, for garnish

1. In a medium bowl, toss together the oil, cauliflower, cumin, chili pepper, salt, and black pepper. Place the cauliflower in the Cook & Crisp Basket and place the basket in pot. Close crisping lid.
2. Select AIR CRISP, set temperature to 390°F (199°C), and set time to 15 minutes. Select START/STOP to begin.
3. After 8 minutes, open lid, then lift the basket and shake the cauliflower. Lower basket back into pot and close lid. Continue cooking, until the cauliflower reaches your desired crispiness.
4. When cooking is complete, remove basket from pot. Place the cauliflower in a bowl and mix with the tomatoes.
5. Lay the tortillas on a work surface. Divide the cauliflower-
6. tomato mixture between the tortillas and roll them up. Place the filled tortillas seam-side down in the pot. Pour the enchilada sauce on top.
7. Close crisping lid. Select BROIL and set time to 10 minutes. Select START/STOP to begin.
8. After 5 minutes, open lid and add the cheese on top. Close lid and continue cooking until cheese is golden brown.
9. When cooking is complete, add cilantro and serve.

Italian Caprese Elbow Salad

Prep time: 10 minutes | Cook time: 3 minutes | Serves 8

1 (16-ounce / 454-g) box elbow pasta
4 cups water
1 tablespoon sea salt
2 tablespoons extra-virgin olive oil
½ cup red bell pepper, diced
1 cup cherry tomatoes, sliced
¼ cup black olives, sliced
½ pound (227 g) fresh Mozzarella, diced
½ cup chopped fresh basil
½ cup Italian dressing

1. Place the pasta, water, and salt in the pot. Assemble pressure lid, making sure the pressure release valve is in the SEAL position.
2. Select PRESSURE and set to HI. Set time to 3 minutes. Select START/STOP to begin.
3. When pressure cooking is complete, allow pressure to naturally release for 10 minutes. After 10 minutes, quick release remaining pressure by moving the pressure release valve to the VENT position. Carefully remove lid when unit has finished releasing pressure.
4. Drain the pasta in a colander. Place the pasta in a large bowl and toss with the olive oil. Set aside to cool for 20 minutes.
5. Stir in the bell pepper, cherry tomatoes, olives, Mozzarella, and basil. Gently fold in the Italian seasoning.
6. Serve immediately or cover and refrigerate for later.

Sumptuous Vegetable and Penne Primavera

Prep time: 10 minutes | Cook time: 18 minutes | Serves 6

½ red onion, sliced
1 carrot, thinly sliced
1 head broccoli, cut into florets
1 red bell pepper, thinly sliced
1 yellow squash, halved lengthwise and sliced into half
   moons
1 zucchini, halved lengthwise and sliced into half moons
¼ cup extra-virgin olive oil
½ teaspoon dried basil
½ teaspoon dried oregano
½ teaspoon dried parsley
¼ teaspoon dried rosemary
¼ teaspoon crushed red pepper flakes
1 (16-ounce / 454-g) box penne pasta
4 cups water
2 tablespoons freshly squeezed lemon juice
½ cup grated Parmesan cheese, divided

1. Place Cook & Crisp Basket in pot. Close crisping lid. Select AIR CRISP, set temperature to 390°F (199°C), and set time to 5 minutes. Select START/STOP to begin preheating.
2. In a large bowl, combine the red onion, carrot, broccoli, bell pepper, yellow squash, zucchini, olive oil, basil, oregano, parsley, rosemary, and red pepper flakes, and toss to combine.
3. Once unit has preheated, add the vegetable mixture to the basket. Close lid.
4. Select AIR CRISP, set temperature to 390°F (199°C), and set time to 15 minutes. Select START/STOP to begin.
5. When cooking is complete, remove the vegetables and basket, and set aside.
6. Add the pasta and water. Assemble pressure lid, making sure the pressure release valve is in the SEAL position.
7. Select PRESSURE and set to HI. Set time to 3 minutes. Select START/STOP to begin.
8. When pressure cooking is complete, allow pressure to naturally release for 10 minutes. After 10 minutes, quick release remaining pressure by moving the pressure release valve to the VENT position. Carefully remove lid when unit has finished releasing pressure.
9. Add vegetables to pasta. Add the lemon juice and ¼ cup of Parmesan cheese and stir. Serve and top with remaining cheese.

Carrot and Celery Potpie

Prep time: 10 minutes | Cook time: 22 minutes | Serves 6

4 tablespoons unsalted butter
½ large onion, diced
1½ cups diced carrot (about 2 large carrots)
1½ cups diced celery (about 3 celery stalks)
2 garlic cloves, minced
3 cups red potatoes, diced
1 cup vegetable broth
½ cup frozen peas
½ cup frozen corn
1 tablespoon chopped fresh Italian parsley
2 teaspoons fresh thyme leaves
¼ cup all-purpose flour
½ cup heavy (whipping) cream
Salt
Freshly ground black pepper
1 prepared piecrust

1. Select SEAR/SAUTÉ and set temperature to MD:HI. Set the time to 5 minutes to preheat. Select START/STOP to begin.
2. Add the butter to the pot to melt. Add the onion, carrot, and celery to the melted butter. Sauté for about 3 minutes until softened.
3. Stir in the garlic and cook, stirring constantly, for about 30 seconds until fragrant. Select START/STOP to end the function.
4. Add the potatoes and vegetable broth to pot and stir to combine.
5. Assemble the pressure lid, making sure the pressure release valve is in the SEAL position.
6. Select PRESSURE and set to HI. Set the time to 5 minutes. Select START/STOP to begin.
7. When pressure cooking is complete, quick release the pressure by turning the pressure release valve to the VENT position. Carefully remove the lid when the unit has finished releasing pressure.
8. Add the peas, corn, parsley, and thyme to the pot. Season with salt and pepper. Sprinkle the flour over the top and stir to mix well. Stir in the heavy cream.
9. Select SEAR/SAUTÉ and set temperature to MD:HI. Select START/STOP to begin. Cook for 2 to 3 minutes, stirring constantly, until the sauce thickens and is hot. Select START/STOP to end the function.
10. Place the piecrust over the vegetable mixture. Fold over the edges of the crust to fit the pot. Make a small slit in the center of the crust for steam to release. Close the crisping lid.
11. Select BROIL. Set the time to 10 minutes. Select START/STOP to begin.
12. After the cooking is complete, carefully transfer the inner pot to a heat-proof surface. Let the potpie sit for 10 minutes before serving.

Tomato and Leek Galette

Prep time: 15 minutes | Cook time: 40 minutes | Serves 4

½ pound (227 g) mixed tomatoes, cut into ¼-inch slices
3 inches of leek, thinly sliced
2 garlic cloves, diced
Kosher salt
1 store-bought refrigerated pie crust
2 tablespoons bread crumbs
4 tablespoons shredded Parmesan cheese, divided
4 tablespoons shredded Mozzarella, divided
1 egg, beaten
Freshly ground black pepper

1. Place the tomatoes, leeks, and garlic into large bowl. Sprinkle with salt and set aside for at least 5 minutes to draw out the juices from the vegetables.
2. Strain the excess juice off the tomato mixture and pat down the vegetables with paper towels.
3. Unroll the pie crust and place it in the Ninja Multi-Purpose Pan or a 1½-quart round ceramic baking dish and form it to the bottom of the pan. Lay the extra dough loosely on the sides of the pan.
4. Sprinkle the bread crumbs in a thin layer on the pie crust bottom, then scatter 3 tablespoons each of Parmesan and Mozzarella cheese on top. Place the tomato mixture in a heap in the middle of the dough and top with the remaining 1 tablespoon each of Parmesan and Mozzarella cheese.
5. Fold the edges of the crust over the tomatoes and brush with the egg.
6. Close crisping lid. Select BAKE/ROAST, set temperature to 350°F (177°C), and set time to 45 minutes. Select START/STOP to begin. Let preheat for 5 minutes.
7. Place pan on the Reversible Rack, making sure the rack is in the lower position. Cover galette loosely with aluminum foil (do not seal the pan).
8. Once unit has preheated, open lid and carefully place the rack with pan in the pot. Close crisping lid.
9. After 20 minutes, open lid and remove the foil. Close lid and continue cooking.
10. When cooking is complete, remove rack with pan and set aside to let cool. Cut into slices, season with pepper, and serve.

Bell Pepper and Mushroom Pizza

Prep time: 10 minutes | Cook time: 8 minutes | Makes 1 pizza

1 (7-ounce / 198-g) store-bought pizza dough, rolled into an 8-inch circle
¼ cup traditional pizza sauce
1 teaspoon minced garlic
⅔ cup shredded Mozzarella cheese
¼ cup chopped green bell pepper
¼ cup sliced mushrooms
Crushed red pepper flakes, for garnish

1. Select BAKE/ROAST, set the temperature to 400°F (204°C), and set time to 5 minutes to preheat. Select START/STOP to begin.
2. Place the rolled dough in the Ninja Cook & Crisp Basket. Spread the pizza sauce over the crust, leaving about a 1-inch border uncovered. Sprinkle on the garlic, top with the Mozzarella cheese, and evenly distribute the green bell pepper and mushrooms over the pizza.
3. Place the Cook & Crisp Basket into the pot and close the crisping lid.
4. Select BAKE/ROAST, set the temperature to 400°F (204°C), and set the time to 8 minutes. Select START/STOP to begin.
5. When cooking is complete, carefully open the lid and remove the pizza. Serve, garnished with red pepper flakes, if using.

Tomato-Basil Bread Pizza

Prep time: 2 minutes | Cook time: 10 minutes | Serves 6

6 slices frozen garlic bread or Texas Toast
¾ cup tomato-basil sauce or your favorite tomato sauce
6 slices Mozzarella cheese

1. Insert Cook & Crisp Basket in pot. Close crisping lid. Select AIR CRISP, set temperature to 390°F (199°C), and set time to 5 minutes. Select START/STOP to begin preheating.
2. Once unit has preheated, place three of the garlic bread slices in the basket, and top with half the sauce and 3 slices of cheese. Close crisping lid.
3. Select AIR CRISP, set temperature to 375°F (191°C), and set time to 5 minutes. Select START/STOP to begin.
4. When cooking is complete, remove the pizzas from the basket. Repeat steps 2 and 3 with the remaining slices of garlic bread, sauce, and cheese.

Black Bean and Sweet Potato Tacos

Prep time: 15 minutes | Cook time: 1 hour | Serves 8

For the Black Beans:

1 pound (454 g) dried black beans, rinsed and picked through for debris

2 chipotle chiles from a can of chipotles in adobo sauce

2 garlic cloves, smashed

1 teaspoon ground cumin

1 teaspoon kosher salt

½ teaspoon ground coriander

For the Sweet Potatoes:

3 tablespoons peanut oil or vegetable oil

1 tablespoon sauce from a can of chipotles in adobo sauce

2 teaspoons ground cumin

1 teaspoon kosher salt

3 medium sweet potatoes, peeled and diced

16 to 20 (6-inch) corn tortillas, warmed

Sour cream, for serving (optional)

Salsa or pico de gallo, for serving (optional)

Shredded Mexican-style cheese, for serving (optional)

Chopped fresh cilantro, for serving (optional)

1. Make the black beans: Place the beans, chipotle chiles, garlic, cumin, salt, and coriander along with 6 cups water into the Foodi's inner pot. Lock on the Pressure Lid, making sure the valve is set to Seal, and set to Pressure on High for 25 minutes. When the timer reaches 0, allow the pressure to naturally release for 20 minutes, then quick-release the remaining pressure. Carefully remove the lid. Let the beans cool to room temperature. (If desired, transfer beans to an airtight container along with the cooking liquid and refrigerate for up to 1 week.)
2. Make the sweet potatoes: Clean and dry the inner pot. Place the oil, adobo sauce, cumin, and salt in the pot. Add the sweet potatoes and stir to coat until the potatoes glisten.
3. Transfer the potatoes to the crisping basket and place the basket in the inner pot. Drop the Crisping Lid and set to Air Crisp at 390°F (199°C) for 35 to 45 minutes, depending on how browned and crisp you want the potatoes. While they are cooking, lift the lid and shake the basket periodically to move them about. When cooked and tender, lift the lid and transfer the potatoes to a plate.
4. To serve, place some beans and sweet potatoes onto a tortilla, add the toppings of your choice, and serve.

Cauliflower Steaks

Prep time: 5 minutes | Cook time: 20 minutes | Serves 2

1 large cauliflower

2 tablespoons peanut oil or vegetable oil

Kosher salt, to taste

Freshly ground black pepper, to taste

Grated zest of 1 lemon

1. Place the cauliflower on a cutting board and trim off any leaves. Get a good look at where the stem is connected—that area is going to be the steaks. Trim a ¾-inch slice from each side of the cauliflower (save the trimmed bits for another use) and then cut the cauliflower in half to make two steaks. Rub the oil and a liberal amount of salt and pepper onto both sides of the steaks.
2. Insert the crisping basket into the Foodi's inner pot and arrange the steaks in the basket so they are propped up by the basket sides—they should fit snugly in a vertical position. Drop the Crisping Lid and set the Foodi to Air Crisp at 390°F (199°C) for 20 minutes, until the steaks brown.
3. Lift the lid and remove the basket from the Foodi. Transfer the cauliflower steaks to a platter or individual plates. Sprinkle with the lemon zest and serve.

Parmesan Broccoli Florets

Prep time: 5 minutes | Cook time: 8 minutes | Serves 4

12 ounces (340 g) fresh broccoli florets

1 tablespoon peanut oil or vegetable oil

¼ teaspoon kosher salt

Pinch of freshly ground black pepper

½ cup freshly shredded Parmesan cheese

1. Place the broccoli florets in the crisping basket and set the basket into the Foodi's inner pot along with ½ cup water. Lock on the Pressure Lid, making sure the valve is set to Seal, and set to Pressure on High for 0 minutes. When the timer reaches 0, quick-release the pressure and carefully remove the lid. Transfer the broccoli to a medium bowl. Drain the liquid from the inner pot, wash, and dry it.
2. Add the oil, salt, pepper, and Parmesan to the broccoli in the bowl. Stir to combine. Place the crisping basket back into the inner pot and transfer the broccoli mixture to the basket, scraping any cheese left in the bowl on top of the broccoli. Drop the Crisping Lid and set the Foodi to Air Crisp at 390°F (199°C) for 8 minutes, or until the broccoli is crisped and the cheese is browned. Lift the lid and serve hot.

Refried Black Beans

Prep time: 5 minutes | Cook time: 40 minutes | Serves 6

1 pound (454 g) dried black beans, rinsed and picked through for debris
½ medium yellow onion, diced
2 garlic cloves, minced
1 teaspoon ground cumin
1 teaspoon kosher salt, plus more as needed
2 tablespoons peanut oil or vegetable oil

1. Place the beans, onion, garlic, cumin, salt, and 4 cups water into the Foodi's inner pot. Lock on the Pressure Lid, making sure the valve is set to Seal, and set to Pressure on High for 30 minutes. When the timer reaches 0, allow the Foodi to naturally release for 20 minutes, then quick-release any remaining pressure and carefully remove the lid.
2. Add the oil and mash the beans with a silicone potato masher until they are smooth. Set the Foodi to Sear/Saute on High and cook for 10 minutes, or until very thick and shiny, stirring and mashing every couple of minutes. Season with salt to taste before serving.

Maple-Glazed Carrots

Prep time: 5 minutes | Cook time: 29 minutes | Serves 6

2 tablespoons unsalted butter
1 tablespoon ground cumin
2 pounds (907 g) carrots, cut into 2-inch pieces
½ cup orange juice
¼ cup maple syrup
1 teaspoon kosher salt

1. Place the butter and cumin in the Foodi's inner pot and set the Foodi to Sear/Saute until the butter is bubbling and aromatic, about 6 minutes.
2. Add the carrots and orange juice, then lock on the Pressure Lid, making sure the valve is set to Seal, and set to Pressure on High for 3 minutes. When the timer reaches 0, quick-release the pressure and carefully remove the lid.
3. Stir in the maple syrup and salt. Set the Foodi to Air Crisp at 390°F (199°C) for 20 minutes, or until the carrots are nicely browned. Lift the lid and transfer the carrots to a platter. Serve warm or at room temperature if you want them to be a little stickier.

Ham Hock Braised Collard Greens

Prep time: 10 minutes | Cook time: 13 minutes | Serves 6

2 tablespoons unsalted butter
1 medium yellow onion, diced
2 garlic cloves, minced
1 smoked ham hock
2 cups chicken stock
2 pounds (907 g) collard greens, tough stems and ribs removed, leaves thinly sliced
Juice of 1 lemon
2 teaspoons kosher salt

1. Add the butter to the Foodi's inner pot and set the Foodi to Sear/Saute on High until melted, about 4 minutes. Add the onion and garlic and cook until beginning to soften, about 6 minutes more, stirring occasionally.
2. Add the ham hock and stock and stir once, then add the collard greens (you may really have to jam them in!). Lock on the Pressure Lid, making sure the valve is set to Seal, and set to Pressure on High for 3 minutes. When the timer reaches 0, quick-release the pressure and carefully remove the lid. (If you plan on eating the greens soon after cooking them, turn the Foodi to the Keep Warm setting.)
3. Use tongs to remove the ham hock and set it aside to cool slightly before cutting the meat into chunks (discard the bone). Stir the ham back into the greens, then stir in the lemon juice and salt and serve.

Homemade Ratatouille

Prep time: 15 minutes | Cook time: 22 minutes | Serves 6

For the Sauce:
2 (14½-ounce / 411-g) cans diced tomatoes with juice
1 medium yellow onion, diced
1 red bell pepper, seeded, ribbed, and diced
4 garlic cloves, minced
7 fresh basil leaves
3 tablespoons extra-virgin olive oil
½ teaspoon kosher salt
¼ teaspoon freshly ground black pepper

For the Vegetables:
½ medium Italian eggplant, sliced as thin as possible into rounds
3 vine-ripened tomatoes, sliced as thin as possible into rounds
1 medium yellow squash, sliced as thin as possible into rounds
1 medium zucchini, sliced as thin as possible into rounds
Cooking spray
Kosher salt, to taste
Freshly ground black pepper, to taste
6 sprigs fresh thyme
1 tablespoon fresh torn basil leaves
1 tablespoon finely chopped fresh flat-leaf parsley

Make the Sauce
1. Add the diced tomatoes, onion, bell pepper, garlic, basil, olive oil, salt, pepper, and ½ cup water to the Foodi's inner pot. Lock on the Pressure Lid, making sure the valve is set to Seal, and set to Pressure on High for 2 minutes. When the timer reaches 0, quick-release the pressure and carefully remove the lid.

Make the Vegetables
2. Starting from the center of the Foodi pot, arrange the veggie slices by overlapping them in a spiral, alternating among the different vegetables. The vegetables will shrink as they cook, so really pack them in. It's okay if they are placed vertically once you get near the edge of the pot.
3. Spray the top of the vegetables heavily with cooking spray and season with salt and pepper. Lay the thyme sprigs on top and drop the Crisping Lid. Set the Foodi to Air Crisp at 390°F (199°C) for 20 minutes, or until the veggies begin to brown.
4. Lift the lid and carefully remove the thyme. Shake the dried leaves off the stems, then sprinkle the dried thyme onto the ratatouille along with the fresh basil and parsley. Let the ratatouille cool at least 5 minutes before scooping from the pot and serving.

Twice-Baked Cheese Potatoes

Prep time: 10 minutes | Cook time: 33 minutes | Serves 4

2 medium russet potatoes, poked a few times with a fork
½ teaspoon kosher salt
Cooking spray
1 cup shredded mild Cheddar cheese
2 tablespoons sour cream
1 garlic clove, minced
½ teaspoon smoked paprika
Chopped fresh chives, for garnish
Smoked paprika, for garnish

1. Add ½ cup water and salt to the Foodi's inner pot. Place the reversible rack in the pot in the low position and set the potatoes on the rack. Lock on the Pressure Lid, making sure the valve is set to Seal, and set to Pressure on High for 20 minutes. When the timer reaches 0, allow the pressure to release naturally for 10 minutes, then quick-release the remaining pressure and carefully remove the lid.
2. Use tongs to remove the potatoes from the Foodi and set aside to cool enough to pick up and hold—about 5 minutes for my iron hands (but letting them cool longer won't hurt). Remove the rack from the inner pot but leave the cooking liquid in the pot.
3. Spray a knife with cooking spray and slice the potatoes in half lengthwise. Use a fork to lightly rake and fluff the insides of the potato halves and then use a small spoon to carefully remove the flesh of each, keeping as much of the skin intact as possible. Set the skins aside to stuff later.
4. Add the scooped-out potato flesh to the Foodi's inner pot and combine with the cooking liquid. Add the cheese, sour cream, and garlic to the pot and set the Foodi to Sear/Saute on High. Mash everything together and cook, stirring often, until the cheese is melted, about 3 minutes.
5. Carefully spoon the potato mixture into the potato skins. Place the reversible rack in the Foodi in the high position, and arrange the stuffed potatoes on the rack (it's okay if they are touching). Spray the potatoes with cooking spray, drop the Crisping Lid, and set the Foodi to Broil for 10 minutes, or until the cheesy mixture is browned on top. Lift the lid and sprinkle the potatoes with the smoked paprika, then let cool for 5 minutes before transferring them to plates. Serve sprinkled with chives and paprika

Bread Stuffing

Prep time: 10 minutes | Cook time: 48 minutes | Serves 6

1 loaf French bread, cut into 1-inch cubes
4 tablespoons unsalted butter
1 medium yellow onion, diced
3 celery ribs, diced
1½ cups chicken stock
1 large egg, lightly beaten
2 teaspoons kosher salt
1 teaspoon freshly ground black pepper
1 tablespoon minced fresh thyme leaves
4 fresh sage leaves, minced
Minced fresh parsley, for garnish
Fresh thyme leaves, for garnish

1. Place the bread cubes in the crisping basket and set the crisping basket in the Foodi's inner pot. Drop the Crisping Lid and set the Foodi to Dehydrate at 195°F (91°C) for 15 minutes, or until the bread is dried out. Lift the lid, carefully remove the basket with the bread, and set aside. Use a damp paper towel to wipe out any crumbs that might have fallen into the pot.
2. Add the butter to the inner pot and set the Foodi to Sear/Saute on High until the butter is melted and quite warm (you want the vegetables to sizzle when they are added to the pot), about 5 minutes. Add the onion and celery and cook until they begin to soften, about 8 minutes, stirring often.
3. Meanwhile, in a medium bowl, whisk together the stock, egg, salt, and pepper.
4. Add the dried bread cubes and the fresh thyme and sage to the onion mixture in the inner pot, then stir in the egg mixture, making sure all the bread is moistened. Flatten out the stuffing so the top layer is somewhat even. Drop the Crisping Lid and set the Foodi to Bake/Roast at 375°F (190°C) for 20 minutes, or until browned yet moist, stirring halfway through. Transfer the stuffing to a serving dish and garnish with fresh parsley and thyme.

Roasted Zucchini and Summer Squash

Prep time: 10 minutes | Cook time: 25 minutes | Serves 4

2 medium zucchini, cut into ¼-inch-thick rounds
2 medium yellow summer squash, cut into ¼-inch-thick rounds
½ cup fresh flat-leaf parsley leaves
3 tablespoons peanut oil or vegetable oil
Zest of 1 lemon
2 teaspoons kosher salt
½ teaspoon freshly ground black pepper

1. Place the zucchini, yellow squash, parsley, oil, lemon zest, salt, and pepper into the Foodi's inner pot and stir to evenly coat the squash with the oil. Transfer the squash mixture to the crisping basket and place it in the inner pot. Set the Foodi to Air Crisp at 390°F (199°C) for 25 minutes, stirring occasionally, or until browned.
2. Serve warm.

Brown Sugar-Glazed Brussels Sprouts

Prep time: 10 minutes | Cook time: 23 minutes | Serves 6

3 tablespoons peanut oil or vegetable oil
2 pounds (907 g) Brussels sprouts, stem ends trimmed and scored with an "x"
2 teaspoons kosher salt
½ teaspoon freshly ground black pepper
3 tablespoons light brown sugar
2 tablespoons fish sauce
¼ cup pickled jalapeños, plus ¼ cup pickling liquid
Juice of 1 lime

1. Place the oil, Brussels sprouts, salt, and pepper into the Foodi's inner pot, stirring to fully coat the Brussels sprouts with the oil. Transfer the sprouts to the crisping basket, place the basket in the Foodi pot, and set the Foodi to Air Crisp at 390°F (199°C) for 20 minutes, or until browned. Lift the lid and remove the basket with the sprouts.
2. Add the brown sugar, fish sauce, and jalapeños and pickling liquid to the inner pot. Set the Foodi to Sear/Saute and cook until the brown sugar has melted, about 3 minutes.
3. Add the lime juice to the pot and then return the sprouts to the pot. Toss to coat in the sauce and serve immediately.

Green Beans with Dill

Prep time: 5 minutes | Cook time: 18 minutes | Serves 4

12 ounces (340 g) fresh green beans, ends trimmed
1 tablespoon peanut oil or vegetable oil
¼ teaspoon kosher salt
Zest of 1 lemon
1 tablespoon finely chopped fresh dill, plus more for garnish

1. Place the beans, oil, and salt into the Foodi's inner pot, stirring to coat the beans with the oil. Transfer the beans to the crisping basket and place the basket in the inner pot. Drop the Crisping Lid and set the Foodi to Air Crisp at 390°F (199°C) for 15 minutes. After 12 minutes, lift the lid, add the lemon zest and dill, and shake the basket to coat the beans. Drop the lid again and continue to cook until the beans are blistered, about 3 minutes more.
2. Serve warm.

Canned Pickled Beets

Prep time: 10 minutes | Cook time: 1 minute | Makes 4 pints

8 (2-pound / 907-g) medium beets, scrubbed, trimmed, peeled, and cut into eighths
2 cups apple cider vinegar
1 cup sugar
12 whole cloves
6 allspice berries
6 cardamom pods
1 cinnamon stick
2 tablespoons kosher salt
1 teaspoon black peppercorns

1. Place the beets, vinegar, sugar, cloves, allspice, cardamom, cinnamon stick, salt, and peppercorns in the Foodi's inner pot. Add enough water to just barely cover the beets. Lock on the Pressure Lid, making sure the valve is set to Seal, and set the Foodi to Pressure on High for 1 minute. When the timer reaches 0, quick-release the pressure and carefully remove the lid. Allow the beets to cool in the pickling liquid for 2 to 3 hours.
2. Transfer the beets and the liquid, spices and all, to an airtight container or 4 pint-size glass jars and refrigerate for up to 1 month.

Saffron and Orange Rice Pilaf

Prep time: 10 minutes | Cook time: 20 minutes | Serves 4

3 tablespoons peanut oil or vegetable oil
½ medium yellow onion, diced
1 garlic clove, minced
Pinch of saffron threads
½ teaspoon dried orange peel
2 cups basmati rice
2 cups chicken stock
1 (10-ounce / 283-g) package frozen mixed vegetables
½ teaspoon kosher salt
Thinly sliced scallions, for garnish
Sweet paprika, for garnish
Flat-leaf parsley or mint, for garnish

1. Add the oil to the Foodi's inner pot and set the Foodi to Sear/Saute on High, heating for 5 minutes. Add the onion, garlic, saffron, and orange peel to the pot and cook until aromatic, about 4 minutes, stirring frequently.
2. Stir in the rice and cook until slightly toasted, about 4 minutes, stirring often. Add the stock. Lock on the Pressure Lid, making sure the valve is set to Seal, and set the Foodi to Pressure on High for 3 minutes. When the time reaches 0, allow the pressure to naturally release for 6 minutes, then quick-release the remaining pressure and carefully remove the lid.
3. Add the mixed vegetables. Drop the Crisping Lid and set the Foodi to Air Crisp at 390°F (199°C) for 8 minutes, or until the vegetables are warmed through. Lift the lid and stir in the salt. Serve sprinkled with the scallions, paprika, and parsley.

Fried Rice with Vegetable

Prep time: 10 minutes | Cook time: 18 minutes | Serves 6

2 cups short-grain white rice, rinsed well
2 tablespoons soy sauce
1 tablespoon oyster sauce
1 teaspoon sugar
1 teaspoon freshly ground black pepper
½ teaspoon kosher salt
¼ cup peanut oil or vegetable oil
2 large eggs, lightly beaten
4 garlic cloves, minced
1 (10-ounce / 283-g) package mixed frozen vegetables
3 scallions, trimmed and thinly sliced

1. Place the rice and 2 cups water into the Foodi's inner pot. Lock on the Pressure Lid, making sure the valve is set to Seal, and set to Pressure on High for 3 minutes. When the timer reaches 0, allow the pressure to naturally release for 11 minutes, then quick-release any remaining pressure. Carefully remove the lid. Scoop out the rice from the Foodi and transfer to a bowl to cool. Wash and dry the inner pot.
2. In a small bowl, combine the soy sauce, oyster sauce, sugar, pepper, and salt.
3. Set the Foodi to Sear/Saute on High, add the oil to the Foodi's inner pot, and allow to heat for 2 minutes. Add the eggs to the pot and stir, cooking until just set, about 3 minutes. Stir in the garlic and cook until aromatic, about 3 minutes.
4. Return the rice to the pot and use a silicone spatula to stir and break it up. Cook the rice until it toasts slightly, about 3 minutes, stirring often. Add the soy sauce mixture and cook until the sauce is absorbed, about 2 minutes, continuing to stir often.
5. Make a large well in the center of the rice, pushing the rice to the sides of the pot. Add the vegetables. Drop the Crisping Lid and set the Foodi to Air Crisp at 390°F (199°C) for 5 minutes, or until the vegetables are tender. Lift the lid and give the rice a good stir, then add the scallions and stir again before serving.

Spanish White Quinoa

Prep time: 10 minutes | Cook time: 2 minutes | Serves 6

1 cup white quinoa, rinsed
1 (14-ounce / 397-g) can diced tomatoes with juice
2 garlic cloves, minced
1 teaspoon ground cumin
½ teaspoon chili powder
½ teaspoon kosher salt
1 tablespoon unsalted butter

1. Place the quinoa, tomatoes and juice, garlic, cumin, chili powder, salt, butter, and ½ cup water into the Foodi's inner pot and stir to combine. Lock on the Pressure Lid, set the valve to Seal, and set the Foodi to Pressure on High for 2 minutes. When the timer reaches 0, allow the pressure to naturally release for 10 minutes, then quick-release any remaining pressure and carefully remove the lid.
2. Fluff with a silicone spatula and serve.

Moroccan-Style Couscous

Prep time: 5 minutes | Cook time: 1 minutes | Serves 4

Cooking spray
1 cup Moroccan-style couscous (not Israeli couscous)
2 tablespoons unsalted butter

1. Spray the Foodi's inner pot with cooking spray. Add the couscous, butter, and 1½ cups water. Lock on the Pressure Lid, making sure the valve is set to Seal, and set to Pressure on High for 1 minute. When the timer reaches 0, allow pressure to naturally release, then carefully remove the lid.
2. Fluff the couscous with a fork and serve.

Farro, Fennel and Arugula Salad

Prep time: 5 minutes | Cook time: 10 minutes | Serves 6

1 cup farro
2 fennel bulbs, fronds separated and
    reserved (optional), bulbs halved, cored,
    and diced
1 tablespoon fennel seeds
Zest and juice of 1 lemon
1 teaspoon kosher salt, plus more as needed
2 tablespoons extra-virgin olive oil
5 ounces (142 g) arugula leaves

1. Place the farro, half the fennel, the fennel seeds, lemon zest, and salt into the Foodi's inner pot. Add 1¾ cups water, lock on the Pressure Lid, making sure the valve is set to Seal, and set to Pressure on High for 10 minutes. When the timer reaches 0, allow the pressure to naturally release for 5 minutes, then quick-release any remaining pressure and carefully remove the lid. Allow the farro to cool completely.
2. Chop the fennel fronds, if using, and add them to the cooled farro along with the remaining chopped fennel, the lemon juice, and the olive oil. Toss to coat. Add the arugula and toss once more. Season with salt and serve.

Persian Crunch Rice Tahdig

Prep time: minutes | Cook time: 23 minutes | Serves 4 to 6

2 cups basmati rice
1 teaspoon ground turmeric
1 teaspoon kosher salt
4 tablespoons unsalted butter, at room
    temperature

1. Place the rice, 2 cups water, turmeric, and salt in the Foodi's inner pot. Lock on the Pressure Lid, making sure the valve is set to Seal, and set to Pressure on High for 3 minutes. When the timer reaches 0, allow the pressure to naturally release for 6 minutes, then quick-release any remaining pressure and carefully remove the lid.
2. Make a well in the center of the rice and add 2 tablespoons of the butter. Use a silicone spatula to draw spokes out of the well that extend to the pot sides (so the butter has a route to disperse). Set the Foodi to Sear/Saute on High, and allow the butter to melt—this should take about 2 minutes. Once melted, use the spatula to smooth over the rice, covering the well, then continue to cook the rice until the bottom has crisped (you can slide a silicone spatula under the rice to get a sense of its texture), about 8 minutes more.
3. Use the spatula again to smear the remaining 2 tablespoons of butter over the top of the rice, smoothing and pressing it down on the surface of the rice. Drop the Crisping Lid and set the Foodi to Broil for 10 minutes, or until the top of the rice is crisp. Lift the lid and carefully remove the pot from the Foodi. Run the spatula around the edge of the rice to loosen it before inverting it onto a plate. Serve hot.

Lebanese Tabbouleh

Prep time: 10 minutes | Cook time: 9 minutes | Serves 6

4 tablespoons extra-virgin olive oil
½ teaspoon ground cumin
1 cup whole-grain red bulgur
1 teaspoon kosher salt
Zest and juice of ½ lemon
2 ripe plum tomatoes, halved, seeded, and
    diced
1 English cucumber, seeded and diced
1 tablespoon chopped fresh mint
1 tablespoon chopped fresh flat-leaf parsley
Ground sumac, for garnish
Flat-leaf parsley, for garnish

1. Add 3 tablespoons of the olive oil to the Foodi's inner pot and set the Foodi to Sear/Saute on High. Allow the oil to heat for 3 minutes, then add the cumin and the bulgur and cook until aromatic, about 3 minutes more, stirring often.
2. Add ½ teaspoon of the salt and 2 cups water. Lock on the Pressure Lid, making sure the valve is set to Seal, and set to Pressure on High for 3 minutes. When the timer reaches 0, allow the pressure to release naturally, then carefully remove the lid.
3. Stir the bulgur to fluff it up and then stir in the remaining tablespoon olive oil and half the lemon juice. Transfer to a bowl and allow to cool completely.
4. When ready to serve, add the tomatoes, cucumber, mint, parsley, remaining ½ teaspoon salt, and remaining lemon juice plus the zest. Stir and serve with sumac and parsley.

Parmesan Risotto with Herbs

Prep time: 10 minutes | Cook time: 26 minutes | Serves 4

4 tablespoons unsalted butter
½ medium yellow onion, diced
2 garlic cloves, minced
1 shallot, minced
1 cup arborio rice
1 cup dry white wine
2 cups chicken stock
2 teaspoons kosher salt
1 cup finely grated Parmesan cheese,
    plus more for serving
Finely chopped fresh chives, for garnish
Flat-leaf parsley or fresh basil, for garnish

1. Add the butter to the Foodi's inner pot, set the Foodi to Sear/Saute on High, and allow the butter to melt, about 5 minutes. Add the onion, garlic, and shallot to the pot and cook until slightly softened, about 4 minutes.
2. Stir in the rice, making sure all the grains get coated with butter. Continue cooking until the rice is looking a little translucent, about 4 minutes. Pour in the wine, stir, and cook until the alcohol smell has diminished, about 2 minutes.
3. Add the stock and the salt. Lock on the Pressure Lid, making sure the valve is set to Seal, and set the Foodi to Pressure on Low for 6 minutes. When the timer reaches 0, quick-release the pressure and carefully remove the lid.
4. Set the Foodi to Sear/Saute on High. Stir in the Parmesan cheese and cook until the liquid is absorbed and a starchy texture develops, about 5 minutes, stirring often. Serve immediately with extra cheese and garnished with fresh herbs.

Cajun Red Beans and Rice

Prep time: 15 minutes | Cook time: 47 minutes | Serves 4

For the Rice:
2 cups short-grain white rice,
    rinsed well
½ teaspoon kosher salt

For the Beans:
3 tablespoons peanut oil
    or vegetable oil
3 celery stalks, chopped
1 medium yellow onion, diced
1 green bell pepper, seeded,
    ribbed, and diced
3 garlic cloves, minced
5 sprigs fresh thyme
2 dried bay leaves, or 1 fresh
3 tablespoons Cajun seasoning
1 smoked ham hock
1 pound (454 g) dried red kidney beans
1 teaspoon kosher salt
Fresh thyme leaves, for garnish
Black pepper, for garnish

Make the Rice
1. Add the rice, 2 cups water, and the salt to the Foodi's inner pot. Lock on the Pressure Lid, making sure the valve is set to Seal, and set to Pressure on High for 3 minutes. When the timer reaches 0, allow the pressure to naturally release for 11 minutes, then quick-release any remaining pressure and carefully remove the lid. Transfer the rice to a large bowl. Wash and dry the inner pot.

Make the Beans
2. Add the oil to the inner pot, set the Foodi to Sear/Saute on High, and heat the oil for 5 minutes. Add the celery, onion, and bell pepper and cook until beginning to soften, about 6 minutes, stirring often.
3. Add the garlic, thyme, bay leaves, and Cajun seasoning and cook until aromatic, about 3 minutes, stirring occasionally.
4. Add the ham hock, kidney beans, and 4 cups water and stir. Lock on the Pressure Lid, making sure the valve is set to Seal, and set the Foodi to Pressure on High for 30 minutes. When the timer reaches 0, allow the pressure to naturally release for 15 minutes, then quick-release any remaining pressure and carefully remove the lid. Stir in the salt. Add a ladleful of beans and broth to a bowl, top with a small scoop of rice, and serve with extra thyme and pepper.

Creamy Potato Soup with Crispy Leek

Prep time: 15 minutes | Cook time: 20 minutes | Serves 6

2 tablespoons extra-virgin olive oil, divided
4 leeks, cleaned and thinly sliced, divided
4 garlic cloves, minced
5 Yukon Gold potatoes, peeled and diced
3 thyme sprigs, stems removed
2 bay leaves
5 cups vegetable broth
¾ cup white wine
1½ teaspoons dried oregano
1 teaspoon sea salt
½ teaspoon freshly ground black pepper
1½ cups light cream
½ cup grated Cheddar cheese

1. Select Sear/Sauté and set to Medium High. Select Start/Stop to begin. Allow the pot to preheat for 5 minutes.
2. Put 1 tablespoon of oil and three-quarters of the sliced leeks in the pot. Cook until soft, about 5 minutes. Add the garlic and cook for 1 minute more.
3. Add the potatoes, thyme, bay leaves, vegetable broth, white wine, oregano, salt, and black pepper to the pot. Assemble the Pressure Lid, making sure the pressure release valve is in the Seal position.
4. Select Pressure and set to High. Set the time to 10 minutes, then select Start/Stop to begin.
5. When pressure cooking is complete, quick release the pressure by moving the pressure release valve to the Vent position. Carefully remove the lid when the unit has finished releasing pressure.
6. Remove and discard the bay leaves. Add the cream and use a potato masher to mash the soup to your desired consistency. Evenly top with the cheese.
7. In a small bowl, toss the remaining sliced leeks with the remaining 1 tablespoon of oil. Place the Reversible Rack in the pot in the higher position. Place a sheet of aluminum foil on top of the rack and arrange the leeks on top.
8. Close the Crisping Lid. Select Broil and set the time to 5 minutes. Select Start/Stop to begin.
9. When cooking is complete, check to see if the leeks have reached your desired crispiness. Remove the rack from the pot and serve the crispy leeks over the soup.

Chapter 4: Seafood

Ale and Cod Sandwich

Prep time: 5 minutes | Cook time: 15 minutes | Serves 4

2 eggs
8 ounces (227 g) ale
1 cup cornstarch
1 cup all-purpose flour
½ tablespoon chili powder
1 tablespoon ground cumin
1 teaspoon sea salt
1 teaspoon freshly ground black pepper
4 (5- to 6-ounce / 142- to 170-g) cod fillets, cut into 16 half-inch strips
Cooking spray
Tartar sauce, for garnish
8 slices sandwich bread

1. Insert Cook & Crisp Basket in pot. Close crisping lid. Select AIR CRISP, set temperature to 375ºF (191ºC), and set time to 5 minutes. Select START/STOP to begin preheating.
2. In a shallow bowl, whisk together the eggs and beer. In a medium bowl, whisk together the cornstarch, flour, chili powder, cumin, salt, and pepper.
3. Dip each strip of cod fillet in the egg mixture, then dredge in the flour mixture, coating on all sides.
4. Once unit has preheated, spray the basket with the cooking spray. Place the fish strips in the basket and coat them with cooking spray. Close crisping lid.
5. Select AIR CRISP, set temperature to 375ºF (191ºC), and set time to 15 minutes. Select START/STOP to begin.
6. When cooking is complete, check the fish for your desired crispiness. Remove the fish from the basket.
7. Spread tartar sauce on four slices of bread. Place four fish strips on each slice and top the sandwiches with the four remaining slices. Serve.

Garlicky Shrimp with Broccoli

Prep time: 5 minutes | Cook time: 5 minutes | Serves 4

2 tablespoons unsalted butter
1 shallot, minced
3 garlic cloves, minced
¼ cup white wine
½ cup chicken stock
Juice of ½ lemon
½ teaspoon sea salt
½ teaspoon freshly ground black pepper
1½ pounds (680 g) frozen shrimp, thawed
1 large head broccoli, cut into florets

1. Add the butter. Select SEAR/SAUTÉ and set to MED. Select START/STOP to begin.
2. Once the butter is melted, add the shallots and cook for 3 minutes. Add the garlic and cook for 1 minute.
3. Deglaze the pot by adding the wine and using a wooden spoon to scrape the bits of garlic and shallot off the bottom of the pot. Stir in the chicken stock, lemon juice, salt, pepper, and shrimp.
4. Place the broccoli florets on top of the shrimp mixture. Assemble pressure lid, making sure the pressure release valve is in the SEAL position.
5. Select PRESSURE and set to HI. Set time to 0 minutes. Select START/STOP to begin.
6. When pressure cooking is complete, quick release the pressure by moving the pressure release valve to the VENT position. Carefully remove lid when the unit has finished releasing pressure. Serve immediately.

Country Shrimp Boil

Prep time: 10 minutes | Cook time: 10 minutes | Serves 6

2 pounds (907 g) Red Bliss potatoes, diced
3 ears corn, cut crosswise into thirds
1 (14-ounce / 397-g) package smoked sausage
    or kielbasa, sliced into 1-inch pieces
4 cups water
2½ tablespoons Creole seasoning
1 pound (454 g) medium (21–30 count)
    shrimp, peeled and deveined

1. Place the potatoes, corn, sausage, water, and Creole seasoning into the pot and stir. Assemble pressure lid, making sure the pressure release valve is in the SEAL position.
2. Select PRESSURE and set to HI. Set time to 5 minutes. Select START/STOP to begin.
3. When pressure cooking is complete, quick release the pressure by turning the pressure release valve to the VENT position. Carefully remove lid when unit has finished releasing pressure.
4. Stir in the shrimp.
5. Select SEAR/SAUTÉ and set to MD:LO. Simmer for about 5 minutes, until the shrimp is cooked through.
6. When cooking is complete, serve immediately.

Lobster Lettuce Rolls

Prep time: 10 minutes | Cook time: 20 minutes | Serves 4

4 (4-ounce / 113-g) lobster tails
¼ cup mayonnaise
1 celery stalk, minced
Zest of 1 lemon
Juice of 1 lemon
¼ teaspoon celery seed
Kosher salt
Freshly ground black pepper
4 split-top hot dog buns
4 tablespoons unsalted butter, at room
    temperature
4 leaves butter lettuce

1. Insert Cook & Crisp Basket into the pot and close the crisping lid. Select AIR CRISP, set temperature to 375ºF (191ºC), and set time to 15 minutes. Select START/STOP to begin. Let preheat for 5 minutes.
2. Once unit has preheated, open lid and add the lobster tails to the basket. Close the lid and cook for 10 minutes.
3. In a medium bowl, mix together the mayonnaise, celery, lemon zest and juice, and celery seed, and add salt and pepper.
4. Fill a large bowl with a tray of ice cubes and enough water to cover the ice.
5. When cooking is complete, open lid. Transfer the lobster into the ice bath for 5 minutes. Close lid to keep unit warm.
6. Spread butter on the hot dog buns. Open lid and place the buns in the basket. Close crisping lid.
7. Select AIR CRISP, set temperature to 375ºF (191ºC), and set time to 4 minutes. Select START/STOP to begin.
8. Remove the lobster meat from the shells and roughly chop. Place in the bowl with the mayonnaise mixture and stir.
9. When cooking is complete, open lid and remove the buns. Place lettuce in each bun, then fill with the lobster salad.

Ginger and Scallion Cod Fillets

Prep time: 5 minutes | Cook time: 10 minutes | Serves 4

2 tablespoons rice vinegar
2 tablespoons soy sauce
1 tablespoon chicken stock
1 tablespoon grated fresh ginger
4 skinless cod fillets (about 1½ pounds / 680
    g)
Sea salt
Freshly ground black pepper
Greens of 6 scallions, thinly sliced

1. In a small bowl, mix together the rice vinegar, soy sauce, chicken stock, and ginger.
2. Season the cod fillets on both sides with salt and pepper. Place them in the pot and cover with the vinegar mixture.
3. Select SEAR/SAUTÉ and set to MED. Bring the liquid to a low boil.
4. Once boiling, turn the heat to LO and cover with the pressure lid. Cook for 8 minutes.
5. Remove lid and add the scallion greens to the top of the fish. Cover with the pressure lid and cook for 2 minutes more. Serve.

Tuscan Cod with Red Potatoes

Prep time: 20 minutes | Cook time: 32 minutes | Serves 4

2 tablespoons canola oil, divided
1½ pounds (680 g) baby red potatoes, cut into ½-inch pieces
2½ teaspoons kosher salt, divided
1 teaspoon freshly ground black pepper, divided
1 cup panko bread crumbs
6 tablespoons unsalted butter, divided
2 teaspoons poultry seasoning
Juice of 1 lemon
1 medium onion, thinly sliced
1½ cups cherry tomatoes, halved
4 garlic cloves, quartered lengthwise
⅓ cup Kalamata olives, roughly chopped
4 (6-ounce / 170-g) fresh cod fillets
1 teaspoon fresh mint, finely chopped
1 lemon, cut into wedges

1. Select SEAR/SAUTÉ and set to HI. Select START/STOP to begin. Let preheat for 5 minutes.
2. Add 1 tablespoon of oil and the potatoes. Season with 1½ teaspoons of salt and ½ teaspoon of pepper. Sauté for about 15 minutes, stirring occasionally, until the potatoes are golden brown.
3. While potatoes are cooking, combine the bread crumbs, 4 tablespoons of butter, poultry seasoning, the remaining 1 teaspoon of salt and ½ teaspoon of pepper, and lemon juice in a medium bowl. Stir well.
4. Once the potatoes are browned, carefully remove them from the pot and set aside. Add the remaining 1 tablespoon of oil, then the onion. Sauté for 2 to 3 minutes, until the onions are lightly browned. Add the tomatoes, garlic, and olives and cook for about 2 minutes more, stirring occasionally. Return the potatoes to the pot, stir. Select START/STOP to pause cooking. Close crisping lid to retain heat.
5. Coat the cod on both sides with the remaining 2 tablespoons of butter. Evenly distribute the breadcrumb mixture on top of the cod, pressing the crumbs down firmly.
6. Open lid and place the Reversible Rack in the pot over the potato mixture, making sure it is the higher position. Place the cod fillets on the rack, bread-side up. Close crisping lid.
7. Select BAKE/ROAST, set temperature to 375ºF (191ºC), and set time to 12 minutes. Select START/STOP to begin.
8. When cooking is complete, leave the cod in the pot with the crisping lid closed for 5 minutes to rest before serving. After resting, the internal temperature of the cod should be at least 145ºF (63ºC) and the bread crumbs should be golden brown. Serve with potato mixture and garnish with chopped mint and lemon wedges.

Apricot Salmon with Potatoes

Prep time: 10 minutes | Cook time: 25 minutes | Serves 4

20 ounces (567 g) baby potatoes, whole
1½ cups water
4 (6-ounce / 170-g) frozen skinless salmon fillets
¼ cup apricot preserves
2 teaspoons Dijon mustard
2 tablespoons extra-virgin olive oil
½ teaspoon kosher salt
½ teaspoon freshly ground black pepper

1. Place the potatoes and water in the pot. Put Reversible Rack in pot, making sure it is in the higher position. Place salmon on the rack. Assemble pressure lid, making sure the pressure release valve is in the SEAL position.
2. Select PRESSURE and set to HI. Set time to 5 minutes. Select START/STOP to begin.
3. Mix together the apricot preserves and mustard in a small bowl.
4. When pressure cooking is complete, quick release the pressure by turning the pressure release valve to the VENT position. Carefully remove lid when unit has finished releasing pressure.
5. Carefully remove rack with salmon. Remove potatoes from pot and drain. Place the potatoes on a cutting board and, using the back of a knife, carefully press down to flatten each. Drizzle the flattened potatoes with the olive oil and season with salt and pepper.
6. Place Cook & Crisp Basket in the pot. Place the potatoes into the basket and close crisping lid.
7. Select AIR CRISP, set temperature to 390ºF (199ºC), and set time to 15 minutes. Select START/STOP to begin.
8. After 8 minutes, open lid, and using silicone-tipped tongs, gently flip the potatoes. Lower basket back into pot and close lid to resume cooking.
9. When cooking is complete, remove basket from pot. Return the rack with the salmon to the pot, making sure the rack is in the higher position. Gently brush the salmon with the apricot and mustard mixture.
10. Close crisping lid. Select BROIL and set time to 5 minutes. Select START/STOP to begin.
11. When cooking is complete, remove salmon and serve immediately with the potatoes.

Salmon with Rice and Brussels Sprouts

Prep time: 10 minutes | Cook time: 57 minutes | Serves 2

2 cups brown rice
2½ cups water
2 (4- to 6-ounce / 113- to 170-g) salmon fillets
4 tablespoons everything bagel seasoning, divided
1 pound (454 g) Brussels sprouts, ends trimmed, cut in half
1 tablespoon olive oil
2 tablespoons balsamic glaze

1. Place the rice and water in the cooking pot. Assemble the pressure lid, making sure the pressure release valve is in the SEAL position.
2. Select PRESSURE and set to HI. Set the time to 30 minutes. Select START/STOP to begin.
3. Meanwhile, season both sides of the salmon fillets with the everything bagel seasoning, using one tablespoon per fillet. Set aside.
4. When pressure cooking is complete, allow the pressure to release naturally for 10 minutes. After 10 minutes, quick release any remaining pressure by moving the pressure release valve to the VENT position. Carefully remove the lid when the unit has finished releasing pressure.
5. Season both sides of each salmon fillet with one tablespoon of the everything bagel seasoning.
6. In a medium bowl, combine the Brussels sprouts and olive oil. Toss to coat, and then sprinkle with one tablespoon of the everything bagel seasoning. Toss again to ensure Brussels sprouts are coated.
7. Place the Cook & Crisp Basket into the cooking pot. Close the crisping lid. Select AIR CRISP, set the temperature to 390°F (199°C), and set the time to 16 minutes. Select START/STOP to begin. Allow to preheat for 5 minutes, then add the sprouts to the Cook & Crisp Basket. Close the crisping lid to begin cooking.
8. After 8 minutes, open the crisping lid, lift the basket, and shake the sprouts. Lower the basket back into the pot and close the lid to resume cooking another 8 minutes or until the Brussels sprouts reach your desired crispiness.
9. Once timer is complete, transfer the sprouts to a bowl and toss with remaining tablespoon of seasoning and the balsamic glaze.
10. Close the crisping lid. Select AIR CRISP, set the temperature to 390°F (199°C), and set the time to 11 minutes. Select START/STOP to begin. Allow to preheat for 5 minutes, then add the salmon fillets to the Cook & Crisp basket. Close the lid to begin cooking.
11. Once timer is complete, remove fillets from basket and serve alongside sprouts and rice.

Tilapia with Rice and Avocado Salsa

Prep time: 10 minutes | Cook time: 12 minutes | Serves 4

2 cups white rice, rinsed
2 cups water
¼ cup blackening seasoning
4 (4-ounce / 113-g) tilapia fillets
2 tablespoons freshly squeezed lime juice, divided
1 bunch cilantro, minced
1 tablespoon extra-virgin olive oil
2 avocados, diced
1 large red onion, diced
2 Roma tomatoes, diced
Kosher salt
Freshly ground black pepper

1. Place the rice and water in the pot and stir. Assemble pressure lid, making sure the pressure release valve is in the SEAL position.
2. Select PRESSURE and set to HI. Set time to 2 minutes. Select START/STOP to begin.
3. Place the blackening seasoning on a plate. Dredge the tilapia fillets in the seasoning.
4. When pressure cooking is complete, allow pressure to naturally release for 10 minutes. After 10 minutes, quick release remaining pressure by turning the pressure release valve to the VENT position. Carefully remove lid when unit has finished releasing pressure.
5. Transfer the rice to a large bowl and stir in 1 tablespoon of lime juice and half the cilantro. Cover the bowl with aluminum foil and set aside.
6. Place the Reversible Rack in the pot and arrange tilapia fillets on top. Close crisping lid.
7. Select BROIL and set time to 10 minutes. Select START/STOP to begin.
8. In a medium bowl, stir together the remaining cilantro, remaining 1 tablespoon of lime juice, olive oil, avocado, onion, tomato, and season with salt and pepper.
9. When cooking is complete, open lid and lift the rack out of the pot. Serve the fish over the rice and top with avocado salsa.

White Wine Mussels with Saffron Threads

Prep time: 15 minutes | Cook time: 25 minutes | Serves 4

2 tablespoons vegetable oil

2 shallots, sliced

3 garlic cloves, minced

1 cup cherry tomatoes, halved

2 pounds (907 g) fresh mussels, washed with cold water, strained, scrubbed, and debearded, as needed

2 cups white wine (chardonnay or sauvignon blanc)

2 cups heavy cream

1½ teaspoons cayenne pepper

1½ teaspoons freshly ground black pepper

½ teaspoon saffron threads

1 loaf sourdough bread, cut into slices, for serving

1. Select SEAR/SAUTÉ and set the temperature to HI. Select START/STOP to begin and allow to preheat for 5 minutes.
2. Add oil to the pot and allow to heat for 1 minute. Add the shallots, garlic, and cherry tomatoes. Stir to ensure the ingredients are coated and sauté for 5 minutes.
3. Add the mussels, wine, heavy cream, cayenne, black pepper, and saffron threads to the pot.
4. Assemble the pressure lid, making sure the pressure release valve is in the VENT position.
5. Select STEAM and set the temperature to HI. Set the time to 20 minutes. Select START/STOP to begin.
6. When cooking is complete, carefully remove the lid.
7. Transfer the mussels and broth to bowls or eat straight from the pot. Discard any mussels that have not opened.
8. Serve with the bread and enjoy!

Pineapple Rice with Coconut-Crusted Shrimp

Prep time: 15 minutes | Cook time: 45 minutes | Serves 4

2 tablespoons canola oil

1 (20-ounce / 567-g) can diced pineapple

1 yellow onion, diced

1 cup long-grain white rice

1½ cups chicken stock

½ cup freshly squeezed lime juice

¾ cup all-purpose flour

1 tablespoon kosher salt

½ teaspoon freshly ground black pepper

2 large eggs

½ cup coconut flakes

½ cup plain panko bread crumbs

10 ounces (283 g) deveined shrimp, tails removed

Cooking spray

1. Select SEAR/SAUTÉ and set temperature to HI. Select START/STOP to begin. Let preheat for 5 minutes.
2. Add the oil and heat for 1 minute. Add the pineapple and onion. Cook, stirring frequently, for about 8 minutes, or until the onion is translucent.
3. Add the rice, chicken stock, and lime juice. Assemble pressure lid, making sure the pressure release valve is in the SEAL position.
4. Select PRESSURE and set to HI. Set time to 2 minutes. Select START/STOP to begin.
5. When pressure cooking is complete, allow press to naturally release for 10 minutes. After 10 minutes, quick release remaining pressure by turning the pressure release valve to the VENT position. Carefully remove lid when unit has finished releasing pressure.
6. Transfer the rice mixture to a bowl and cover to keep warm. Clean the cooking pot and return to the unit.
7. Create a batter station with three medium bowls. In the first bowl, mix together the flour, salt and pepper. In the second bowl, whisk the eggs. In the third bowl, combine the coconut flakes and bread crumbs. Dip each shrimp into the flour mixture. Next dip it in the egg. Finally, coat in the coconut mixture, shaking off excess as needed. Once all the shrimp are battered, spray them with cooking spray.
8. Place Cook & Crisp Basket into pot. Place the shrimp in basket and close crisping lid.
9. Select AIR CRISP, set temperature to 390ºF (199ºC), and set time to 10 minutes. Select START/STOP to begin.
10. After 5 minutes, open lid, then lift basket and shake the shrimp. Lower basket back into the pot and close the lid to continue cooking until the shrimp reach your desired crispiness.
11. When cooking is complete, serve the shrimp on top of the rice.

Vodka Shrimp Penne

Prep time: 5 minutes | Cook time: 11 minutes | Serves 6

2 tablespoons extra-virgin olive oil
2 tablespoons minced garlic
1 teaspoon crushed red pepper flakes
1 small red onion, diced
Kosher salt
Freshly ground black pepper
¾ cup vodka
2¾ cups vegetable stock
1 (28-ounce / 794-g) can crushed tomatoes
1 (16-ounce / 454-g) box penne pasta
1 pound (454 g) frozen shrimp, peeled and deveined
1 (8-ounce / 227-g) package cream cheese, cubed
4 cups shredded Mozzarella cheese

1. Select SEAR/SAUTÉ and set to MD:HI. Select START/STOP to begin. Let preheat for 5 minutes.
2. Add the olive oil, garlic, and crushed red pepper flakes. Cook until garlic is golden brown, about 1 minute. Add the onions and season with salt and pepper and cook until translucent, about 2 minutes.
3. Stir in the vodka, vegetable stock, crushed tomatoes, penne pasta, and frozen shrimp. Assemble pressure lid, making sure the pressure release valve is in the SEAL position.
4. Select PRESSURE and set temperature to HI. Set time to 6 minutes. Select START/STOP to begin.
5. When pressure cooking is complete, quick release the pressure by turning the pressure release valve to the VENT position. Carefully remove lid when unit has finished releasing pressure.
6. Stir in the cream cheese until it has melted. Layer the Mozzarella on top of the pasta. Close crisping lid.
7. Select AIR CRISP, set temperature to 400°F (204°C), and set time to 5 minutes. Select START/STOP to begin.
8. When cooking is complete, open lid and serve.

Crab and Rice Cake Casserole

Prep time: 10 minutes | Cook time: 17 minutes | Serves 8

2 tablespoons canola oil
1 large onion, chopped
2 celery stalks, chopped
1 red bell pepper, chopped
1½ cups basmati rice, rinsed
2 cups chicken stock
¼ cup mayonnaise
¼ cup Dijon mustard
3 (8-ounce / 227-g) cans lump crab meat
1 cup shredded Cheddar cheese, divided
1 (5-ounce / 142-g) sleeve butter crackers, crumbled

1. Select SEAR/SAUTÉ and set to HI. Select START/STOP to begin. Let preheat for 5 minutes.
2. Add the oil. Once hot, add the onion, celery, and bell pepper and stir. Cook for 5 minutes, stirring occasionally.
3. Stir in the rice and chicken stock. Assemble pressure lid, making sure the pressure release valve is in the SEAL position.
4. Select PRESSURE and set to HI. Set time to 2 minutes. Select START/STOP to begin.
5. When pressure cooking is complete, allow pressure to naturally release for 10 minutes. After 10 minutes, quick release any remaining pressure by moving the pressure release valve to the VENT position. Carefully remove lid when unit has finished releasing pressure.
6. Stir in the mayonnaise, mustard, crab, and ½ cup of Cheddar cheese. Top evenly with the crackers, then top with remaining ½ cup of cheese. Close crisping lid.
7. Select BAKE/ROAST, set temperature to 350°F (177°C), and set time to 10 minutes. Select START/STOP to begin.
8. When cooking is complete, open lid and serve immediately.

Chorizo and Shrimp Veg Potpie

Prep time: 10 minutes | Cook time: 23 minutes | Serves 6

¼ cup unsalted butter
½ large onion, diced
1 celery stalk, diced
1 carrot, peeled and diced
8 ounces (227 g) chorizo, fully cooked, cut into
    ½-inch wheels
¼ cup all-purpose flour
16 ounces (454 g) frozen tail-off shrimp, cleaned
    and deveined
¾ cup chicken stock
1 tablespoon Cajun spice mix
½ cup heavy (whipping) cream
Sea salt
Freshly ground black pepper
1 refrigerated store-bought pie crust, at room
    temperature

1. Select SEAR/SAUTÉ and set to MD:HI. Select START/STOP to begin. Let preheat for 5 minutes.
2. Add the butter. Once melted, add the onion, celery, carrot, and sausage, and cook until softened, about 3 minutes. Stir in the flour and cook 2 minutes, stirring occasionally.
3. Add the shrimp, stock, Cajun spice mix, and cream and season with salt and pepper. Stir until sauce thickens and bubbles, about 3 minutes.
4. Lay the pie crust evenly on top of the filling, folding over the edges if necessary. Make a small cut in center of pie crust so that steam can escape during baking. Close crisping lid.
5. Select BROIL and set time to 10 minutes. Select START/STOP to begin.
6. When cooking is complete, open lid and remove pot from unit. Let rest 10 to 15 minutes before serving.

Salmon, Almond, and Cranberry Rice Bowl

Prep time: 10 minutes | Cook time: 10 minutes | Serves 4

1½ cups long-grain white rice, rinsed
1½ cups water
⅓ cup dry cranberries
⅓ cup slivered almonds
Kosher salt
4 (4-ounce / 113-g) frozen salmon fillets
⅓ cup dry roasted sunflower seeds
¼ cup Dijon mustard
⅓ cup panko bread crumbs
1 tablespoon honey
1 tablespoon minced parsley

1. Place the rice, water, cranberries, and almonds in the pot. Season with salt and stir. Place Reversible Rack in pot in the higher broil position. Place a circle of aluminum foil on top of the rack, then place the salmon fillets on the foil. Assemble pressure lid, making sure the pressure release valve is in the SEAL position.
2. Select PRESSURE and set to HI. Set time to 2 minutes. Select START/STOP to begin.
3. Add the sunflower seeds, mustard, bread crumbs, honey, and parsley to a small bowl and mix well.
4. When pressure cooking is complete, allow pressure to naturally release for 10 minutes. After 10 minutes, quick release remaining pressure by moving the pressure release valve to the VENT position. Carefully remove lid when unit has finished releasing pressure.
5. Using a spoon, spread a thick, even layer of the sunflower mixture across the top of each fillet. Close crisping lid.
6. Select BROIL and set time to 8 minutes. Select START/STOP to begin. When cooking is complete, open lid and remove the rack and salmon. Use a silicone-coated spatula to fluff the rice. Serve the salmon fillets over the rice.

Bang Bang Popcorn Shrimp

Prep time: 10 minutes | Cook time: 11 minutes | Serves 4

1 cup long-grain white rice
1 cup water
16 ounces (454 g) frozen
    popcorn shrimp
½ cup mayonnaise

¼ cup sweet chili sauce
½ teaspoon Sriracha
2 tablespoons sliced scallions,
    for garnish

1. Put the rice and water in the pot and stir to combine. Assemble the Pressure Lid, making sure the pressure release valve is in the Seal position. Select Pressure and set to High. Set the time to 2 minutes, then select Start/Stop to begin.
2. When pressure cooking is complete, quick release the pressure by moving the pressure release valve to the Vent position. Carefully remove the lid when the pressure has finished releasing.
3. Place the Reversible Rack inside the pot over the rice, making sure the rack is in the higher position. Place the shrimp on the rack.
4. Close the Crisping Lid. Select Air Crisp, set the temperature to 390°F (199°C), and set the time to 9 minutes. Select Start/Stop to begin.
5. Meanwhile, in a medium mixing bowl, stir together the mayonnaise, sweet chili sauce, and Sriracha to create the sauce.
6. After 5 minutes of Air Crisping time, use tongs to flip the shrimp. Close the lid to resume cooking.
7. After cooking is complete, check for desired crispiness and remove the rack from the pot. Toss the shrimp in the sauce to coat evenly. Plate the rice and shrimp, garnish with the scallions, and serve.

Breathtaking Cod Fillets

Prepping time: 10 minutes| Cooking time: 5-10 minutes |For 4 servings

1 pound frozen cod fish fillets
2 garlic cloves, halved
1 cup chicken broth
½ cup packed parsley
2 tablespoons oregano
2 tablespoons almonds, sliced½ teaspoon paprika

1. Take the fish out of the freezer and let it defrost
2. Take a food processor and stir in garlic, oregano, parsley, paprika, 1 tablespoon almond and process. Set your Ninja Foodi to "SAUTE" mode and add olive oil, let it heat up
3. Add remaining almonds and toast, transfer to a towel. Pour broth in a pot and add herb mixture
4. Cut fish into 4 pieces and place in a steamer basket, transfer steamer basket to the pot
5. Lock lid and cook on HIGH pressure for 3 minutes. Quick release pressure once has done
6. Serve steamed fish by pouring over the sauce.Enjoy!

Lemon And Pepper Salmon Delight

Prepping time: 5 minutes| Cooking time: 6 minutes |For 4 servings

¾ cup of water
Sprigs of parsley, basil, tarragon
1 pound salmon, skin on
3 teaspoons ghee
¾ teaspoon salt
½ teaspoon pepper
½ lemon, sliced
1 red bell pepper, julienned
1 carrot, julienned

1. Set your Ninja Foodi to Saute mode and add water and herbs
2. Place a steamer rack and add the salmon. Drizzle ghee on top of the salmon
3. Season with pepper and salt. Cover lemon slices on top
4. Lock up the lid and cook on HIGH pressure for 3 minutes
5. Release the pressure naturally over 10 minutes
6. Transfer the salmon to a platter. Add veggies to your pot and set the pot to Saute mode
7. Cook for 1-2 minutes. Serve the cooked vegetables with salmon. Enjoy!

Fresh Steamed Salmon

Prepping time: 5 minutes| Cooking time: 5 minutes |For 4 servings

2 salmon fillets
¼ cup onion, chopped
2 stalks green onion stalks, chopped
1 whole egg
Almond meal
Salt and pepper to taste
2 tablespoons olive oil

1. Add a cup of water to your Ninja Foodi and place a steamer rack on top
2. Place the fish. Season the fish with salt and pepper and lock up the lid
3. Cook on HIGH pressure for 3 minutes. Once done, quick release the pressure
4. Remove the fish and allow it to cool
5. Break the fillets into a bowl and add egg, yellow and green onions
6. Add ½ a cup of almond meal and mix with your hand. Divide the mixture into patties
7. Take a large skillet and place it over medium heat. Add oil and cook the patties.Enjoy!

Spiced Up Cajun Style Tilapia

Prepping time: 10 minutes| Cooking time: 5 minutes |For 4 servings

4 tilapia fillets, 6 ounces each
1 cup ghee
2 teaspoons cayenne pepper
2 tablespoons smoked paprika
2 teaspoons garlic powder
2 teaspoons onion powder
Pinch of salt
1 teaspoon dried oregano
1 teaspoon dried thyme
1 cup of water

1. Take a small bowl and add cayenne pepper, smoked paprika, garlic powder, onion powder, salt, pepper, dried oregano, dried thyme and ghee
2. Dip the fillets into the seasoned ghee mix. Add 1 cup of water to your Ninja Foodi
3. Place steamer rack and place the fillets on the rack
4. Lock lid and cook on HIGH pressure for 5 minutes. Release naturally over 10 minutes
5. Transfer to serving platter and garnish with parsley. Serve and enjoy!

Delightful Salmon Fillets

Prepping time: 5 minutes| Cooking time: 5 minutes |For 4 servings

2 salmon fillets
¼ cup onion, chopped
2 stalks green onion stalks, chopped
1 whole egg
Almond meal as needed
Salt and pepper to taste
2 tablespoons olive oil

1. Add a cup of water to your Ninja Foodi and place a steamer rack on top
2. Place the fish. Season the fish with salt and pepper and lock up the lid
3. Cook on HIGH pressure for 3 minutes. Once done, quick release the pressure
4. Remove the fish and allow it to cool
5. Break the fillets into a bowl and add egg, yellow and green onions
6. Add ½ a cup of almond meal and mix with your hand. Divide the mixture into patties
7. Take a large skillet and place it over medium heat. Add oil and cook the patties.Enjoy!

A Pot Full Of Shellfish

Prepping time: 15 minutes |Cooking time: 1 minute |For 4 servings

3 pounds mussels
1 tablespoon extra-virgin olive oil
4 garlic cloves, minced
1 large roasted bell pepper
¾ cup fish stock
½ cup white wine vinegar
1/8 teaspoon red pepper flakes
2 tablespoons cashew cream
3 tablespoons parsley, chopped

1. Clean the mussels well and scrub them, debeard if needed. Make a steaming liquid
2. Set your Ninja Foodi to Saute mode and add olive oil, allow it to heat up
3. Add garlic and cook for 1 minute
4. Add roasted red pepper, vinegar, fish stock, red pepper flakes and stir
5. Add mussels to the Ninja Foodi and lock up the lid
6. Cook on HIGH pressure for 1 minute and quick release the pressure
7. Remove the lid and check the mussels, if they are open then enjoy
8. If not, lock up the lid and steam for 1 minute more.Garnish with a bit of parsley. Enjoy!

Orange Sauce And Salmon

Prepping time: 30 minutes| Cooking time: 15 minutes |For 4 servings

1 pound salmon
1 tablespoon coconut amino
2 teaspoons ginger, minced
1 teaspoon garlic, minced
1 teaspoon salt
2 tablespoons sugar
   marmalade

1. Take a zip bag and add the Salmon. Take a bowl and add all of the   and mix well
2. Pour the mixture into the salmon container bag and mix well to ensure that the salmon is coated well. Allow it to marinate for 30 minutes
3. Add 2 cups of water to the Ninja Foodi. Carefully put a steamer rack/trivet on top of your Foodi
4. Add the marinated salmon and sauce on the rack
5. Lock up the lid and cook on LOW pressure for 3 minutes
6. Allow the pressure to release naturally.Serve or broil for 3-4 minutes for a brown texture
7. Alternatively, you may bake the salmon at 350 degrees Fahrenheit for a slightly flaky fish. Enjoy!

Cucumber And Salmon Mix

Prepping time: 5 minutes| Cooking time: 5 minutes |For 4 servings

1 pound salmon steaks
½ cup plain low-fat Greek yogurt
½ cup cucumber, peeled and diced
1 tablespoon fresh dill, chopped
1 tablespoon olive oil
½ teaspoon ground coriander
1 teaspoon fresh lemon juice
1 cup of water
Salt and pepper to taste

1. Mix in low-fat Greek yogurt, dill, cucumber, a pinch of salt and pepper each, mix well and put in the fridge
2. Brush salmon steaks with olive oil, season salmon with salt, pepper and coriander and lemon juice. Add water to Ninja Foodi and place a steamer rack
3. Add fish fillets on rack and lock lid. Cook on HIGH pressure for 3 minutes
4. Release pressure naturally over 10 minutes . Open the lid and serve salmon with cucumber sauce. Enjoy!

The Ginger Flavored Tilapia

Prepping time: 10 minutes| Cooking time: 5 minutes |For 4 servings

1 pound Tilapia fish fillets
3 tablespoons low-sodium coconut
   aminos
2 tablespoons white vinegar
2 fresh garlic cloves, minced
Pinch of salt and pepper
1 tablespoon olive oil
2 tablespoons fresh ginger,
   julienned
¼ cup fresh scallions, julienned
¼ cup fresh cilantro, chopped

1. Take a bowl and add coconut aminos, white vinegar, minced garlic, salt, white pepper and mix well. Add tilapia fish and carefully spoon the sauce over and coat it
2. Marinate for 2 hours. Add 2 cups of water to the Ninja Foodi
3. Add steamer rack to the Ninja Foodi and remove fillets from marinade, transfer them to Steamer Rack. Lock lid and cook on LOW pressure for 2 minutes
4. Quick release pressure. Transfer fillets to serving the dish and discard water
5. Set your pot to Saute mode and add olive oil, let it heat up
6. Add julienned ginger and Saute for a few seconds
7. Add scallions, cilantro and Saute for 2 minutes. Stir in remaining marinade and let it heat up
8. Spoon the sauce over fish. Enjoy!

Favorite Salmon Stew

Prepping time: 5 minutes| Cooking time: 11 minutes |For 4 servings

1 cup fish broth
Salt and pepper to taste
1 medium onion, chopped
1-2 pounds salmon fillets, cubed
1 tablespoon butter

1. Add the listed   to a large-sized bowl and let the shrimp marinate for 30-60 minutes
2. Grease the inner pot of the Ninja Foodi with butter and transfer marinated shrimp to the pot
3. Lock the lid and select "Bake/Roast" mode and bake for 15 minutes at 355 degrees F
4. Once done, serve and enjoy!

Tilapia And Asparagus Delight

Prepping time: 5 minutes| Cooking time: 2 hours |For 4 servings

1 bunch asparagus
4-6 tilapia fillets
8-12 tablespoons lemon juice
Pepper for seasoning
Lemon juice for seasoning
½ tablespoons for clarified butter, for each fillet

1. Cut single pieces of foil for the fillets
2. Divide the bundle of asparagus into even number depending on the number of your fillets
3. Lay the fillets on each of the pieces of foil and sprinkle pepper and add a teaspoon of lemon juice. Add clarified butter and top with asparagus
4. Fold the foil over the fish and seal the ends.Repeat with all the fillets and transfer to Ninja Foodi
5. Cook on SLOW COOK MODE (HIGH) for 2 hours. Enjoy!

Asian Salmon And Veggie Meal

Prepping time: 5 minutes| Cooking time: 2 hours |For 4 servings

For Fish

2 medium salmon fillets
1 garlic cloves, diced
2 teaspoons ginger, grated
¼ a long red chili, diced
Salt as needed
2 tablespoons coconut aminos
1 teaspoon agave nectar

For Veggies

½ pound mixed green veggies
1 large carrot, sliced
1 garlic clove, diced
½ lime, juice
1 tablespoon tamari sauce
1 tablespoon olive oil
½ teaspoon sesame oil

1. Add 1 cup of water to your Ninja Foodi and place a trivet inside
2. Place fish fillets inside a heatproof tin (small enough to fit inside the pot) and sprinkle diced garlic, chili, and ginger on top. Season with salt and pepper
3. Take a small bowl and create a mixture of tamari and agave nectar
4. Pour the mixture over the fillets. Place tin with salmon on top of the trivet
5. Lock up the lid and cook on HIGH pressure for 3 minutes and perform a quick release
6. Cut the vegetables and place the veggies in a steam basket. Sprinkle garlic
7. Place the steamer basket with veggies on top of the salmon tin and drizzle lime juice, olive oil, tamari, sesame oil. Season with salt and pepper
8. Lock up the lid and cook on HIGH pressure for 0 minutes (just the time required for the pressure to build up). Quick release the remove the and basket and tin
9. Transfer the salmon to a plate alongside veggies and pour any remaining sauce over the salmon, enjoy!

All-Time Favorite Codes

Prepping time: 5 minutes| Cooking time: 8 minutes |For 4 servings

4 garlic cloves, minced
2 teaspoons coconut aminos
¼ cup butter
6 whole eggs
2 small onions, chopped
3 (4 ounces each) skinless cod fish fillets, cut into rectangular pieces
2 green chilies, chopped
Salt and pepper to taste

1. Take a shallow dish and add all   except cod, beat the mixture well
2. Dip each fillet into the mixture and keep it on the side
3. Transfer prepared fillets to your Ninja Foodi Crisping basket and transfer basket to Pot
4. Lock Crisping lid and cook on "Air Crisp" mode for 8 minutes at 330 degrees F.Serve and enjoy!

The Great Poached Salmon

Prepping time: 10 minutes| Cooking time: 5 minutes |For 4 servings

16-ounce salmon fillet, skin on
4 scallions, chopped
Zest of 1 lemon
½ a teaspoon of fennel seeds
1 teaspoon white wine vinegar
1 bay leaf
½ cup dry white wine
2 cups chicken broth
¼ cup fresh dill
Salt and pepper

1. Add the listed   to your Ninja Foodi, stir well
2. Lock lid and cook on HIGH pressure for 4 minutes. Release pressure naturally over 10 minutes
3. Serve and enjoy!

Great Seafood Stew

Prepping time: 10 minutes| Cooking time: 10 minutes |For 4 servings

3 tablespoons extra virgin olive oil
2 bay leaves
2 teaspoons paprika
1 small onion, sliced
1 small green bell pepper
2 garlic cloves, mashed
Salt and pepper to taste
1 cup fish stock
1 and ½ pound meat fish
1 pound shrimp, cleaned and deveined
12 neck clams
¼ cup cilantro, garnish
1 tablespoon extra- virgin olive oil

1. Set your Ninja Foodi to Saute mode and add olive oil
2. Add bay leaves and paprika and Saute for 30 seconds
3. Add onion, bell pepper, tomatoes, 2 tablespoons of cilantro, garlic and season with salt and pepper. Stir for a few minutes . Add fish stock
4. Season fish with salt and pepper and Nestle the clams and shrimp among the veggies in the Ninja Foodi. Add fish on top
5. Lock up the lid and cook on HIGH pressure for 10 minutes
6. Release the pressure over 10 minutes
7. Divide the stew amongst bowls and drizzle 1 tablespoon of olive oil
8. Sprinkle 2 tablespoon of cilantro and serve. Enjoy!

Garlic Sauce And Mussels

Prepping time: 15 minutes |Cooking time: 1 minute |For 4 servings

3 pounds mussels
1 tablespoon extra-virgin olive oil
4 garlic cloves, minced
1 large roasted bell pepper
¾ cup fish stock
½ cup white wine vinegar
1/8 teaspoon red pepper flakes
2 tablespoons cashew cream
3 tablespoons parsley, chopped

1. Clean the mussels well and scrub them, debeard if needed. Make a steaming liquid
2. Set your Ninja Foodi to Saute mode and add olive oil, allow it to heat up
3. Add garlic and cook for 1 minute
4. Add roasted red pepper, vinegar, fish stock, red pepper flakes and stir
5. Add mussels to the Ninja Foodi and lock up the lid
6. Cook on HIGH pressure for 1 minute and quick release the pressure
7. Remove the lid and check the mussels, if they are open then enjoy
8. If not, lock up the lid and steam for 1 minute more. Garnish with a bit of parsley. Enjoy!

Shrimp And Tomato Delight

Prepping time: 10 minutes| Cooking time: 5 minutes |For 4 servings

3 tablespoons unsalted butter
1 tablespoon garlic
½ teaspoon red pepper flakes
1 and ½ cup onion, chopped
1 can (14 and ½ ounces tomatoes, diced
1 teaspoon dried oregano
1 teaspoon salt
1 pound frozen shrimp, peeled
1 cup crumbled feta cheese
½ cup black olives, sliced
½ cup parsley, chopped

1. Pre-heat your Ninja Foodi by setting in in the Saute mode on HIGH settings, add butter and let it melt. Add garlic, pepper flakes, cook for 1 minute
2. Add onion, tomato, oregano, salt and stir well. Add frozen shrimp
3. Lock lid and cook on HIGH pressure for 1 minute. Quick release pressure
4. Mix shrimp with tomato broth, let it cool and serve with a sprinkle of feta, olives, and parsley
5. Enjoy!

Juicy Mediterranean Cod

Prepping time: 5 minutes| Cooking time: 15 minutes |For 4 servings

6 Fresh Cod
3 tablespoons clarified butter
1 lemon, juiced
1 onion, sliced
1 teaspoon salt
½ teaspoon pepper
1 teaspoon oregano
1 can (28 ounces tomatoes, diced

1. Set your pot to Saute mode and add clarified butter
2. Once the butter is hot, add the rest of the   and stir (except fish).Saute for 10 minutes
3. Arrange the fish portions in the sauce and spoon the sauce over the fish to coat it
4. Lock up the lid and cook under HIGH pressure for 5 minutes. Perform a quick release and serve!

Medi-Bass Stew

Prepping time: 10 minutes| Cooking time: 28 minutes |For 6 servings

1 pound sea bass fillets, patted dry and cut into 2 inch chunks
3 tablespoons Cajun seasoning, divided
½ teaspoon salt
2 tablespoons extra virgin olive oil
2 yellow onion, diced
2 bell peppers, diced
4 celery stalks, diced
1 can (28 ounces diced tomatoes, drained
¼ cup tomato paste
1 and ½ cups veggie broth
2 pounds large shrimp, peeled and deveined

1. Set your Pot to Saute mode at a temperature of Medium-HIGH heat, let it pre-heat for 5 minutes
2. Season sea bass on both sides with 1 and ½ tablespoons Cajun seasoning and ¼ teaspoon salt. Put 1 tablespoon oil and sea bass in your pre-heated pot. Saute for 4 minutes
3. Add remaining 1 tablespoon oil and onions to the pot and cook for 3 minutes, add bell peppers, celery, and 1 and ½ tablespoons Cajun seasoning to the pot. Cook for 2 minutes more
4. Add sea bass, diced tomatoes, tomato paste, broth to the pot, place the lid and seal the valves
5. Cook on HIGH pressure for 5 minutes, quick release the pressure once did
6. Set your pot to Saute mode again with the temperature set at Medium-HIGH mode and add shrimp. Place lid and seal the pressure valve, cook for 4 minutes until the shrimp is opaque
7. Season with ¼ teaspoon salt and serve, enjoy!

Delicious Smoked Salmon And Spinach Frittata

Prepping time: 10 minutes| Cooking time: 8 hours |For 4 servings

10 whole eggs
¼ cup unsweetened almond milk
1 teaspoon garlic powder
1 teaspoon orange-chili-garlic sauce
½ teaspoon of sea salt
¼ teaspoon freshly ground black pepper
8 ounces smoked salmon, flaked
8 ounces shiitake mushrooms, sliced
2 cups baby spinach
Oil for greasing

1. Take a large sized bowl and add eggs, orange chili garlic sauce, almond milk, garlic powder and season with salt and pepper. Fold in smoked salmon, spinach and mushrooms
2. Mix well. Grease Ninja Foodi with oil. Pour egg mix in Ninja Foodi
3. Close lid and cook on SLOW COOK Mode (LOW) for 8 hours. Serve and enjoy!

Dijon Flavored Lemon Whitefish

Prepping time: 5 minutes| Cooking time: 2 minutes |For 4 servings

1 pound whitefish fillets
2 tablespoons Dijon mustard
1 teaspoon horseradish, grated
1 tablespoon fresh lemon juice
1 teaspoon fresh ginger, grated
½ teaspoon salt and black pepper (each)
1 lemon, sliced
½ tablespoon olive oil
1 cup of water

1. Mix in Dijon mustard, lemon juice and horseradish in a bowl
2. Season white fish fillets with salt and pepper, add Dijon marinade
3. Let it marinate for 20 minutes. Add water to your Ninja Foodi and place a steamer rack inside
4. Put fillets on the rack and pour marinade on top
5. Lock lid and cook on HIGH pressure for 20 minutes
6. Release pressure naturally over 10 minutes. Enjoy!

Very Low Carb Clam Chowder

Prepping time: 5 minutes| Cooking time: 4 hours 20 minutes |For 6 servings

13 slices bacon, thick cut
2 cups chicken broth
1 cup celery, chopped
1 cup onion, chopped
6 cups baby clams, with juice
2 cups heavy whipping cream
1 teaspoon salt
1 teaspoon ground thyme
1 teaspoon pepper

1. Take a skillet and place it over medium heat, cook bacon until crispy
2. Drain and crumble the bacon. Chop onion, celery and add them to the pan
3. Once tender add veggies alongside remaining   to your Ninja Foodi
4. Lock lid and cook on SLOW COOK MODE(LOW) for 4-6 hours. Serve and enjoy!

Chapter 5: Soups and Stews

Pumpkin Soup

Prep time: 10 minutes | Cook time: 23 minutes | Serves 8

¼ cup unsalted butter
½ small onion, diced
1 celery stalk, diced
1 carrot, diced
2 garlic cloves, minced
1 (15-ounce / 425-g) can pumpkin purée
1½ teaspoons poultry spice blend
3 cups chicken stock
1 (8-ounce / 227-g) package cream cheese
1 cup heavy (whipping) cream
¼ cup maple syrup
Sea salt
Freshly ground black pepper

1. Select SEAR/SAUTÉ and set to HI. Select START/STOP to begin. Let preheat for 5 minutes.
2. Add the butter. Once melted, add the onions, celery, carrot, and garlic. Cook, stirring occasionally, for 3 minutes
3. Add the pumpkin, poultry spice, and chicken stock. Assemble pressure lid, making sure the pressure release valve is in the SEAL position.
4. Select PRESSURE and set to HI. Set time to 15 minutes. Select START/STOP to begin.
5. When pressure cooking is complete, quick release the pressure by turning the pressure release valve to the VENT position. Carefully remove lid when the unit has finished releasing pressure.
6. Whisk in the cream cheese, heavy cream, and maple syrup. Season with salt and pepper. Using an immersion blender, purée the soup until smooth.

Beef and Potato Goulash

Prep time: 15 minutes | Cook time: 55 minutes | Serves 6

½ cup all-purpose flour
1 tablespoon kosher salt
½ teaspoon freshly ground black pepper
2 pounds (907 g) beef stew meat
2 tablespoons canola oil
1 medium red bell pepper, seeded and chopped
4 garlic cloves, minced
1 large yellow onion, diced
2 tablespoons smoked paprika
1½ pounds (680 g) small Yukon Gold potatoes, halved
2 cups beef broth
2 tablespoons tomato paste
¼ cup sour cream
Fresh parsley, for garnish

1. Select SEAR/SAUTÉ and set to HI. Select START/STOP to begin. Let preheat for 5 minutes.
2. Mix together the flour, salt, and pepper in a small bowl. Dip the pieces of beef into the flour mixture, shaking off any extra flour.
3. Add the oil and let heat for 1 minute. Place the beef in the pot and brown it on all sides, about 10 minutes.
4. Add the bell pepper, garlic, onion, and smoked paprika. Sauté for about 8 minutes or until the onion is translucent.
5. Add the potatoes, beef broth, and tomato paste and stir. Assemble pressure lid, making sure the pressure release valve is in the SEAL position.
6. Select PRESSURE and set to LO. Set time to 30 minutes. Select START/STOP to begin.
7. When pressure cooking is complete, quick release the pressure by moving the pressure release valve to the VENT position. Carefully remove lid when unit has finished releasing pressure.
8. Add the sour cream and mix thoroughly. Garnish with parsley, if desired, and serve immediately.

Rice and Mushroom Soup

Prep time: 10 minutes | Cook time: 30 minutes | Serves 6

5 medium carrots, chopped
5 celery stalks, chopped
1 onion, chopped
3 garlic cloves, minced
1 cup wild rice
8 ounces (227 g) fresh mushrooms, sliced
6 cups vegetable broth
1 teaspoon kosher salt
1 teaspoon poultry seasoning
½ teaspoon dried thyme

1. Place all the ingredients in the pot. Assemble pressure lid, making sure the pressure release valve is in the SEAL position.
2. Select PRESSURE and set to HI. Set time to 30 minutes. Select START/STOP to begin.
3. When pressure cooking is complete, quick release the pressure by turning the pressure release valve to the VENT position. Carefully remove lid when unit has finished releasing pressure.
4. Serve.

Bacon and Cheddar Potato Soup

Prep time: 15 minutes | Cook time: 30 minutes | Serves 6

5 slices bacon, chopped
1 onion, chopped
3 garlic cloves, minced
4 pounds (1.8 kg) Russet potatoes, peeled and chopped
4 cups chicken broth
1 cup whole milk
½ teaspoon sea salt
½ teaspoon freshly ground black pepper
1½ cups shredded Cheddar cheese
Sour cream, for serving (optional)
Chopped fresh chives, for serving (optional)

1. Select SEAR/SAUTÉ and set to HI. Select START/STOP to begin. Let preheat for 5 minutes.
2. Add the bacon, onion, and garlic. Cook, stirring occasionally, for 5 minutes. Set aside some of the bacon for garnish.
3. Add the potatoes and chicken broth. Assemble pressure lid, making sure the pressure release valve is in the SEAL position.
4. Select PRESSURE and set to HI. Set time to 10 minutes, then select START/STOP to begin.
5. When pressure cooking is complete, quick release the pressure by moving the pressure release valve to the VENT position. Carefully remove lid when unit has finished releasing pressure.
6. Add the milk and mash the ingredients until the soup reaches your desired consistency. Season with the salt and black pepper. Sprinkle the cheese evenly over the top of the soup. Close crisping lid.
7. Select BROIL and set time to 5 minutes. Select START/STOP to begin.
8. When cooking is complete, top with the reserved crispy bacon and serve with sour cream and chives (if using).

Italian Sausage Soup

Prep time: 10 minutes | Cook time: 18 minutes | Serves 8

1 tablespoon extra-virgin olive oil
1½ pounds (680 g) hot Italian sausage, ground
1 pound (454 g) sweet Italian sausage, ground
1 large yellow onion, diced
2 tablespoons minced garlic
4 large Russet potatoes, cut in ½-inch thick quarters
5 cups chicken stock
2 tablespoons Italian seasoning
2 teaspoons crushed red pepper flakes
Salt
Freshly ground black pepper
6 cups kale, chopped
½ cup heavy (whipping) cream

1. Select SEAR/SAUTÉ. Set temperature to MD:HI. Select START/STOP to begin. Let preheat for 5 minutes.
2. Add the olive oil and hot and sweet Italian sausage. Cook, breaking up the sausage with a spatula, until the meat is cooked all the way through, about 5 minutes.
3. Add the onion, garlic, potatoes, chicken stock, Italian seasoning, and crushed red pepper flakes. Season with salt and pepper. Stir to combine. Assemble pressure lid, making sure the pressure release valve is in the SEAL position.
4. Select PRESSURE and set to HI. Set time to 10 minutes. Select START/STOP to begin.
5. When pressure cooking is complete, quick release the pressure by turning the pressure release valve to the VENT position. Carefully remove lid when the unit has finished releasing pressure.
6. Stir in the kale and heavy cream. Serve.

Butternut Squash and Orzo Soup

Prep time: 10 minutes | Cook time: 28 minutes | Serves 8

4 slices uncooked bacon, cut into ½-inch pieces
12 ounces (340 g) butternut squash, peeled and cubed
1 green apple, cut into small cubes
Kosher salt
Freshly ground black pepper
1 tablespoon minced fresh oregano
2 quarts (1.8 kg) chicken stock
1 cup orzo

1. Select SEAR/SAUTÉ and set temperature to HI. Select START/STOP to begin. Let preheat for 5 minutes.
2. Place the bacon in the pot and cook, stirring frequently, about 5 minutes, or until fat is rendered and the bacon starts to brown. Using a slotted spoon, transfer the bacon to a paper towel-lined plate to drain, leaving the rendered bacon fat in the pot.
3. Add the butternut squash, apple, salt, and pepper and sauté until partially soft, about 5 minutes. Stir in the oregano.
4. Add the bacon back into the pot along with the chicken stock. Bring to a boil for about 10 minutes, then add the orzo. Cook for about 8 minutes, until the orzo is tender. Serve.

Pork, Bean, and Hominy Stew

Prep time: 15 minutes | Cook time: 30 minutes | Serves 8

2 pounds (907 g) boneless pork shoulder, cut into 1-inch pieces
¼ cup all-purpose flour
¼ cup unsalted butter
½ small onion, diced
1 carrot, diced
1 celery stalk, diced
2 garlic cloves, minced
1 tablespoon tomato paste
1 tablespoon cumin
1 tablespoon smoked paprika
4 cups chicken stock
1 (10-ounce / 283-g) can diced tomatoes with chiles
1 (15-ounce / 425-g) can black beans, rinsed and drained
1 (15-ounce / 425-g) can hominy, rinsed and drained
Sea salt
Freshly ground black pepper

1. In a large bowl, coat the pork pieces with the flour.
2. Select SEAR/SAUTÉ and set to HI. Select START/STOP to begin. Let preheat for 5 minutes.
3. Add the butter. Once melted, add the pork and sear for 5 minutes, turning the pieces so they begin to brown on all sides.
4. Add the onion, carrot, celery, garlic, tomato paste, cumin, and paprika and cook, stirring occasionally, for 3 minutes.
5. Add the chicken stock and tomatoes. Assemble pressure lid, making sure the pressure release valve is in the SEAL position.
6. Select PRESSURE and set to HI. Set time to 15 minutes. Select START/STOP to begin.
7. When pressure cooking is complete, quick release the pressure by turning the pressure release valve to the VENT position. Carefully remove lid when the unit has finished releasing pressure.
8. Select SEAR/SAUTÉ and set to HI. Select START/STOP to begin.
9. Whisk in the beans and hominy. Season with salt and pepper and cook for 2 minutes. Serve.

Haddock and Biscuit Chowder

Prep time: 15 minutes | Cook time: 30 minutes | Serves 8

5 strips bacon, sliced
1 white onion, chopped
3 celery stalks, chopped
4 cups chicken stock
2 Russet potatoes, rinsed and cut in 1-inch pieces
4 (6-ounce / 170-g) frozen haddock fillets

Kosher salt
½ cup clam juice
⅓ cup all-purpose flour
2 (14-ounce / 397-g) cans evaporated milk
1 (14-ounce / 397-g) tube refrigerated biscuit dough

1. Select SEAR/SAUTÉ and set to HI. Select START/STOP to begin. Let preheat for 5 minutes.
2. Add the bacon and cook, stirring frequently, for 5 minutes. Add the onion and celery and cook for an additional 5 minutes, stirring occasionally.
3. Add the chicken stock, potatoes, and haddock filets. Season with salt. Assemble pressure lid, making sure the pressure release valve is in the SEAL position.
4. Select PRESSURE and set to HI. Set time to 5 minutes. Select START/STOP to begin.
5. Whisk together the clam juice and flour in a small bowl, ensuring there are no flour clumps in the mixture.
6. When pressure cooking is complete, quick release the pressure by moving the pressure release valve to the VENT position. Carefully remove lid when unit has finished releasing pressure.
7. Select SEAR/SAUTÉ and set to MED. Select START/STOP to begin. Add the clam juice mixture, stirring well to combine. Add the evaporated milk and continue to stir frequently for 3 to 5 minutes, until chowder has thickened to your desired texture.
8. Place the Reversible Rack in the pot in the higher position. Place the biscuits on the rack; it may be necessary to tear the last biscuit or two into smaller pieces in order to fit them all on the rack. Close crisping lid.
9. Select BAKE/ROAST, set temperature to 350°F (177°C), and set time to 12 minutes. Select START/STOP to begin.
10. After 10 minutes, check the biscuits for doneness. If desired, cook for up to an additional 2 minutes.
11. When cooking is complete, open lid and remove rack from pot. Serve the chowder and top each portion with biscuits.

Coconut Shrimp and Pea Bisque

Prep time: 10 minutes | Cook time: 15 minutes | Serves 4

¼ cup red curry paste
2 tablespoons water
1 tablespoon extra-virgin olive oil
1 bunch scallions, sliced
1 pound (454 g) medium (21-30 count) shrimp, peeled and deveined
1 cup frozen peas
1 red bell pepper, diced
1 (14-ounce / 397-g) can full-fat coconut milk
Kosher salt

1. In a small bowl, whisk together the red curry paste and water. Set aside.
2. Select SEAR/SAUTÉ and set to MED. Select START/STOP to begin. Let preheat for 3 minutes.
3. Add the oil and scallions. Cook for 2 minutes.
4. Add the shrimp, peas, and bell pepper. Stir well to combine. Stir in the red curry paste. Cook for 5 minutes, until the peas are tender.
5. Stir in coconut milk and cook for an additional 5 minutes until shrimp is cooked through and the bisque is thoroughly heated.
6. Season with salt and serve immediately.

Shrimp and White Fish Stew

Prep time: 10 minutes | Cook time: 46 minutes | Serves 6

2 tablespoons extra-virgin olive oil
1 yellow onion, diced
1 fennel bulb, tops removed and bulb diced
3 garlic cloves, minced
1 cup dry white wine
2 (14½-ounce / 411-g) cans fire-roasted tomatoes
2 cups chicken stock
1 pound (454 g) medium (21-30 count) shrimp, peeled and deveined
1 pound (454 g) raw white fish (cod or haddock), cubed
Salt
Freshly ground black pepper
Fresh basil, torn, for garnish

1. Select SEAR/SAUTÉ and set to MED. Select START/STOP to begin. Let preheat for 3 minutes.
2. Add the olive oil, onions, fennel, and garlic. Cook for about 3 minutes, until translucent.
3. Add the white wine and deglaze, scraping any stuck bits from the bottom of the pot using a silicone spatula. Add the roasted tomatoes and chicken stock. Simmer for 25 to 30 minutes. Add the shrimp and white fish.
4. Select SEAR/SAUTÉ and set to MD:LO. Select START/STOP to begin.
5. Simmer for 10 minutes, stirring frequently, until the shrimp and fish are cooked through. Season with salt and pepper.
6. Ladle into bowl and serve topped with torn basil.

Chicken and Black Bean Enchilada Soup

Prep time: 5 minutes | Cook time: 30 minutes | Serves 8

1 tablespoon extra-virgin olive oil
1 small red onion, diced
2 (10-ounce / 283-g) cans fire-roasted tomatoes with chiles
1 (15-ounce / 425-g) can corn
1 (15-ounce / 425-g) can black beans, rinsed and drained
1 (10-ounce / 283-g) can red enchilada sauce
1 (10-ounce / 283-g) can tomato paste
3 tablespoons taco seasoning
2 tablespoons freshly squeezed lime juice
2 (8-ounce / 227-g) boneless, skinless chicken breasts
Salt
Freshly ground black pepper

1. Select SEAR/SAUTÉ and set temperature to MD:HI. Select START/STOP to begin. Let preheat for 5 minutes.
2. Place the olive oil and onion in the pot. Cook until the onions are translucent, about 2 minutes.
3. Add the tomatoes, corn, beans, enchilada sauce, tomato paste, taco seasoning, lime juice, and chicken. Season with salt and pepper and stir. Assemble pressure lid, making sure the pressure release valve is in the SEAL position.
4. Select PRESSURE and set to HI. Set time to 9 minutes. Select START/STOP to begin.
5. When pressure cooking is complete, allow pressure to naturally release for 10 minutes. After 10 minutes, quick release remaining pressure by moving the pressure release valve to the VENT position. Carefully remove lid when unit has finished releasing pressure.
6. Transfer the chicken breasts to a cutting board. Using two forks, shred the chicken. Return the chicken back to the pot and stir. Serve in a bowl with toppings of choice, such as shredded cheese, crushed tortilla chips, sliced avocado, sour cream, cilantro, and lime wedges, if desired.

Chicken and Egg Noodle Soup

Prep time: 10 minutes | Cook time: 19 minutes | Serves 8

2 tablespoons unsalted butter
1 large onion, chopped
2 carrots, chopped
2 celery stalks, chopped
2 pounds (907 g) boneless chicken breast
4 cups chicken broth
4 cups water
1 tablespoon chopped fresh parsley
1 teaspoon dried thyme
1 teaspoon dried oregano
½ teaspoon sea salt
½ teaspoon freshly ground black pepper
5 ounces (142 g) egg noodles

1. Select SEAR/SAUTÉ and set to HI. Select START/STOP to begin. Let preheat for 5 minutes.
2. Add the butter. Once melted, add the onion, carrots, and celery. Cook, stirring occasionally, for 5 minutes.
3. Add the chicken, chicken broth, water, parsley, thyme, oregano, salt, and pepper. Assemble pressure lid, making sure the pressure release valve is in the SEAL position.
4. Select PRESSURE and set to HI. Set time to 8 minutes. Select START/STOP to begin.
5. When pressure cooking is complete, quick release the pressure by moving the pressure release valve to the VENT position. Carefully remove lid when unit has finished releasing pressure.
6. Remove the chicken from the soup and shred it with two forks. Set aside.
7. Add the egg noodles. Select SEAR/SAUTÉ and set to MED. Select START/STOP to begin.
8. Cook for 6 minutes, uncovered, or until the noodles are tender. Stir the shredded chicken back into the pot. Serve.

Chicken and Mixed Vegetable Potpie Soup

Prep time: 15 minutes | Cook time: 1 hour | Serves 6

4 (8-ounce / 227-g) chicken breasts
2 cups chicken stock
2 tablespoons unsalted butter
1 yellow onion, diced
16 ounces (454 g) frozen mixed vegetables
1 cup heavy (whipping) cream
1 (10½-ounce / 298-g) can condensed cream of chicken
    soup
2 tablespoons cornstarch
2 tablespoons water
Salt
Freshly ground black pepper
1 (16.3-ounce / 462-g) tube refrigerated biscuit dough

1. Place the chicken and stock in the pot. Assemble pressure lid, making sure the pressure release valve is in the SEAL position.
2. Select PRESSURE and set to HI. Set time to 15 minutes. Select START/STOP to begin.
3. Once pressure cooking is complete, quick release the pressure by turning the pressure release valve to the VENT position. Carefully remove lid when the unit has finished releasing pressure.
4. Using a silicone-tipped utensil, shred the chicken.
5. Select SEAR/SAUTÉ and set to MED. Add the butter, onion, mixed vegetables, cream, and condensed soup and stir. Select START/STOP to begin. Simmer for 10 minutes.
6. In a small bowl, whisk together the cornstarch and water. Slowly whisk the cornstarch mixture into the soup. Set temperature to LO and simmer for 10 minutes more. Season with salt and pepper.
7. Carefully arrange the biscuits on top of the simmering soup. Close crisping lid.
8. Select BAKE/ROAST, set temperature to 325°F (163°C), and set time to 15 minutes. Select START/STOP to begin.
9. When cooking is complete, remove the biscuits. To serve, place a biscuit in a bowl and ladle soup over it.

Chicken and Corn Tortilla Soup

Prep time: 10 minutes | Cook time: 20 minutes | Serves 8

1 tablespoon extra-virgin olive oil
1 onion, chopped
1 pound (454 g) boneless, skinless chicken breasts
6 cups chicken broth
1 (12-ounce / 340-g) jar salsa
4 ounces (113 g) tomato paste
1 tablespoon chili powder
2 teaspoons cumin
½ teaspoon sea salt
½ teaspoon freshly ground black pepper
1 pinch of cayenne pepper
1 (15-ounce / 425-g) can black beans, rinsed and drained
2 cups frozen corn
Tortilla strips, for garnish

1. Select SEAR/SAUTÉ and set to temperature to HI. Select START/STOP to begin. Let preheat for 5 minutes.
2. Place the olive oil and onions into the pot and cook, stirring occasionally, for 5 minutes.
3. Add the chicken breast, chicken broth, salsa, tomato paste, chili powder, cumin, salt, pepper, and cayenne pepper. Assemble pressure lid, making sure the pressure release valve is in the SEAL position.
4. Select PRESSURE and set to HI. Set time to 10 minutes. Select START/STOP to begin.
5. When pressure cooking is complete, allow pressure to naturally release for 10 minutes. After 10 minutes, quick release remaining pressure by moving the pressure release valve to the VENT position. Carefully remove lid when unit has finished releasing pressure.
6. Transfer the chicken breasts to a cutting board and shred with two forks. Set aside.
7. Add the black beans and corn. Select SEAR/SAUTÉ and set to MD. Select START/STOP to begin. Cook until heated through, about 5 minutes.
8. Add shredded chicken back to the pot. Garnish with tortilla strips, serve, and enjoy!

Tomatillo Chicken Thigh Stew

Prep time: 15 minutes | Cook time: 46 minutes | Serves 4

3 medium onions, quartered

3 garlic cloves, whole

2 poblano peppers, seeded and quartered

½ pound (227 g) tomatillos

2 small jalapeño peppers, seeded and quartered (optional)

2 tablespoons canola oil, divided

Kosher salt

Freshly ground black pepper

2½ pounds (1.1 kg) boneless, skinless chicken thighs (6 to 8 pieces)

1 cup chicken stock

1 teaspoon cumin

1 tablespoon oregano

1 tablespoon all-purpose flour

1 cup water

1. Place Cook & Crisp Basket in pot and close crisping lid. Select AIR CRISP and set to HIGH. Set time to 25 minutes. Select START/STOP to begin. Let preheat for 5 minutes.
2. Place the onions, garlic, poblano peppers, tomatillos, jalapeños, 1 tablespoon of canola oil, salt, and pepper in a medium-sized bowl and mix until vegetables are evenly coated.
3. Once unit has preheated, open lid and place the vegetables in the basket. Close lid and cook for 20 minutes.
4. After 10 minutes, open lid, then lift basket and shake the vegetables or toss them with silicone-tipped tongs. Lower basket back into pot and close lid to continue cooking.
5. When cooking is complete, remove basket and vegetables and set aside.
6. Select SEAR/SAUTÉ and set to HI. Select START/STOP to begin. Let preheat for 5 minutes.
7. Season the chicken thighs with salt and pepper.
8. After 5 minutes, add the remaining 1 tablespoon of oil and chicken. Sear the chicken, about 3 minutes on each side.
9. Add the chicken stock, cumin, and oregano. Scrape the pot with a rubber or wooden spoon to release any pieces that are sticking to the bottom. Assemble pressure lid, making sure the pressure release valve is in the SEAL position.
10. Select PRESSURE and set to HI. Set time to 10 minutes. Select START/STOP to begin.
11. Remove the vegetables from the basket and roughly chop.
12. In a small bowl, add the flour and water and stir.
13. When pressure cooking is complete, quick release the pressure by turning the pressure release valve to the VENT position. Carefully remove lid when unit has finished releasing pressure.
14. Remove the chicken and shred it using two forks.
15. Select SEAR/SAUTÉ and set to MED. Select START/STOP to begin. Return the chicken and vegetables and stir with a rubber or wooden spoon, being sure to scrape the bottom of the pot. Slowly stir in the flour mixture. Bring to a simmer and cook for 10 minutes, or until the broth becomes clear and has thickened.
16. When cooking is complete, serve as is or garnish with sour cream, lime, cilantro, and a flour tortilla for dipping.

Jamaican Jerk Chicken and Cabbage Stew

Prep time: 15 minutes | Cook time: 28 minutes | Serves 6

2 tablespoons canola oil

6 boneless, skinless chicken thighs, cut in 2-inch

pieces

2 tablespoons Jamaican jerk spice

1 white onion, peeled and chopped

2 red bell peppers, chopped

½ head green cabbage, core removed and cut into 2-inch pieces

1½ cups wild rice blend, rinsed

4 cups chicken stock

½ cup prepared Jamaican jerk sauce

Kosher salt

1. Select SEAR/SAUTÉ and set to HI. Select START/STOP to begin. Let preheat for 5 minutes.
2. Add the oil, chicken, and jerk spice and stir. Cook for 5 minutes, stirring occasionally.
3. Add the onions, bell pepper, and cabbage and stir. Cook for 5 minutes, stirring occasionally.
4. Add the wild rice and stock, stirring well to combine. Assemble pressure lid, making sure the pressure release valve is in the SEAL position.
5. Select PRESSURE and set to HI. Set time to 18 minutes. Select START/STOP to begin.
6. When pressure cooking is complete, allow pressure to naturally release for 10 minutes. After 10 minutes, quick release any remaining pressure by moving the pressure release valve to the VENT position. Carefully remove lid when unit has finished releasing pressure.
7. Add the jerk sauce to pot, stirring well to combine. Let the stew sit for 5 minutes, allowing it to thicken. Season with salt and serve.

Chapter 6: Appetizers and Snacks

Vegetable Tamales

Prep time: 15 minutes | Cook time: 23 minutes | Makes 2 dozen tamales

For the Squash and Pepper Filling:

3 tablespoons vegetable oil

2 medium yellow summer squash, finely diced

1 red bell pepper, seeded, ribbed, and finely diced

1 jalapeño, seeded and finely diced

4 garlic cloves, minced

1 medium yellow onion, finely diced

1 teaspoon chili powder

1 teaspoon ground cumin

1 (15-ounce / 425-g) can tomato sauce

1 cup vegetable broth

2 teaspoons kosher salt

For the Tamales:

24 dried corn husks

4½ cups instant yellow corn masa flour (see Note, this page)

3¾ teaspoons kosher salt

3 teaspoons baking powder

¾ cup vegetable shortening, at room temperature

Make the Filling

1. Set the Foodi to Sear/Saute on High. Add the oil to the inner pot and heat for 4 minutes. Add the squash and cook until softened, about 6 minutes, stirring once halfway through. Stir in the bell pepper, jalapeño, and garlic and continue to cook until softened, about 4 minutes, stirring often. Add the onion, chili powder, and cumin and cook until softened and aromatic, about 4 minutes more, stirring once.

2. Add the tomato sauce, vegetable broth, and salt. Lock on the Pressure Lid, making sure the valve is set to Seal, and set to Pressure on High for 1 minute. When the timer reaches 0, quick-release the pressure and carefully remove the lid. Transfer the squash and bell pepper mixture to a medium bowl and set aside to cool to room temperature. Wash and dry the Foodi's inner pot.

Make the Tamales

3. Arrange the corn husks vertically in the crisping basket (see this page), folding the edges in, and place the basket in the Foodi's inner pot. Add 3 cups water and lock on the Pressure Lid, making sure the valve is set to Seal, then set the Foodi to Pressure on High for 0 minutes. When the timer reaches 0, quick-release the pressure and carefully remove the lid. Remove the crisping basket and set aside. Leave the water in the pot.

4. Place the masa in a medium bowl and whisk in the salt and baking powder. Add the vegetable shortening and pinch it into the flour mixture (as you would if making pie dough), rubbing the shortening into the flour until there aren't any fat bits larger than a pea. Add the water from the inner pot and use a spoon to stir the mixture until it forms a batter of sorts.

5. Place a corn husk on your work surface, ribbed side down, and unfold the husk so it lies flat. Gently spread about 3 tablespoons of the masa dough on the husk in an even layer all the way to the edges of the husk. Add about 2 tablespoons of the filling to the middle of the masa and spread it, leaving a ¼-inch border around the edges. Fold in the sides of the tamale, followed by the bottom. Set the tamale into the crisping basket (it's easiest to place the crisping basket on its side; see photograph on right), seam side down, like a little package. Repeat with the remaining husks, dough, and filling.

6. Place 2 cups water in the Foodi's inner pot. Arrange the tamales in the crisping basket so that the folded ends are at the bottom of the basket and the open tops are pointing upward. Place the basket in the Foodi, then lock on the Pressure Lid, making sure the valve is set to Seal, and set to Pressure on High for 10 minutes. When the timer reaches 0, quick-release the pressure and carefully remove the lid. Allow the tamales to cool slightly before serving or store them, when completely cooled, in an airtight container.

Artichokes with Melted Butter

Prep time: 5 minutes | Cook time: 12 minutes | Serves 6

3 globe artichokes, stems and top leaves trimmed, if
   desired
2 teaspoons kosher salt
1 lemon, halved
4 tablespoons butter, melted

1. Add ½ cup water, the artichokes, and the salt to the Foodi's inner pot. Squeeze the lemon halves over the artichokes and then add them to the pot as well. Lock on the Pressure Lid, making sure the valve is set to Seal, and set to Pressure on High for 12 minutes. When the timer reaches 0, quick-release the pressure and carefully open the lid.
2. Serve the artichokes with melted butter.

Chicken Wings

Prep time: 5 minutes | Cook time: 40 minutes | Serves 2

1½ cups hot sauce
6 whole chicken wings, split into drumettes and flats
½ teaspoon kosher salt
Celery sticks, for garnish (optional)
Carrot sticks, for garnish (optional)
Blue cheese dressing, for garnish (optional)
Ranch dressing, for garnish (optional)

1. Place ½ cup of the hot sauce and 1 cup water in the Foodi's inner pot and stir to combine. Place the wings in the crisping basket and set the basket into the inner pot. Lock on the Pressure Lid, making sure the valve is set to Seal, and set to Pressure on High for 2 minutes. When the timer reaches 0, quick-release the pressure and carefully remove the lid.
2. Sprinkle the wings with the salt. Drop the Crisping Lid and set the Foodi to Air Crisp at 390°F (199°C) for 40 minutes, or until crisp and blistered.
3. Lift the lid and remove the basket with the wings. Add the remaining 1 cup hot sauce to the pot, and toss the wings with the sauce in the pot. Transfer the wings to a platter and serve with your favorite accoutrements.

Hot Blackberry Chicken Wing Sauce

Prep time: 5 minutes | Cook time: 8 minutes | Makes 1 cup

4 tablespoons unsalted butter
6 ounces (170 g) fresh blackberries
2 serrano chiles, roughly chopped (for less heat,
   remove the seeds and membranes)
1 teaspoon freshly ground black pepper

1. Place the butter, blackberries, chiles, pepper, and ½ cup water into the Foodi's inner pot. Lock on the Pressure Lid, making sure the valve is set to Seal, and set to Pressure on High for 2 minutes. When the timer reaches 0, quick-release the pressure and carefully remove the lid.
2. Use a silicone potato masher to mash the blackberries until they are uniformly pulverized. Set the Foodi to Sear/Saute on High and cook the mixture until thickened, about 6 minutes.
3. Strain the sauce through a fine-mesh sieve and into a bowl, pressing on the mixture to extract as much juice as possible. Discard the seeds and remaining bits of pepper in the sieve. Immediately toss the sauce with unsauced chicken wings or transfer to an airtight container and refrigerate for up to 1 week before warming, stirring, and adding to wings.

Homemade Hummus

Prep time: 10 minutes | Cook time: 30 minutes | Makes 6 cup

1 pound (454 g) dried chickpeas
4 teaspoons cumin seeds
Zest of 1 lemon and juice of 2
    lemons
¾ cup tahini
1 cup extra-virgin olive oil
1 tablespoon toasted sesame oil
2 garlic cloves, minced
2 teaspoons kosher salt
Pita, for serving (optional)
Bread, for serving (optional)
Vegetable sticks, for serving
    (optional)

1. Place the chickpeas into the Foodi's inner pot. Add 5 cups water, half the cumin seeds, and the lemon zest to the pot. Lock on the Pressure Lid, making sure the valve is set to Seal, and set to Pressure on High for 30 minutes. When the timer reaches 0, turn off the Foodi and let the pressure naturally release for 15 minutes, then quick-release any remaining pressure and carefully remove the lid.
2. Drain the chickpeas (reserve the cooking liquid) using the crisping basket as a colander. Add the cooked chickpeas to the Foodi's inner pot.
3. While the chickpeas are still hot, add the remaining cumin seeds, tahini, olive oil, sesame oil, garlic, lemon juice, and salt. Use a silicone potato masher or silicone spatula to smash and stir everything together. (Alternatively, you can transfer everything to a food processor or blender and process until smooth.) Use the reserved cooking liquid as needed to thin the mash to your desired thickness—I usually end up adding about 1 cup of cooking liquid. Transfer the hummus to an airtight container and refrigerate until cool. Serve with pita, bread, or vegetable sticks.

Breaded Jalapeño Poppers

Prep time: 5 minutes | Cook time: 10 minutes | Makes 24 poppers

1½ cups breadcrumbs
3 large eggs
1 (8-ounce / 227-g) package
    cream cheese, transferred
    to a zippered plastic bag to
    warm to room temperature
1 (26-ounce / 737-g) can
    whole pickled jalapeños,
    drained, stemmed, halved
    lengthwise, and seeds and
    ribs removed
Cooking spray

1. Place the breadcrumbs in a medium bowl. Add the eggs to another small bowl and lightly whisk.
2. Snip off one of the bottom corners of the cream cheese–filled bag and use it like a pastry bag to fill the jalapeños to their rims with cream cheese.
3. Line a freezer-safe container with plastic wrap. Spray the plastic wrap with cooking spray.
4. Dip the filled jalapeños in the egg, then roll them in the breadcrumbs, then repeat with the egg and breadcrumbs so the jalapeños get a double coating.
5. Place the stuffed jalapeños in the prepared container without overlapping (though the sides can touch). If you run out of space in the container, spray the jalapeños with cooking spray, cover with plastic wrap, spray the wrap, and add another layer. Cover the container with plastic wrap and freeze for at least 4 hours or up to 1 week.
6. Insert the crisping basket into the Foodi's inner pot and spray with cooking spray. Add 9 poppers to the basket and spray the tops of the poppers. Drop the Crisping Lid and set the Foodi to Air Crisp at 390°F (199°C) for 10 minutes, or until the poppers are browned and bubbling. Lift the lid and remove the basket from the Foodi pot. Repeat for the remaining poppers. Cool for 5 minutes before eating

Mexican Cheese Chicken Taquitos

Prep time: 5 minutes | Cook time: 15 minutes | Makes 6 taquitos

1½ cups shredded cooked chicken
1½ cups shredded Mexican-style
    cheese
¼ cup your favorite salsa
6 (8-inch) flour tortillas
Cooking spray
Sour cream, for garnish (optional)
Salsa, for garnish (optional)
Nacho cheese, for garnish
    (optional)

1. Combine the chicken, cheese, and salsa in a medium bowl, mashing until it holds together.
2. Shape ¼ cup of the chicken mixture into a log and place in the center of a tortilla, then tightly roll it up, securing it with a toothpick. Repeat with the remaining filling and tortillas.
3. Place the crisping basket in the Foodi's inner pot, spray it with cooking spray, and place 3 taquitos in the basket. Add the small rack to the basket, spray the rack (and the top of the taquitos) with cooking spray, and add the other 3 taquitos. Spray the tops of the second taquito layer.
4. Drop the Crisping Lid and set to Air Crisp at 390°F (199°C) for 15 minutes, or until the taquitos are golden and crisp, rotating the positioning of the taquitos every 5 minutes. Lift the lid and carefully remove the taquitos from the Foodi. Allow them to cool slightly before serving with salsa, sour cream, or nacho cheese for dipping.

Gruyère Cheese Fondue

Prep time: 5 minutes | Cook time: 5 minutes | Serves 4

1 garlic clove, crushed
1½ cups dry white wine
1 tablespoon cornstarch
1 pound (454 g) Gruyère cheese, cubed
Toasted cubes of bread, for serving (optional)
Steamed and cooled broccoli florets, for serving (optional)
Roasted baby potatoes, for serving (optional)
Grapes, for serving (optional)
Strawberries, for serving (optional)

1. Rub the garlic all over the inside of the Foodi's inner pot and then discard.
2. Mix ½ cup of the wine with the cornstarch. Add the remaining wine to the Foodi's inner pot and set the Foodi to Sear/Saute on High. When the wine begins to simmer, after about 5 minutes, whisk in the cornstarch mixture and return the mixture to a simmer.
3. Slowly add small handfuls of the cheese, allowing it to melt and incorporate before adding the next handful, whisking constantly to prevent the cheese from clumping.
4. When all the cheese is added, allow the fondue to come to a boil, stirring often to prevent it from scorching, then transfer to a fondue pot. (If you want to serve it directly out of the Foodi, set it to Keep Warm so the cheese doesn't cool too much between dips.) Serve with your favorite fondue accoutrements.

Spicy Harissa

Prep time: 10 minutes | Cook time: 6 minutes | Makes 1 cup

2 ounces dried red chiles
4 garlic cloves, minced
1 tablespoon coriander seeds
2 teaspoons ground cumin
¼ cup peanut oil or vegetable oil
1 tablespoon tomato paste
1 teaspoon kosher salt
1 tablespoon fresh lemon juice

1. Use kitchen shears to snip off the stem ends from the chiles and carefully shake out the seeds, using a paring knife to slice away any bits of tough veining inside the chiles. Use the kitchen shears to cut the chiles into tiny pieces over the Foodi's inner pot. Add the garlic, coriander, cumin, oil, and ¾ cup water. Whisk in the tomato paste until it is dissolved.
2. Lock on the Pressure Lid, making sure the valve is set to Seal, and set to Pressure on High for 1 minute. When the timer reaches 0, turn off the Foodi and quick-release the pressure. Carefully remove the lid—be careful not to get steam in your eyes!
3. Set the Foodi to Sear/Saute on High and cook until thickened, about 5 minutes. Turn off the Foodi and stir in the salt and lemon juice. Transfer the harissa to a storage container and allow to cool to room temperature before covering and refrigerating. (The harissa can be refrigerated for up to 1 week.)

Patatas Bravas

Prep time: 10 minutes | Cook time: 31 minutes | Serves 4

2 tablespoons unsalted butter
2 teaspoons sweet paprika
1 teaspoon hot smoked paprika
1½ cups canned tomato sauce
1 tablespoon minced fresh oregano
1 tablespoon sugar
1 tablespoon hot sauce of choice
½ teaspoon onion powder
¼ teaspoon garlic powder
1 teaspoon kosher salt
1½ pounds (680 g) baby yellow potatoes
2 tablespoons peanut oil or vegetable oil

1. Add the butter and both paprikas to the Foodi's inner pot and set the Foodi to Sear/Saute on High. Stir until the butter is bubbling, about 3 minutes.
2. Add the tomato sauce, oregano, sugar, hot sauce, onion powder, garlic powder, and ½ teaspoon of the salt. Stir and cook until the mixture returns to a simmer, about 3 minutes. Pour the sauce from the pot into a heat-safe mixing bowl and set aside.
3. Add the potatoes to the inner pot along with the oil and the remaining ½ teaspoon salt. Stir to coat the potatoes with the oil and then transfer them to the Crisping Basket. Set the basket into the inner pot, drop the Crisping Lid, and set the Foodi to Air Crisp at 390°F (199°C) for 25 minutes, or until the potatoes are crisp and browned. Serve hot with the sauce.

Ultimate Layered Nachos

Prep time: 5 minutes | Cook time: 18 minutes | Serves 4

Cooking spray
8 (6-inch) corn tortillas, cut into sixths (like a pie)
Kosher salt
8 ounces (227 g) Mexican-style cheese, shredded
Refried Black Beans, for garnish (optional)
Sliced pickled jalapeños, for garnish (optional)
Diced red onion, for garnish (optional)
Pitted and sliced black olives, for garnish (optional)
Guacamole, for garnish (optional)
Sour cream, for garnish (optional)
Cilantro, for garnish (optional)
Salsa, for garnish (optional)

Spray the crisping basket with cooking spray, add the tortillas to the basket, and place in the Foodi's inner pot. Spray the tortillas liberally with cooking spray. Drop the Crisping Lid and set to Air Crisp at 390°F (199°C) for 15 minutes, or until the tortillas are brown and crispy.

Lift the lid and season the chips with salt. Remove the crisping basket and spray the bottom and sides of the Foodi's inner pot with cooking spray. Add a handful of cheese to the pot, then a handful of the chips, another handful of cheese, another handful of chips, and so on, making the last layer cheese.

Drop the Crisping Lid and set the Foodi to Bake/Roast at 375°F (190°C)for 3 minutes, or until cheese is melted throughout.

Lift the lid and carefully remove the inner pot from the Foodi. Flip the chips out and onto a platter. Add your choice of toppings and serve with plenty of salsa and your fave nacho accoutrements.

Pão de Queijo

Prep time: 10 minutes | Cook time: 20 minutes | Makes 8 large rolls

1¼ cups whole milk
6 tablespoons vegetable oil
2 teaspoons kosher salt
4 cups tapioca flour
2 large eggs
1½ cups finely grated Pecorino cheese
1 cup packaged shredded Mozzarella (not fresh)
Cooking spray

1. Place the milk, ½ cup water, the oil, and salt in the Foodi's inner pot. Set the Foodi to Sear/Saute on High and cook until the liquid is boiling, about 5 minutes.
2. Place the tapioca flour in a large bowl. Using a silicone spatula, slowly beat the hot milk mixture into the tapioca flour until it is super sticky, like lumpy glue. Don't be scared. Add 2 of the eggs to the batter, one at a time, followed by the cheeses, beating until the batter is well combined.
3. Spray the Foodi's inner pot with cooking spray. Drop the Crisping Lid and set the Foodi to Bake/Roast at 375°F (190°C)for 5 minutes to preheat.
4. Lift the lid. Spray a ¼-cup measuring cup with cooking spray, and use it to place 4 scoops of batter into the inner pot, spacing them far enough apart so they don't touch. Drop the Crisping Lid and set the Foodi to Bake/Roast at 375°F (190°C)for 10 minutes, or until the rolls are browned. Lift the lid and transfer the rolls to a plate. Continue baking in batches until all the dough is used up. The extra rolls can be rewarmed using the Air Crisp function at 390°F (199°C) for 5 to 10 minutes.

Golden Brown Potato Chips

Prep time: 5 minutes | Cook time: 14 minutes | Serves 2

1 large russet potato, peeled
Cooking spray
Kosher salt, to taste

1. Fill a medium bowl with water and use a vegetable peeler to shave thin slices off the potato, adding them to the water as you peel (so they don't discolor). Let the slices soak at least 20 minutes and up to 1 hour, then drain the potato slices and pat them dry.
2. Spray the crisping basket with cooking spray, add the potatoes to the basket, and place the basket in the Foodi's inner pot. Spray the potatoes liberally with cooking spray, tossing them around to ensure the spray gets on every slice.
3. Drop the Crisping Lid and set to Air Crisp at 390°F (199°C) for 14 to 18 minutes (14 minutes for golden brown chips and 18 minutes for darker, earthier chips), until golden brown. Lift the lid and toss the chips often while cooking. Lift the lid when finished and season the chips with salt while hot. Serve warm or at room temperature.

Crispy Fries

Prep time: 5 minutes | Cook time: 40 minutes | Serves 2

3 large russet potatoes
2 teaspoons kosher salt, plus more as needed
Cooking spray

1. Place the potatoes in the Foodi's crisping basket and set the basket into the Foodi's inner pot. Fill the pot with water to reach the maximum fill line. Then remove the potatoes, one at a time, to peel them before returning them to the water. Once the potatoes are peeled, put one on a cutting board and cut it into ½-inch fries (thicker than McDonald's, about the size of Wendy's). Return the cut potato to the water and repeat with the remaining 2 potatoes (keeping the potatoes in water prevents them from turning brown).
2. Reserve ½ cup of the water from the inner pot and drain the potatoes. Return the reserved ½ cup water to the potatoes in the Foodi's inner pot and add the salt. Lock on the Pressure Lid, making sure the valve is set to Seal, and set to Pressure on High for 0 minutes. When the timer reaches 0, quick-release the pressure and carefully remove the lid. Transfer the potatoes to a kitchen towel-lined baking sheet and blot them dry with another kitchen towel.
3. Spray the potatoes heavily with cooking spray, tossing gently to evenly coat them. Add them to the crisping basket, insert the basket into the Foodi inner pot, drop the Crisping Lid, and set the Foodi to Air Crisp at 275°F (135°C) for 10 minutes, or until the fries are limp and pale.
4. Lift the lid and spray the fries with more oil. Drop the Crisping Lid again and set the Foodi to Air Crisp at 400°F (205°C) for 30 minutes, or until the fries are browned and crisp. Lift the lid and sprinkle with more salt if you like, then serve hot

Dried Watermelon Jerky

Prep time: 5 minutes | Cook time: 12 hours | Makes ½ cup

1 cup seedless watermelon (1-inch) cubes

1. Arrange the watermelon cubes in a single layer in the Cook & Crisp™ Basket. Place the basket in the pot and close the Crisping Lid.
2. Press Dehydrate, set the temperature to 135°F (57°C), and set the time to 12 hours. Select Start/Stop to begin.
3. When dehydrating is complete, remove the basket from the pot and transfer the jerky to an airtight container.

Dehydrated Mango

Prep time: 5 minutes | Cook time: 8 hours | Serves 2

½ mango, peeled, pitted, and cut into ⅜-inch slices

1. Arrange the mango slices flat in a single layer in the Cook & Crisp™ Basket. Place in the pot and close the Crisping Lid.
2. Press Dehydrate, set the temperature to 135°F (57°C), and set the time to 8 hours. Select Start/Stop to begin.
3. When dehydrating is complete, remove the basket from the pot and transfer the mango slices to an airtight container.

Dried Beet Chips

Prep time: 5 minutes | Cook time: 8 hours | Makes ½ cup

½ beet, peeled and cut into ⅛-inch slices

1. Arrange the beet slices flat in a single layer in the Cook & Crisp™ Basket. Place in the pot and close the Crisping Lid.
2. Press Dehydrate, set the temperature to 135ºF (57ºC), and set the time to 8 hours. Select Start/Stop to begin.
3. When dehydrating is complete, remove the basket from the pot and transfer the beet chips to an airtight container.

Candied Maple Bacon

Prep time: 5 minutes | Cook time: 20 minutes | Makes 12 slices

½ cup maple syrup
¼ cup brown sugar
Nonstick cooking spray
1 pound (454 g) (454 g) thick-cut bacon

1. Place the Reversible Rack in the pot. Close the Crisping Lid. Preheat the unit by selecting Air Crisp, setting the temperature to 400ºF (205ºC), and setting the time to 5 minutes.
2. Meanwhile, in a small mixing bowl, mix together the maple syrup and brown sugar.
3. Once the Ninja Foodi has preheated, carefully line the Reversible Rack with aluminum foil. Spray the foil with cooking spray.
4. Arrange 4 to 6 slices of bacon on the rack in a single layer. Brush them with the maple syrup mixture.
5. Close the Crisping Lid. Select Air Crisp and set the temperature to 400ºF (205ºC). Set the time to 10 minutes, then select Start/Stop to begin.
6. After 10 minutes, flip the bacon and brush with more maple syrup mixture. Close the Crisping Lid, select Air Crisp, set the temperature to 400ºF (205ºC), and set the time to 10 minutes. Select Start/Stop to begin.
7. Cooking is complete when your desired crispiness is reached. Remove the bacon from the Reversible Rack and transfer to a cooling rack for 10 minutes. Repeat steps 4 through 6 with the remaining bacon.

Spicy Ranch Chicken Wings

Prep time: 10 minutes | Cook time: 20 minutes | Serves 4

½ cup water
½ cup hot pepper sauce
2 tablespoons unsalted butter, melted
1½ tablespoons apple cider vinegar
2 pounds (907 g) frozen chicken wings
½ (1-ounce / 28-g) envelope ranch salad dressing mix
½ teaspoon paprika
Nonstick cooking spray

1. Pour the water, hot pepper sauce, butter, and vinegar into the pot. Place the wings in the Cook & Crisp™ Basket and place the basket in the pot. Assemble the Pressure Lid, making sure the pressure release valve is in the Seal position.
2. Select Pressure and set to High. Set the time to 5 minutes. Select Start/Stop to begin.
3. When pressure cooking is complete, quick release the pressure by turning the pressure release valve to the Vent position. Carefully remove the lid when the unit has finished releasing pressure.
4. Sprinkle the chicken wings with the dressing mix and paprika. Coat with cooking spray.
5. Close the Crisping Lid. Select Air Crisp, set the temperature to 375ºF (190ºC), and set the time to 15 minutes. Select Start/Stop to begin.
6. After 7 minutes, open the Crisping Lid, then lift the basket and shake the wings. Coat with cooking spray. Lower the basket back into the pot and close the lid to resume cooking until the wings reach your desired crispiness.

Breaded Parmesan Arancini

Prep time: 10 minutes | Cook time: 28 minutes | Serves 6

½ cup extra-virgin olive oil, plus 1 tablespoon
1 small yellow onion, diced
2 garlic cloves, minced
5 cups chicken broth
½ cup white wine
2 cups arborio rice
1½ cups grated Parmesan cheese, plus more for garnish
1 cup frozen peas
1 teaspoon sea salt
1 teaspoon freshly ground black pepper
2 cups fresh bread crumbs
2 large eggs

1. Select Sear/Sauté and set to Medium High. Select Start/Stop to begin. Allow the pot to preheat for 5 minutes.
2. Add 1 tablespoon of oil and the onion to the preheated pot. Cook until soft and translucent, stirring occasionally. Add the garlic and cook for 1 minute.
3. Add the broth, wine, and rice to the pot; stir to incorporate. Assemble the Pressure Lid, making sure the pressure release valve is in the Seal position.
4. Select Pressure and set to High. Set the time to 7 minutes. Press Start/Stop to begin.
5. When pressure cooking is complete, allow pressure to naturally release for 10 minutes, then quick release any remaining pressure by turning the pressure release valve to the Vent position. Carefully remove the lid when the unit has finished releasing pressure.
6. Add the Parmesan cheese, frozen peas, salt, and pepper. Stir vigorously until the rice begins to thicken. Transfer the risotto to a large mixing bowl and let cool.
7. Meanwhile, clean the pot. In a medium mixing bowl, stir together the bread crumbs and the remaining ½ cup of olive oil. In a separate mixing bowl, lightly beat the eggs.
8. Divide the risotto into 12 equal portions and form each one into a ball. Dip each risotto ball in the beaten eggs, then coat in the bread crumb mixture.
9. Arrange half of the arancini in the Cook & Crisp™ Basket in a single layer.
10. Close the Crisping Lid. Select Air Crisp, set the temperature to 400°F (205°C), and set the time to 10 minutes. Select Start/Stop to begin.
11. Repeat steps 9 and 10 to cook the remaining arancini.

Spaghetti Squash And Chicken Parmesan

Prepping time: 10 minutes| Cooking time: 20 minutes |For 4 servings

1 spaghetti squash
1 cup marinara sauce (Keto Friendly)
1 pound chicken, cooked and cubed
16 ounces mozzarella

1. Split up the squash in halves and remove the seeds
2. Add 1 cup of water to the Ninja Foodi and place a trivet on top
3. Add the squash halves on the trivet. Lock up the lid and cook for 20 minutes at HIGH pressure
4. Do a quick release. Remove the squashes and shred them using a fork into spaghetti portions
5. Pour sauce over the squash and give it a nice mix
6. Top them up with the cubed up chicken and top with mozzarella
7. Broil for 1-2 minutes and broil until the cheese has melted

Spice Lover's Jar Of Chili

Prepping time: 10 minutes| Cooking time: 11 minutes |For 4 servings

1 pound green chilies
1 and ½ cups apple cider vinegar
1 teaspoon pickling salt
1 and ½ teaspoons date paste
¼ teaspoon garlic powder

1. Add the above-mentioned   to the Ninja Foodi
2. Lock up the lid and cook on HIGH pressure for 10 minutes
3. Release the pressure naturally
4. Spoon the mix into washed jars and cover the slices with a bit of cooking liquid
5. Add vinegar to submerge the chilly. Enjoy!

Easy To Swallow Beet Chips

Prepping time: 10 minutes| Cooking time: 8 hours |For 8 servings

½ beet, peeled and cut into 1/8 inch slices

Arrange beet slices in single layer in the Cook and Crisp baske. Place the basket in the pot and close the crisping lid. Press the Dehydrate button and let it dehydrate for 8 hours at 135 degrees F. Once the dehydrating is done, remove the basket from pot and transfer slices to your Air Tight container, serve and enjoy!

Bacon Samba Bok Choy

Prepping time: 10 minutes| Cooking time:3 minutes |For 4 servings

½ tablespoons fresh lemon juice
1 medium ripe avocado, peeled and pitted, chopped
6 organic eggs, boiled, peeled and cut half
Salt to taste
½ cup fresh watercress, trimmed

1. Place a steamer basket at the bottom of your Ninja Foodi
2. Add water and put watercress on the basket, lock lid and pressure cook for 3 minutes
3. Quick release pressure. Remove egg yolk and transfer to a bowl
4. Add watercress, avocado, lemon juice, salt, and mash well
5. Place egg whites in serving the dish and fill whites with watercress, mix well and enjoy!

Sour Cream Mushroom Appetizer

Prepping time: 10 minutes| Cooking time: 20 minutes |For 6 servings

24 mushrooms, caps and stems diced
1 cup cheddar cheese, shredded
½ orange bell pepper, diced
½ onion, diced
4 bacon slices, diced
½ cup sour cream

1. Set your Ninja Foodie to Saute mode and add mushroom stems, onion, bacon, bell pepper and Saute for 5 minutes. Add 1 cup cheese, sour cream and cook for 2 minutes more
2. Stuff mushrooms with cheese and vegetable mixture and top with cheddar cheese
3. Transfer them to your Crisping Basket and lock Air Crisping lid
4. Air Crisp for 8 minutes at 350 degrees F. Serve and enjoy!

Tasty Brussels

Prepping time: 10 minutes| Cooking time: 3 minutes |For 4 servings

1 pound Brussels sprouts
¼ cup pine nuts
1 tablespoon extra -virgin olive oil
1 pomegranate
½ teaspoon salt
1 pepper, grated

1. Remove outer leaves and trim the stems off the washed Brussels sprouts
2. Cut the largest ones in uniform halves
3. Add 1 cup of water to the Ninja Foodi
4. Place steamer basket and add sprouts in the basket
5. Lock up the lid and cook on HIGH pressure for 3 minutes
6. Release the pressure naturally
7. Transfer the sprouts to serving dish and dress with olive oil, pepper, and salt
8. Sprinkle toasted pine nuts and pomegranate seeds! Serve warm and enjoy!

Visible Citrus And Cauli Salad

Prepping time: 10 minutes| Cooking time: 10 minutes |For 4 servings

1 small sized cauliflower with the florets divided
1 Romanesco cauliflower with the florets divided
1 pound of broccoli florets
2 seedless oranges peeled up and sliced thinly
For vinaigrette
1 zested and squeezed orange
4 anchovies
1 hot pepper sliced up and chopped
1 tablespoon of capers
4 tablespoon of extra virgin olive oil
Salt as needed
Pepper as needed

1. Add broccoli, cauliflower florets to your Ninja Foodi
2. Lock up the lid and cook on HIGH pressure for 7 minutes
3. Make the vinaigrette by combining the hot pepper, anchovies, olive oil, capers, pepper, salt and mix well. Quick release the pressure
4. Strain the veggies out and mix with vinaigrette and the orange slices. Enjoy!

Faithful Roasted Garlic

Prepping time: 10 minutes| Cooking time: 20 minutes |For 4 servings

3 large garlic bulbs
1 cup of water

1. Slice off ¼ of the garlic bulb from the top, keeping the bulb intact
2. Add water to your Ninja Foodi and a steamer trivet
3. Transfer garlic bulb on rack and lock lid, cook on HIGH pressure for 5-6 minutes
4. Naturally, release the pressure over 10 minutes
5. Transfer the soft garlic to grill rack in your oven and roast for 5 minutes. Serve and enjoy!

Feisty Chicken Thighs

Prepping time: 5 minutes| Cooking time:6-8 hours |For 6 servings

3 pounds boneless chicken thighs, skinless
2 tablespoons apple cider vinegar
½ cup agave nectar
2 teaspoon garlic powder
2 teaspoon paprika
1 teaspoon chili powder
1 teaspoon red pepper flakes
1 teaspoon black pepper
2 teaspoon salt

1. Take a bowl and add garlic pepper, paprika, chili powder, red pepper flakes, salt, and pepper. Take another bowl and mix in agave nectar, vinegar and keep the mix on the side
2. Use the seasoning mix to properly coat the chicken thigh
3. Pour nectar, vinegar mix over chicken. Transfer the mix to Ninja Foodi
4. Lock lid and cook on SLOW COOK MODE (LOW) for 6-8 hours
5. Once done, unlock the lid. Drizzle the glaze on top and serve. Enjoy!

Garlic And Tomato "Herbed" Chicken Thighs

Prepping time: 10 minutes| Cooking time: 5-7 hours |For 4 servings

3 pounds boneless, skinless chicken thighs
½ cup low-sodium chicken broth
2 cups cherry tomatoes, halved
4 garlic cloves, minced
2 teaspoons garlic salt
¼ teaspoon ground white pepper
2 tablespoons fresh basil, chopped
2 tablespoons fresh oregano, chopped

1. Add listed   to your Ninja Foodi and gently stir. Lock lid and cook on SLOW COOK mode for 5-7 hours. Serve and enjoy!

The Kool Poblano Cheese Frittata

Prepping time: 10 minutes| Cooking time: 25 minutes |For 4 servings

4 whole eggs
1 cup half and half
10 ounces canned green chilies
½ -1 teaspoon salt
½ teaspoon ground cumin
1 cup Mexican blend shredded cheese
¼ cup cilantro, chopped

1. Take a bowl and beat eggs and a half and half
2. Add diced green chilis, salt, cumin and ½ cup of shredded cheese
3. Pour the mixture into 6 inches greased metal pan and cover with foil
4. Add 2 cups of water to the Ninja Foodi. Place trivet in the pot and place the pan in the trivet
5. Lock up the lid and cook on HIGH pressure for 20 minutes
6. Release the pressure naturally over 10 minutes
7. Scatter half cup of the cheese on top of your quiche and broil for a while until the cheese has melted. Enjoy!

The Divine Fudge Meal

Prepping time: 10 minute + chill times|Cooking time: 10-20 minutes |For 20 servings

½ teaspoon organic vanilla extract
1 cup heavy whip cream
2 ounces butter, soft
2 ounces 70% dark chocolate, finely chopped

1. Set your Ninja Foodi to Saute mode and add vanilla, heavy cream. Saute for 5 minutes
2. Add butter and chocolate and Saute for 2 minutes. Transfer to serving the dish
3. Chill for few hours and enjoy!

The Original Braised Kale And Carrot Salad

Prepping time: 5 minutes| Cooking time: 30 minutes |For 4 servings

10 ounces kale, roughly chopped
1 tablespoon ghee
1 medium onion, sliced
3 medium carrots, cut into half inch pieces
5 garlic clove, peeled and chopped
½ cup chicken broth
Fresh ground pepper
Vinegar as needed
½ teaspoon red pepper flakes

1. Set your pot to Saute mode and add ghee, allow the ghee to melt
2. Add chopped onion and carrots and Saute for a while
3. Add garlic and Saute for a while. Pile the kale on top
4. Pour chicken broth and season with pepper
5. Lock up the lid and cook on HIGH pressure for 8 minutes
6. Release the pressure naturally over 10 minutes. Open and give it a nice stir
7. Add vinegar and sprinkle a bit more pepper flakes. Enjoy!

Delicious Bacon-Wrapped Drumsticks

Prepping time: 10 minutes| Cooking time: 8 hours |For 6 servings

12 chicken drumsticks
12 slices thin cut bacon

1. Wrap each chicken drumsticks in bacon. Place drumsticks in your Ninja Foodi
2. Place lid and cook SLOW COOK mode (LOW) for 8 hours. Serve and enjoy!

Stuffed Chicken Mushrooms

Prepping time: 10 minutes| Cooking time: 15 minutes |For 4 servings

12 large fresh mushrooms, stems removed

Stuffing

1 cup chicken meat, cubed
½ pound, imitation crabmeat, flaked
2 cups butter
Garlic powder to taste
2 garlic cloves, peeled and minced

1. Take a non-stick skillet and place it over medium heat, add butter and let it heat up
2. Stir in chicken and Saute for 5 minutes. Add   for stuffing and cook for 5 minutes
3. Remove heat and let the chicken cool down. Divide filling into mushroom caps
4. Place stuffed mushroom caps in your Crisping basket and transfer basket to Foodi
5. Lock Crisping Lid and Air Crisp for 10 minutes at 375 degrees F. Serve and enjoy!

A Hot Buffalo Wing Platter

Prepping time: 10 minutes| Cooking time: 6 hours |For 4 servings

1 bottle of (12 ounces hot pepper sauce
½ cup melted ghee
1 tablespoons dried oregano
2 teaspoons garlic powder
1 teaspoon onion powder
5 pounds chicken wing sections

Take a large bowl and mix in hot sauce, ghee, garlic powder, oregano, onion powder and mix well. Add chicken wings and toss to coat. Pour mix into Ninja Foodi and cook on LOW for 6 hours. Serve and enjoy!

Garlic And Mushroom Crunchies

Prepping time: 10 minutes| Cooking time: 8 hours |For 4 servings

¼ cup vegetable stock
2 tablespoons extra virgin olive oil
1 tablespoon Dijon mustard
1 teaspoon dried thyme
1 teaspoon of sea salt
½ teaspoon dried rosemary
¼ teaspoon fresh ground black pepper
2 pounds cremini mushrooms, cleaned
6 garlic cloves, minced
¼ cup fresh parsley, chopped

1. Take a small bowl and whisk in vegetable stock, mustard, olive oil, salt, thyme, pepper and rosemary. Add mushrooms, garlic and stock mix to your Ninja Foodi
2. Close lid and cook on SLOW COOK Mode (LOW) for 8 hours
3. Open the lid and stir in parsley. Serve and enjoy!

Delicious Cocoa Almond Bites

Prepping time: 10 minutes| Cooking time: 2 hours |For 6 servings

3 cups of raw almonds
3 tablespoons coconut oil, melted
Kosher salt
¼ cup Erythritol
1 tablespoon unsweetened cocoa powder
1 tablespoon ground cinnamon

1. Add almonds coconut oil to the Ninja Foodi and stir until coated
2. Season with salt. Mix in Erythritol, cocoa powder, cinnamon, and cover
3. Cook on SLOW COOK MODE(HIGH) for 2 hours, making sure to stir every 30 minutes
4. Transfer nuts to a large baking sheet and spread them out to cool. Serve and enjoy!

Chicken Crescent Wraps

Prepping time: 10 minutes| Cooking time: 15 minutes |For 4 servings

3 (10 ounceso cans, almond flour crescent roll dough
6 tablespoons butter
2 cooked chicken breast, skinless boneless, cubed
3 tablespoons onion, chopped
¾ (8 ounces package cream cheese
3 garlic cloves, peeled and minced

1. Take a skillet to place it over medium heat, add oil and let it heat up
2. Add onion and garlic ad Saute until tender
3. Add chicken, cream cheese, butter, onion garlic to food processor and blend until smooth Spread dough over a flat surface and slice into 12 equal sized rectangles
4. Spoon chicken blend at the center of each dough piece
5. Roll piece while wrapping inner filling completely
6. Place wrapped balls in Crisping basket
7. Insert basket to your ninja Foodi and lock Air Crisp Lid, Air Crisp for 15 minutes at 360 degrees F. Serve and enjoy!

Diced And Spiced Up Paprika Eggs

Prepping time: 10 minutes| Cooking time: 5 minutes |For 4 servings

½ teaspoon paprika
6 whole eggs
¼ teaspoon salt
Pinch of pepper
1 and ½ cups of water

1. Add water to Ninja Foodi. Crack an egg into a baking dish
2. Cover dish with foil and place on a rack, place the rack in Ninja Foodie
3. Lock lid and cook on HIGH pressure for 4 minutes
4. Quick release pressure. Remove loaf of eggs and finely dice
5. Stir in spices and serve. Enjoy!

Faux Daikon Noodles

Prepping time: 10 minutes| Cooking time: 15 minutes |For 6 servings

2 tablespoons coconut oil
1 pound boneless and skinless chicken thigh
1 cup celery, diced
1 cup carrots, diced
¾ cup green onion, chopped
6 cups chicken stock
½ teaspoon dried basil
1 teaspoon salt
1/6 teaspoon fresh ground pepper
2 cups daikon noodles, spiralized

1. Set the Ninja Foodi to Saute mode and add coconut oil, allow the oil to warm up
2. Add chicken thigh and Saute for about 10 minutes
3. Take the chicken out and shred it up
4. Add carrots, onions to the pot and cook for 2 minutes
5. Add the rest of the   and lock up the lid (make sure to return the chicken as well)
6. Cook for 15 minutes on HIGh pressure
7. Do a quick release carefully. Enjoy your "Faux" noodles!

Simple Vegetable Stock

Prepping time: 10 minutes| Cooking time: 30 minutes |For 4 servings

1-2 onions, chopped
2-3 celery ribs, chopped
2 carrots, chopped
1 leek, green parts only, rinsed and chopped
1-2 garlic cloves, chopped
3-4 sprigs parsley
1-2 sprigs rosemary
1-3 sprigs thyme
2 bay leaves
1 teaspoon black peppercorn
12 cups water

1. Add the listed   to your Ninja Foodi
2. Lock up the lid and cook on HIGH pressure for 30 minutes
3. Release the pressure naturally
4. Strain the stock through a strainer
5. Use immediately when needed or store in fridges

Chapter 7: Desserts and Breads

Classic Dinner Rolls

Prep time: 10 minutes | Cook time: 15 minutes | Serves 6

4 tablespoons plus 1 tablespoon cold unsalted butter, plus more at room temperature for greasing

3½ cups all-purpose flour

1 cup whole milk

1 tablespoon extra-virgin olive oil

1 tablespoon coconut oil

½ package active dry yeast

Nonstick cooking spray

¼ teaspoon sea salt

1. In a large mixing bowl, use a pastry cutter or two forks to cut the butter into the flour, breaking up the cold butter into little pieces, until the mixture resembles coarse cornmeal.
2. Put the milk, olive oil, and coconut oil in the pot. Select Sear/Sauté and set to Medium High. Select Start/Stop to begin. Bring to a gentle simmer, about 5 minutes, then press the Start/Stop button to turn off Sear/Sauté.
3. Pour the milk mixture into the flour mixture and stir in the yeast. Mix together until a dough forms.
4. Transfer the dough to a clean work surface dusted with flour and knead it by hand for about 5 minutes.
5. Wipe out the pot, then lightly grease it with butter. Place the kneaded dough in the pot. Cover the dough with plastic wrap and let it rise in a warm place until doubled in size, about 1 hour. Knead the dough again for about 5 minutes, then let it rise a second time for 30 minutes.
6. Turn the dough out onto a floured work surface and divide it evenly into 6 or 12 pieces. Shape each piece into a small ball and place in the Multi-Purpose Pan or an 8-inch baking pan greased with nonstick cooking spray. The rolls should be touching.
7. Close the Crisping Lid. Preheat the unit by selecting Bake/Roast, setting the temperature to 360ºF (182ºC), and setting the time to 5 minutes. Select Start/Stop to begin.
8. Place the pan on the Reversible Rack, making sure the rack is in the lower position. Place the rack with the pan in the preheated pot.
9. Sprinkle the rolls with the salt, then close the Crisping Lid. Select Bake/Roast, set the temperature to 360ºF (182ºC), and set the time to 15 minutes. Select Start/Stop to begin.
10. When cooking is complete, allow the rolls to cool, then pull apart and serve.

Garlicky Bread

Prep time: 5 minutes | Cook time: 8 minutes | Serves 8

2 eggs

¼ cup milk

½ French baguette, cut into 8 pieces

2 tablespoons extra-virgin olive oil

2 teaspoons garlic purée

1 teaspoon dried parsley

1. Place the Reversible Rack in the pot and close the Crisping Lid. Preheat the pot by selecting Air Crisp, setting the temperature to 375ºF (190ºC), and setting the time to 3 minutes. Press Start/Stop to begin.
2. Meanwhile, in a large mixing bowl, whisk together the eggs and milk. Place the bread in the egg mixture and coat each piece on both sides. In a small mixing bowl, mix together the olive oil, garlic purée, and parsley.
3. Place 4 pieces of bread on the preheated rack. Brush the top of each piece with the garlic mixture.
4. Close the Crisping Lid. Select Air Crisp, set the temperature to 375ºF (190ºC), and set the time to 2 minutes. Press Start/Stop to begin.
5. Open the lid and flip the bread. Brush with more of the garlic mixture. Close the lid and select Air Crisp, set the temperature to 375ºF (190ºC), and set the time to 2 minutes. Press Start/Stop to begin.
6. When cooking is complete, remove the garlic bread from the pot and transfer to a plate.
7. Repeat steps 3 through 6 with the remaining pieces of bread. Serve immediately while the garlic bread is warm.

Baked Zucchini Bread

Prep time: 10 minutes | Cook time: 40 minutes | Serves 6

2 eggs
8 tablespoons unsalted butter, melted
1⅓ cups sugar
1 teaspoon vanilla extract
1 teaspoon ground cinnamon
⅛ teaspoon ground nutmeg
½ teaspoon baking soda
¼ teaspoon baking powder
½ teaspoon sea salt
1½ cups all-purpose flour
1 cup grated zucchini
Nonstick cooking spray

1. Close the Crisping Lid. Preheat the unit by selecting Bake/Roast, setting the temperature to 325ºF (163ºC), and setting the time to 5 minutes. Select Start/Stop to begin.
2. Meanwhile, in a large mixing bowl, combine the eggs, butter, sugar, and vanilla. Add the cinnamon, nutmeg, baking soda, baking powder, and salt and stir to combine. Add the flour, a little at a time, stirring until combined.
3. Wring out the excess water from the zucchini and fold it into the batter.
4. Grease the Loaf Pan or another loaf pan with cooking spray and pour in the batter. Place the pan on the Reversible Rack, making sure the rack is in the lower position. Place the rack in the pot.
5. Close the Crisping Lid. Select Bake/Roast, set the temperature to 325ºF (163ºC), and set the time to 40 minutes. Select Start/Stop to begin.
6. When cooking is complete, remove the loaf pan from the pot and place it on a cooling rack. Allow the zucchini bread to cool for 30 minutes before slicing and serving.

Cinnamon-Sugar Dough Balls

Prep time: 10 minutes | Cook time: 10 minutes | Serves 4

⅓ cup all-purpose flour
⅓ cup whole-wheat flour
3 tablespoons sugar, divided
½ teaspoon baking powder
¼ teaspoon ground cinnamon, plus ½ tablespoon
¼ teaspoon sea salt
2 tablespoons cold unsalted butter, cut into small pieces
¼ cup plus 1½ tablespoons whole milk
Nonstick cooking spray

1. Mix together the all-purpose flour, whole-wheat flour, 1 tablespoon of sugar, the baking powder, ¼ teaspoon of cinnamon, and the salt in a medium mixing bowl.
2. Use a pastry cutter or two forks to cut in the butter, breaking it up into little pieces until the mixture resembles coarse cornmeal. Add the milk and continue to mix together until the dough forms a ball.
3. Place the dough on a floured work surface and knead it until a smooth ball forms, about 30 seconds. Divide the dough into 8 equal pieces and roll each piece into a ball.
4. Place the Cook & Crisp™ Basket in the pot. Close the Crisping Lid. Preheat the unit by selecting Air Crisp, setting the temperature to 350ºF (180ºC), and setting the time to 3 minutes. Press Start/Stop to begin.
5. Coat the preheated Cook & Crisp™ Basket with cooking spray. Place the dough balls in the basket, leaving room between each, and spray them with cooking spray.
6. Close the Crisping Lid. Select Air Crisp, set the temperature to 350ºF (180ºC), and set the time to 10 minutes. Press Start/Stop to begin.
7. In a medium mixing bowl, combine the remaining 2 tablespoons of sugar and ½ tablespoon of cinnamon.
8. When cooking is complete, toss the dough balls with the cinnamon sugar. Serve immediately.

Apple Pies

Prep time: 10 minutes | Cook time: 24 minutes | Serves 8

2 apples, peeled, cored, and diced
Juice of 1 lemon
3 tablespoons sugar
1 teaspoon vanilla extract
¼ teaspoon sea salt
1 teaspoon cornstarch
1 package refrigerated piecrusts, at room temperature
Nonstick cooking spray

1. In a large mixing bowl, combine the apples, lemon juice, sugar, vanilla, and salt. Let the mixture stand for 10 minutes, then drain, reserving 1 tablespoon of the liquid.
2. In a small mixing bowl or glass, whisk the cornstarch into the reserved 1 tablespoon of liquid. Stir this mixture into the apple mixture.
3. Place the Cook & Crisp™ Basket in the pot and close the Crisping Lid. Preheat the unit by selecting Air Crisp, setting the temperature to 350ºF (180ºC), and setting the time to 5 minutes. Press Start/Stop to begin.
4. Place the piecrusts on a lightly floured surface and cut them into 8 (4-inch-diameter) circles. Spoon 1 tablespoon of apple mixture into the center of each dough circle, leaving a ½-inch border. Brush the edges of the dough with water. Fold the dough over the filling and press the edges with a fork to seal.
5. Cut 3 small slits in the top of each pie. Coat each pie well with cooking spray and arrange 4 pies in the preheated Cook & Crisp™ Basket in a single layer.
6. Close the Crisping Lid. Select Air Crisp, set the temperature to 350ºF (180ºC), and set the time to 12 minutes. Press Start/Stop to begin. Once cooking is complete, check for your desired crispiness, then place the pies on a wire rack to cool.
7. Repeat steps 5 and 6 to cook the remaining hand pies.

Vanilla Icing Strawberry Toaster Pastries

Prep time: 5 minutes | Cook time: 20 minutes | Serves 4

1 refrigerated piecrust, at room temperature
¼ cup Simple Strawberry Jam
Nonstick cooking spray
Vanilla icing, for frosting
Rainbow sprinkles, for topping

1. Place the Cook & Crisp™ Basket in the pot and close the Crisping Lid. Preheat the unit by selecting Air Crisp, setting the temperature to 350ºF (180ºC), and setting the time to 5 minutes.
2. On a lightly floured surface, roll out the piecrust into a large rectangle. Cut the dough into 8 rectangles.
3. Spoon 1 tablespoon of strawberry jam into the center of each of 4 dough rectangles, leaving a ½-inch border. Brush the edges of the filled dough rectangles with water. Top each with one of the remaining 4 dough rectangles. Press the edges with a fork to seal.
4. Carefully place the pastries in the preheated basket. Coat each pastry well with cooking spray and arrange 2 pastries in the Cook & Crisp™ Basket in a single layer.
5. Close the Crisping Lid and select Air Crisp, set the temperature to 350ºF (180ºC), and set the time to 10 minutes. Press Start/Stop to begin. Once cooking is complete, check for your desired crispiness, then place the pastries on a wire rack to cool. Repeat steps 1 through 5 with the remaining 2 pastries.
6. Frost the pastries with vanilla icing, then top with sprinkles.

S'Mores

Prep time: 5 minutes | Cook time: 4 minutes | Serves 4

4 graham crackers
4 marshmallows
2 (1½-ounce / 42.5-g) chocolate bars

1. Place the Cook & Crisp™ Basket in the pot and close the Crisping Lid. Preheat the unit by selecting Air Crisp, setting the temperature to 350ºF (180ºC), and setting the time to 5 minutes. Press Start/Stop to begin.
2. Break a graham cracker in half. Place half a chocolate bar on one half of the graham cracker. Add a marshmallow and top with the remaining graham cracker half to create a s'more. Repeat with the remaining ingredients to create 4 s'mores.
3. Using aluminum foil, wrap each s'more individually. Place all 4 foil-wrapped s'mores in the preheated Cook & Crisp™ Basket.
4. Close the Crisping Lid. Select Air Crisp, set the temperature to 350ºF (180ºC), and set the time to 4 minutes. Press Start/Stop to begin.
5. When cooking is complete, carefully unwrap the s'mores and serve.

Blackberry and Blueberry Crumble

Prep time: 10 minutes | Cook time: 20 minutes | Serves 6

1 (16-ounce / 454-g) package frozen blackberries

1 (16-ounce / 454-g) package frozen blueberries

2 tablespoons cornstarch

½ cup water, plus 1 tablespoon

1 teaspoon freshly squeezed lemon juice

5 tablespoons granulated sugar, divided

½ cup all-purpose flour

½ cup rolled oats

⅔ cup brown sugar

⅓ cup cold unsalted butter, cut into pieces

1 teaspoon ground cinnamon

1. Place the blackberries and blueberries in the Multi-Purpose Pan or a 1½-quart round ceramic baking dish.
2. In a small mixing bowl, stir together the cornstarch, 1 tablespoon of water, the lemon juice, and 3 tablespoons of granulated sugar. Pour this mixture over the fruit.
3. Place the pan on the Reversible Rack, making sure the rack is in the lower position. Cover the pan with aluminum foil. Pour the remaining ½ cup of water into the pot and add the rack with the pan to the pot. Assemble the Pressure Lid, making sure the pressure release valve is in the Seal position.
4. Select Pressure and set to High. Set the time to 10 minutes, then select Start/Stop to begin.
5. In a medium mixing bowl, combine the flour, oats, brown sugar, butter, cinnamon, and remaining 2 tablespoons of granulated sugar until a crumble forms.
6. When pressure cooking is complete, quick release the pressure by moving the pressure release valve to the Vent position. Carefully remove the lid when the pressure has finished releasing.
7. Remove the foil and stir the fruit mixture. Evenly spread the crumble topping over the fruit.
8. Close the Crisping Lid. Select Air Crisp, set the temperature to 400ºF (205ºC), and set the time to 10 minutes. Select Start/Stop to begin. Cook until the top is browned and the fruit is bubbling.
9. When cooking is complete, remove the rack with the pan from the pot and serve.

New York-Style Cheesecake

Prep time: 15 minutes | Cook time: 35 minutes | Serves 6

Nonstick cooking spray

1½ cups finely crushed graham crackers

4 tablespoons unsalted butter, melted

2 tablespoons granulated sugar

16 ounces (454 g) cream cheese, at room temperature

½ cup light brown sugar

¼ cup sour cream

1 tablespoon all-purpose flour

½ teaspoon sea salt

1½ teaspoons vanilla extract

2 eggs

1 cup water

1. Spray a 7-inch springform pan lightly with cooking spray. Cut a piece of parchment paper to fit the bottom of the pan and spray it with cooking spray. Cover the bottom of the pan tightly with aluminum foil so there are no air gaps.
2. In a medium mixing bowl, combine the graham cracker crumbs, butter, and granulated sugar. Press the mixture firmly into the bottom and up the side of the prepared pan.
3. Using a stand mixer or in a large bowl using an electric hand mixer, beat the cream cheese and brown sugar until combined. Add the sour cream and mix until smooth. Add the flour, salt, and vanilla, scraping down the side of the bowl as necessary.
4. Add the eggs and mix until smooth, being sure not to over-mix. Pour the cream cheese mixture into the prepared crust.
5. Pour the water into the pot. Place the springform pan on the Reversible Rack, making sure the rack is in the lower position. Place the rack in the pot.
6. Assemble the Pressure Lid, making sure the pressure release valve is in the Seal position. Select Pressure and set to High. Set the time to 35 minutes, then select Start/Stop to begin.
7. When pressure cooking is complete, allow the pressure to naturally release for 10 minutes, then quick release any remaining pressure by moving the pressure release valve to the Vent position. Carefully remove the lid when the pressure has finished releasing.
8. Remove the rack from the pot and let the cheesecake cool for 1 hour. Cover the cheesecake with foil and refrigerate to chill for at least 4 hours.

Chocolate Lava Cakes

Prep time: 10 minutes | Cook time: 20 minutes | Serves 4

Nonstick cooking spray
8 tablespoons (1 stick) unsalted butter, cut into pieces
¼ cup dark chocolate chips
¼ cup peanut butter chips
2 eggs
3 egg yolks
1¼ cups confectioners' sugar
1 teaspoon vanilla extract
½ cup all-purpose flour

1. Preheat the unit by selecting Bake/Roast, setting the temperature to 300°F (150°C), and setting the time to 5 minutes. Press Start/Stop to begin.
2. Meanwhile, grease 4 ramekins with cooking spray and set aside.
3. In a microwave-safe medium bowl, combine the butter, chocolate chips, and peanut butter chips. Microwave on high until melted, checking and stirring every 15 to 20 seconds.
4. Add the eggs, egg yolks, confectioners' sugar, and vanilla to the chocolate mixture and whisk until smooth. Stir in the flour a little at a time until combined and incorporated.
5. Divide the batter among the ramekins and wrap each with aluminum foil. Place the ramekins on the Reversible Rack, making sure the rack is in the lower position. Place the rack in the pot.
6. Close the Crisping Lid. Select Bake/Roast, set the temperature to 300°F (150°C), and set the time to 20 minutes. Select Start/Stop to begin.
7. When cooking is complete, remove the rack from the pot. Remove the foil and allow the ramekins to cool for 1 to 2 minutes.
8. Invert the lava cakes onto a plate and serve immediately.

Egg and Ham Pockets

Prep time: 10 minutes | Cook time: 29 minutes | Serves 4

5 large eggs, divided
1 tablespoon extra-virgin olive oil
Sea salt
Freshly ground black pepper
1 (8-ounce / 227-g) tube refrigerated crescent rolls
4 ounces (113 g) thinly sliced ham
1 cup shredded Cheddar cheese
Cooking spray

1. Select SEAR/SAUTÉ and set to MD:HI. Select START/STOP and let preheat for 5 minutes.
2. Lightly whisk 4 eggs in a medium bowl.
3. Once unit has preheated, add the oil and beaten eggs. Season with salt and pepper. Whisk the eggs until they just begin to set, cooking until soft and translucent, 3 to 5 minutes. Remove the eggs from the pot and set aside.
4. In a small bowl, whisk the remaining egg.
5. Remove the crescent rolls from the tube and divide them into 4 rectangles. Gently roll out each rectangle until it is 6-by-4 inches. Top one half of each rectangle with ham, cheese, and scrambled eggs, leaving about a ½-inch border.
6. Brush the edges of the filled dough with water. Fold over the rectangle and press firmly to seal. Brush the top of each pocket with the egg.
7. Place Cook & Crisp Basket in pot. Coat 2 pastries well on both sides with cooking spray and arrange them in the basket in a single layer. Close crisping lid.
8. Select AIR CRISP, set temperature to 375°F (191°C), and set time to 12 minutes. Select START/STOP to begin.
9. After 6 minutes, open lid, remove basket, and use silicone-tipped tongs to flip the breakfast pockets. Lower basket back into pot and close lid to continue cooking, until golden brown.
10. When cooking is complete, check for your desired crispiness. Place the pockets on a wire rack to cool. Repeat steps 7, 8, and 9 with the remaining 2 pastries.

Hazelnut and Chocolate Toaster Pastries

Prep time: 15 minutes | Cook time: 14 minutes | Serves 4

All-purpose flour
1 refrigerated piecrust, at room temperature
¼ cup chocolate hazelnut spread
Cooking spray
Vanilla icing, for frosting
Chocolate sprinkles, for topping

1. Place the Cook & Crisp Basket in the pot and close crisping lid. Select AIR CRISP, set temperature to 350°F (177°C), and set time to 5 minutes. Press START/STOP to preheat.
2. On a lightly floured surface, roll out the piecrust into a large rectangle. Cut the dough into 8 rectangles.
3. Spoon 1 tablespoon of chocolate hazelnut spread into the center of each of 4 dough rectangles, leaving a ½-inch border. Brush the edges of the filled dough rectangles with water. Top each with one of the remaining 4 dough rectangles. Press the edges with a fork to seal.
4. Once unit is preheated, carefully place two pastries in the basket in a single layer. Coat each pastry well with cooking spray. Close crisping lid.
5. Select AIR CRISP, set temperature to 350°F (177°C), and set time to 7 minutes. Select START/STOP to begin.
6. Once cooking is complete, check for your desired crispiness. Place the pastries on a wire rack to cool. Repeat steps 4 and 5 with the remaining 2 pastries.
7. Frost the pastries with vanilla icing, then top with sprinkles.

Simple Cinnamon Donuts

Prep time: 10 minutes | Cook time: 10 minutes | Serves 4

⅔ cup all-purpose flour, plus additional for dusting
3 tablespoons granulated sugar, divided
½ teaspoon baking powder
¼ teaspoon, plus ½ tablespoon cinnamon
¼ teaspoon sea salt
2 tablespoons cold unsalted butter, cut into small pieces
¼ cup plus 1½ tablespoons whole milk
Cooking spray

1. In a medium bowl, mix together the flour, 1 tablespoon of sugar, baking powder, ¼ teaspoon of cinnamon, and salt.
2. Use a pastry cutter or two forks to cut in the butter, breaking it up into little pieces until the mixture resembles coarse cornmeal. Add the milk and continue to mix together until the dough forms a ball.
3. Place the dough on a lightly floured work surface and knead it until a smooth ball forms, about 30 seconds. Divide the dough into 8 equal pieces and roll each piece into a ball.
4. Place the Cook & Crisp Basket in the pot. Close crisping lid. Select AIR CRISP, set temperature to 350°F (177°C), and set time to 3 minutes. Press START/STOP to begin.
5. Once preheated, coat the basket with cooking spray. Place the dough balls in the basket, leaving room between each. Spray them with cooking spray. Close crisping lid.
6. Select AIR CRISP, set temperature to 350°F (177°C), and set time to 10 minutes. Press START/STOP to begin.
7. In a medium bowl, combine the remaining 2 tablespoons of sugar and ½ tablespoon of cinnamon.
8. When cooking is complete, open lid. Place the dough balls in the bowl with the cinnamon sugar and toss to coat. Serve immediately.

Banana and Chocolate Bundt Cake

Prep time: 15 minutes | Cook time: 40 minutes | Serves 8

2 cups all-purpose flour
1 teaspoon baking soda
¼ teaspoon cinnamon
¼ teaspoon sea salt
1 stick (½ cup) unsalted butter, at room temperature
½ cup dark brown sugar
¼ cup granulated sugar
2 eggs, beaten
1 teaspoon vanilla extract
3 ripe bananas, mashed
1 cup semisweet chocolate chips
Cooking spray

1. Close crisping lid. Select BAKE/ROAST, set temperature to 325°F (163°C), and set time to 5 minutes. Select START/STOP to begin preheating.
2. In a medium bowl, stir together the flour, baking soda, cinnamon, and salt.
3. In a large bowl, beat together the butter, brown sugar, and granulated sugar. Stir in the eggs, vanilla, and bananas.
4. Slowly add the dry mixture to wet mixture, stirring until just combined. Fold in chocolate chips.
5. Use cooking spray to grease the Ninja Tube Pan or a 7-inch Bundt pan. Pour the batter into the pan.
6. Once preheated, place pan on the Reversible Rack in the lower position. Close crisping lid.
7. Select BAKE/ROAST, set temperature to 325°F (163°C), and set time to 40 minutes. Select START/STOP to begin.
8. After 30 minutes, open lid and check doneness by inserting a toothpick into the cake. If it comes out clean, it is done. If not, continue baking until done.
9. When cooking is complete, remove pan from pot and place on a cooling rack for 30 minutes before serving.

Breakfast Cinnamon Monkey Bread

Prep time: 5 minutes | Cook time: 20 minutes | Serves 8

¼ cup whole milk
1 teaspoon vanilla extract
½ teaspoon cinnamon
Cooking spray
2 (12½-ounce / 354-g) tubes refrigerated cinnamon rolls with icing, quartered

1. In a medium bowl, whisk together the eggs, milk, vanilla, and cinnamon.
2. Lightly coat the pot with cooking spray, then place the cinnamon roll pieces in the pot. Pour the egg mixture over the dough. Close crisping lid.
3. Select BAKE/ROAST, set temperature to 350°F (177°C), and set time to 20 minutes. Select START/STOP to begin.
4. When cooking is complete, remove pot from unit and place it on a heat-resistant surface. Remove lid. Let cool for 5 minutes, then top with the icing from the cinnamon rolls and serve.

Super Cheesy Pull Apart Bread

Prep time: 10 minutes | Cook time: 25 minutes | Serves 6

½ pound (227 g) store-bought pizza dough
3 tablespoons unsalted butter, melted
4 garlic cloves, minced
¼ cup shredded Parmesan cheese
¼ cup shredded Mozzarella cheese
¼ cup minced parsley
½ teaspoon kosher salt
½ teaspoon garlic powder
Cooking spray
Marinara sauce, for serving

1. Cut the pizza dough into 1-inch cubes. Roll each cube into a ball. Place the dough balls in a large bowl. Add the butter, garlic, Parmesan cheese, Mozzarella cheese, parsley, salt, and garlic powder. Toss, ensuring everything is evenly coated and mixed. Set aside.
2. Close crisping lid. Select BAKE/ROAST, set temperature to 325°F (163°C), and set time to 30 minutes. Select START/STOP to begin. Let preheat for 5 minutes.
3. Coat the Ninja Multi-Purpose Pan with cooking spray. Place the dough balls in the pan and place pan on Reversible Rack, making sure it is in the lower position.
4. Once unit has preheated, open lid and insert the rack in pot. Close lid and cook for 25 minutes.
5. Once cooking is complete, open lid and let the bread cool slightly. Serve with marinara sauce for dipping.

Cookie Pizza

Prep time: 10 minutes | Cook time: 35 minutes | Serves 6

22 ounces (624 g) premade sugar cookie dough
5 tablespoons unsalted butter, at room temperature
1 (8-ounce / 227-g) package cream cheese, at room temperature
2 cups confectioners' sugar
1 teaspoon vanilla extract

1. Select BAKE/ROAST, set temperature to 325°F (163°C), and set time to 40 minutes. Select START/STOP to begin. Let preheat for 5 minutes.
2. Press the cookie dough into the Ninja Multi-Purpose Pan in an even layer.
3. Once unit is preheated, place the pan on the Reversible Rack and place rack in the pot. Close crisping lid and cook for 35 minutes.
4. Once cooking is complete, remove the pan from the pot. Let cool in the refrigerator for 30 minutes.
5. In a large bowl, whisk together the butter, cream cheese, confectioners' sugar, and vanilla.
6. Once the cookie is chilled, carefully remove it from the pan. Using a spatula, spread the cream cheese mixture over cookie. Chill in the refrigerator for another 30 minutes.
7. Decorate with toppings of choice, such as sliced strawberries, raspberries, blueberries, blackberries, sliced kiwi, sliced mango, or sliced pineapple. Cut and serve.

Peanut Butter and Chocolate Bars

Prep time: 5 minutes | Cook time: 10 minutes | Serves 12

1 cup light corn syrup
1 cup granulated sugar
1 teaspoon vanilla extract
1 (10-ounce / 283-g) bag mini marshmallows
1 cup crunchy peanut butter
1 (9-ounce / 255-g) bag potato chips with ridges, slightly crushed
1 cup pretzels, slightly crushed
1 (10-ounce / 283-g) bag hard-shelled candy-coated chocolates

1. Select SEAR/SAUTÉ and set temperature to MD:HI. Select START/STOP to begin. Let preheat for 5 minutes.
2. Add the corn syrup, sugar, and vanilla and stir until the sugar is melted.
3. Add the marshmallows and peanut butter and stir until the marshmallows are melted.
4. Add the potato chips and pretzels and stir until everything is evenly coated in the marshmallow mixture.
5. Pour the mixture into a 9-by-13-inch pan and place the chocolate candies on top, slightly pressing them in. Let cool, then cut into squares and serve.

Arborio Rice and Coconut Milk Pudding

Prep time: 5 minutes | Cook time: 8 minutes | Serves 6

¾ cup arborio rice
1 (15-ounce / 425-g) can unsweetened full-fat coconut milk
1 cup milk
1 cup water
¾ cup granulated sugar
½ teaspoon vanilla extract

1. Rinse the rice under cold running water in a fine-mesh strainer.
2. Place the rice, coconut milk, milk, water, sugar, and vanilla in the pot and stir. Assemble pressure lid, making sure the pressure release valve is in the SEAL position.
3. Select PRESSURE and set to HI. Set time to 8 minutes. Select START/STOP to begin.
4. When pressure cooking is complete, allow pressure to naturally release for 10 minutes. After 10 minutes, quick release remaining pressure by moving the pressure release valve to the VENT position. Carefully remove lid when unit has finished releasing pressure.
5. Press a layer of plastic wrap directly on top of the rice (it should be touching) to prevent a skin from forming on top of the pudding. Let pudding cool to room temperature, then refrigerate overnight to set.

Cream Cheese Babka

Prep time: 25 minutes | Cook time: 30 minutes | Serves 8

For the Dough:

1 (31-ounce / 879-g) packet dry active yeast

¼ cup water, warmed to 110°F (43°C)

¼ cup, plus ¼ teaspoon granulated sugar, divided

2 cups all-purpose flour

2 large eggs, divided

½ teaspoon kosher salt

3 tablespoons unsalted butter, at room temperature

¼ cup milk

For the Filling:

8 ounces (227 g) cream cheese

¼ cup granulated sugar

1 tablespoon sour cream

1 tablespoon all-purpose flour

½ teaspoon vanilla extract

Zest of 1 lemon

Cooking spray

All-purpose flour, for dusting

3 tablespoons water

To Make the Dough

1. In a small bowl, combine the yeast, warm water, and ¼ teaspoon of sugar. Let sit 10 minutes until foamy.
2. Place the flour, yeast mixture, remaining ¼ cup of sugar, 1 egg, salt, butter, and milk into the bowl of stand mixer. Using the dough hook attachment, mix on medium-low speed until the dough is smooth and elastic, about 10 minutes.

To Make the Filling

3. In a medium bowl, whisk together all the filling ingredients until smooth.

To Make the Babka

4. Spray the cooking pot with the cooking spray. Place the dough in the pot. Cover the dough with plastic wrap and let it rise in a warm place until doubled in size, about 1 hour.
5. Spray the Ninja Multi-Purpose Pan or 8-inch baking pan with cooking spray.
6. Turn the dough out onto a floured work surface. Punch down the dough. Using a rolling pin, roll it out into a 10-by-12-inch rectangle. Spread the cheese filling evenly on top of the dough. From the longer edge of the dough, roll it up like a jelly roll.

7. Cut the roll evenly into 12 pieces. Place each piece cut-side up in the prepared pan. The rolls should be touching but with visible gaps in between.
8. Beat the remaining egg with 1 teaspoon of water. Gently brush the tops of the rolls with this egg wash.
9. Place the remaining 3 tablespoons of water in the pot. Place the pan on the Reversible Rack, making sure the rack is in the lower position. Then place the rack with pan in the pot.
10. Select SEAR/SAUTÉ and set to LO. Select START/STOP to begin.
11. After 5 minutes, select START/STOP to turn off the heat. Let the rolls rise for another 15 minutes in the warm pot.
12. Remove the rack and pan from the pot. Close crisping lid.
13. Select BAKE/ROAST, set temperature to 325°F (163°C), and set time to 30 minutes. Select START/STOP to begin. Let preheat for 5 minutes.
14. Place the rack with pan in the pot. Close lid and cook for 25 minutes.
15. Once cooking is complete, open lid and remove rack and pan. Let the babka completely cool before serving.

Coconut, Almond, and Chocolate Bars

Prep time: 8 minutes | Cook time: 20 minutes | Serves 8

1¼ cups all-purpose flour

6 tablespoons unsalted butter, melted

2 tablespoons granulated sugar

½ cup unsweetened shredded coconut, divided

½ cup chopped almonds, divided

Cooking spray

1 package instant vanilla pudding

1 cup milk

1 cup heavy (whipping) cream

4 tablespoons finely chopped dark chocolate, divided

1. Select BAKE/ROAST, set temperature to 375°F (191°C), and set time to 15 minutes. Select START/STOP to begin. Let preheat for 5 minutes.
2. To make the crust, combine the flour, butter, sugar, ¼ cup of coconut, and ¼ cup of almonds in a large bowl and stir until a crumbly dough forms.
3. Grease the Ninja Multi-Purpose Pan or an 8-inch round baking dish with cooking spray. Place the dough in the pan and press it into an even layer covering the bottom.
4. Once unit has preheated, place pan on Reversible Rack, making sure the rack is in the lower position. Open lid and place rack in pot. Close crisping lid. Reduce temperature to 325°F (163°C).
5. Place remaining ¼ cup each of almonds and coconut in a Ninja Loaf Pan or any small loaf pan and set aside.
6. When cooking is complete, remove rack with pan and let cool for 10 minutes.

7. Quickly place the loaf pan with coconut and almonds in the bottom of the pot. Close crisping lid.
8. Select AIR CRISP, set temperature to 350°F (177°C), and set time to 10 minutes. Select START/STOP to begin.
9. While the nuts and coconut toast, whisk together the instant pudding with the milk, cream, and 3 tablespoons of chocolate.
10. After 5 minutes, open lid and stir the coconut and almonds. Close lid and continue cooking for another 5 minutes.
11. When cooking is complete, open lid and remove pan from pot. Add the almonds and coconut to the pudding. Stir until fully incorporated. Pour this in a smooth, even layer on top of the crust.
12. Refrigerate for about 10 minutes. Garnish with the remaining 1 tablespoon of chocolate, cut into wedges, and serve.

Peach, Rhubarb, and Raspberry Cobbler

Prep time: 20 minutes | Cook time: 40 minutes | Serves 6

1 cup all-purpose flour, divided
¾ cup granulated sugar
½ teaspoon kosher salt, divided
2½ cups diced fresh rhubarb
2½ cups fresh raspberries
2½ cups fresh peaches, peeled and sliced into ¾-inch pieces
Cooking spray
¾ cup brown sugar
½ cup oat flakes (oatmeal)
1 teaspoon cinnamon
Pinch ground nutmeg
6 tablespoons unsalted butter, sliced, at room temperature
½ cup chopped pecans or walnuts

1. Select BAKE/ROAST, set temperature to 400°F (204°C), and set time to 30 minutes. Select START/STOP to begin. Let preheat for 5 minutes.
2. In a large bowl, whisk together ¼ cup of flour, granulated sugar, and ¼ teaspoon of salt. Add the rhubarb, raspberries, and peach and mix until evenly coated.
3. Grease a Ninja Multi-Purpose Pan or a 1½-quart round ceramic baking dish with cooking spray. Add the fruit mixture to the pan.
4. Place pan on Reversible Rack, making sure the rack is in the lower position. Cover pan with aluminum foil.
5. Once unit has preheated, place rack in pot. Close crisping lid and adjust temperature to 375°F (191°C). Cook for 25 minutes.
6. In a medium bowl, combine the remaining ¾ cup of flour, brown sugar, oat flakes, cinnamon, remaining ¼ teaspoon of salt, nutmeg, butter, and pecans. Mix well.
7. When cooking is complete, open lid. Remove the foil and stir the fruit. Spread the topping evenly over the fruit. Close crisping lid.
8. Select BAKE/ROAST, set temperature to 400°F (204°C), and set time to 15 minutes. Select START/STOP to begin. Cook until the topping is browned and the fruit is bubbling.
9. When cooking is complete, remove rack with pan from pot and serve.

Cinnamon Apple Crisp

Prep time: 15 minutes | Cook time: 20 minutes | Serves 8

4 to 5 Granny Smith apples, peeled and cut into 1-inch cubes
1 tablespoon cornstarch
½ cup, plus 1 tablespoon water
2 teaspoons cinnamon, divided
1 teaspoon freshly squeezed lemon juice
5 tablespoons granulated sugar, divided
½ cup all-purpose flour
½ cup rolled oats
⅔ cup brown sugar
⅓ cup unsalted butter, melted

1. Place the apples in the Ninja Multi-Purpose Pan or a 1½-quart round ceramic baking dish.
2. In a small bowl, stir together the cornstarch, 1 tablespoon of water, 1 teaspoon of cinnamon, lemon juice, and 3 tablespoons of granulated sugar. Pour this mixture over the apples.
3. Place pan on Reversible Rack, making sure the rack is in the lower position. Cover the pan with aluminum foil. Pour the remaining ½ cup of water into the pot. Insert rack with pan in pot. Assemble pressure lid, making sure the pressure release valve is in the SEAL position.
4. Select PRESSURE and set to HI. Set time to 0 minutes. Select START/STOP to begin.
5. In a medium bowl, combine the flour, oats, brown sugar, butter, remaining 1 teaspoon of cinnamon, and remaining 2 tablespoons of granulated sugar until a crumble forms.
6. When pressure cooking is complete, allow the pressure to naturally release for 10 minutes. After 10 minutes, quick release remaining pressure by moving the pressure release valve to the VENT position. Carefully remove lid when pressure has finished releasing.
7. Remove the foil and stir the fruit mixture. Evenly spread the crumble topping over the apples. Close crisping lid.
8. Select AIR CRISP, set temperature to 375°F (191°C), and set time to 10 minutes. Select START/STOP to begin.
9. Cooking is complete when the top is browned and the fruit is bubbling. Remove rack with the pan from the pot and serve.

Chapter 8: Staples

Air Crisp Bacon

Prep time: 2 minutes | Cook time: 25 minutes | Makes 1 pound bacon

1 pound (454 g) bacon

1. Place Cook & Crisp Basket in pot. Place the bacon in the basket. Close crisping lid.
2. Select AIR CRISP, set temperature to 390°F (199°C), and set time to 25 minutes. Select START/STOP to begin.
3. After 8 minutes, open lid and stir to separate the bacon slides. Close lid and continue cooking. After another 8 minutes, open lid and separate the bacon to ensure the strips are cooked evenly. Close lid and continue cooking.
4. When cooking is complete, open lid and remove bacon. Serve.

Boiled Eggs

Prep time: 2 minutes | Cook time: 15 minutes | Makes 2 to 12 eggs

1 cup water
2 to 12 eggs

1. Place Reversible Rack in pot, making sure it is in the lower position. Add the water to the pot. Arrange the eggs on the rack in a single layer. Assemble pressure lid, making sure the pressure release valve is in the SEAL position.
2. Select PRESSURE and set to LO. Set time to 8 minutes. Select START/STOP to begin.
3. Prepare a large bowl of ice water.
4. When pressure cooking is complete, quick release the pressure by moving the pressure release valve to the VENT position. Carefully remove lid when unit has finished releasing pressure.
5. Using a slotted spoon, immediately transfer the eggs to the ice water bath and let cool for 5 minutes.

Strawberry Jam

Prep time: 10 minutes | Cook time: 42 minutes | Makes 1½ cups

2 pounds (907 g) strawberries, hulled and halved
Juice of 2 lemons
1½ cups granulated sugar

1. Place ingredients in the pot. Using a silicone potato masher, mash together to begin to release the strawberry juices. Assemble pressure lid, making sure the pressure release valve is in the SEAL position.
2. Select PRESSURE and set to HI. Set time to 1 minute. Select START/STOP to begin.
3. When pressure cooking is complete, allow pressure to naturally release for 10 minutes. After 10 minutes, quick release remaining pressure by moving the pressure release valve to the VENT position. Cover the vent with a cloth in case of any spraying. Carefully remove lid when pressure has finished releasing.
4. Select SEAR/SAUTÉ and set to MD:HI. Select START/STOP to begin. Let the jam reduce for 10 to 20 minutes, stirring frequently, until it tightens.
5. When cooking is complete, mash the strawberries together using the silicone potato masher for a textured jam, or transfer the strawberry mixture to a food processor and purée for a smooth consistency. Let the jam cool, pour it into a glass jar with a tight-fitting lid, and refrigerate for up to 2 weeks.

Maple Applesauce

Prep time: 5 minutes | Cook time: 8 minutes | Serves 6

6 apples, peeled, cored, and chopped
2 tablespoons maple syrup
1 tablespoon brown sugar
¼ cup apple cider
½ teaspoon cinnamon

1. Place all the ingredients in the pot. Assemble pressure lid, making sure the pressure release valve is in the SEAL position.
2. Select PRESSURE and set to HI. Set time for 8 minutes. Select START/STOP to begin.
3. When pressure cooking is complete, quick release the pressure by moving the pressure release valve to the VENT position. Carefully remove lid when unit has finished releasing pressure.
4. Use a wooden spoon to stir and break any remaining chunks of apple into smaller pieces.
5. Serve warm or cool to room temperature. Store in an airtight container in the refrigerator.

Fluffy Quinoa

Prep time: 1 minutes | Cook time: 8 minutes | Serves 6

1 cup quinoa, rinsed
1½ cups water

1. Place the quinoa and water in the pot. Assemble pressure lid, making sure the pressure release valve is in the SEAL position.
2. Select PRESSURE and set to HI. Set time for 8 minutes. Select START/STOP to begin.
3. When pressure cooking is complete, quick release the pressure by moving the pressure release valve to the VENT position. Carefully remove lid when unit has finished releasing pressure.
4. Serve hot, or store in an airtight container in the refrigerator to use throughout the week.

Herbed Chicken Wing Stock

Prep time: 5 minutes | Cook time: 45 minutes | Makes 3 quarts

3 pounds (1.4 kg) chicken wings
1 carrot, peeled
2 ribs celery, halved
1 large onion, halved
1 head garlic, halved
4 sprigs fresh thyme
2 bay leaves
1 teaspoon black peppercorns
1 teaspoon kosher salt

1. Place all the ingredients in the pot. Cover with enough water to reach the max fill line. Assemble pressure lid, making sure the pressure release valve is in the SEAL position.
2. Select PRESSURE and set to HI. Set time for 45 minutes. Select START/STOP to begin.
3. When pressure cooking is complete, allow pressure to naturally release for 25 minutes. After 25 minutes, quick release any remaining pressure by moving the pressure release valve to the VENT position. Carefully remove lid when unit has finished releasing pressure.
4. Strain the chicken stock through a fine-mesh sieve and discard the solid pieces. Use a spoon to skim any remaining fat from surface and discard. Let cool, then transfer to airtight containers. The stock can last in the freezer for up to 3 months.

Barbecue Baked Three Beans with Bacon

Prep time: 15 minutes | Cook time: 25 minutes | Serves 8

5 bacon strips, thinly sliced
2 green bell peppers, chopped
1 white onion, chopped
2 cups barbecue sauce
½ cup molasses
½ cup dark brown sugar
½ cup apple cider vinegar
1 (15-ounce / 425-g) can kidney beans, rinsed and drained
2 (15-ounce / 425-g) cans cannellini beans, rinsed and drained
1 (15-ounce / 425-g) can black beans, rinsed and drained

1. Select SEAR/SAUTÉ and set to HI. Select START/STOP to begin. Let preheat for 5 minutes.
2. Add the bacon and cook for 5 minutes, stirring frequently. Add the bell peppers and onion and cook for an additional 5 minutes, stirring occasionally.
3. Add the barbecue sauce, molasses, brown sugar, vinegar, kidney beans, cannellini beans, and black beans and stir well. Assemble pressure lid, making sure the pressure release valve is in the SEAL position.
4. Select PRESSURE and set to LO. Set time to 15 minutes. Select START/STOP to begin.
5. When pressure cooking is complete, quick release the pressure by moving the pressure release valve to the VENT position. Carefully remove lid when unit has finished releasing pressure.
6. Serve.

Simple Cooked Black Beans

Prep time: 2 minutes | Cook time: 25 minutes | Makes 6 cups

2 cups dry black beans
6 cups water

1. Place the beans and water in the pot. Assemble pressure lid, making sure the pressure release valve is in the SEAL position.
2. Select PRESSURE and set to HI. Set time for 25 minutes. Select START/STOP to begin.
3. When pressure cooking is complete, allow pressure to naturally release for 20 minutes. After 20 minutes, quick release remaining pressure by moving the pressure release valve to the VENT position. Carefully remove lid when unit has finished releasing pressure.
4. Drain the beans and store them in an airtight container until ready to use.

Chapter 9: 20 Minutes Ninja Foodi Recipes

Baked Paprika Delight

Prepping time: 5 minutes| Cooking time: 15 minutes |For 4 servings

1 teaspoon smoked paprika
3 tablespoons butter
1 pound tiger shrimps
Salt, to taste

1. Add listed   in large bowl and marinate shrimps
2. Grease Ninja Foodi pot with butter and add seasoned shrimps
3. Lock lid and BAKE/ROAST for 15 minutes at 355 degrees F. Serve and enjoy!

The Good Eggs De Provence

Prepping time: 2 minutes| Cooking time: 18 minutes |For 4 servings

6 whole eggs
1 cup cooked ham
1 small onion, chopped
1 cup cheddar cheese
½ cup heavy cream
Salt to taste
Ground black pepper to taste
1 cup of water

1. Add water to your Ninja Foodi. Place a trivet
2. Take a medium bowl and whisk in eggs, heavy cream
3. Add remaining   and mix thoroughly. Transfer mix to a heatproof dish
4. Cover and place in your Ninja Foodi. Lock lid and cook on HIGH pressure for 18 minutes
5. Release pressure naturally over 10 minutes. Serve and enjoy!

Spiced Up Brussels

Prepping time: 10 minutes| Cooking time: 5 minutes |For 4 servings

2 pounds Brussels sprouts, halved
¼ cup coconut aminos
2 tablespoons sriracha sauce
1 tablespoon vinegar
2 tablespoons sesame oil
1 tablespoon almonds, chopped
1 teaspoon red pepper flakes
2 teaspoons garlic powder
1 teaspoon onion powder
1 tablespoon smoked paprika
½ tablespoons cayenne pepper
Salt and pepper to taste

1. Set your Ninja Foodi to Saute mode and add almonds. Toast them for a while
2. Take a bowl and add the remaining   (except the Brussels and give it a nice mix
3. Add the Brussels to the pot alongside the prepped mixture
4. Stir well and lock up the lid. Cook on HIGH pressure for 3 minutes
5. Release the pressure naturally and serve!

The Epic French Egg

Prepping time: 10 minutes| Cooking time: 8 minutes |For 4 servings

4 whole eggs
4 slices of your desired meat/vegetable
4 slices cheese
Fresh herbs, for garnish
Olive oil
1 cup of water

1. Place trivet to your Ninja Foodi
2. Prepare ramekins by drizzling drop of olive oil and greasing them
3. Add meat/veggies to the ramekin. Break an egg and drop it into the ramekins
4. Top with cheese. Place into a steamer basket and lock lid
5. Cook on LOW pressure for 4 minutes. Release pressure naturally over 10 minutes
6. Remove ramekins and serve. Enjoy!

Quick Avocado And Coconut Pudding

Prepping time: 10 minutes| Cooking time: 5 minutes |For 4 servings

2 avocados, pitted, peeled and chopped
2 teaspoons vanilla extract
2 tablespoons coconut sugar
1 tablespoon lime juice
14 ounces of coconut milk
1 and ½ cup of water

1. Take a bowl and add coconut milk, avocado, vanilla extract, sugar, lime juice, and blend well. Pour the mix into a ramekin. Add water to your pot
2. Add a steamer basket and place the ramekin in the pot
3. Close lid and cook on HIGH pressure for 5 minutes
4. Release pressure naturally over 10 minutes. Serve cold and enjoy!

Juicy Glazed Carrots

Prepping time: 5 minutes| Cooking time: 4 minutes |For 4 servings

2 pounds carrots
¼ cup raisins
Pepper as needed
1 cup of water
1 tablespoon butter
1 tablespoon sugar-free Keto-Friendly Maple Syrup

1. Wash, peel the skin and slice the carrots diagonally
2. Add the carrots, raisins, water to your Instant Pot
3. Lock up the lid and cook on HIGH pressure for 4 minutes
4. Perform a quick release. Strain the carrots
5. Add butter and maple syrup to the warm Instant Pot and mix well
6. Transfer the strained carrots back to the pot and stir to coat with maple sauce and butter
7. Serve with a bit of pepper. Enjoy!

All-Round Pumpkin Puree

Prepping time: 5 minutes| Cooking time: 13-15 minutes |For 2 servings

2 pounds small sized pumpkin, halved and seeded
½ cup of water
Salt and pepper to taste

1. Add water to your Ninja Foodi, place a steamer rack in the pot
2. Add pumpkin halves to the rack and lock lid, cook on HIGH pressure for 13-15 minutes
3. Once done, quick release pressure and let the pumpkin cool
4. Once done, scoop out flesh into a bowl
5. Blend using an immersion blender and season with salt and pepper. Serve and enjoy!

Broccoli And Scrambled Egg Ala Gusto

Prepping time: 10 minutes| Cooking time: 5 minutes |For 4 servings

1 pack, 12 ounces frozen broccoli florets
2 tablespoons butter
salt and pepper as needed
8 whole eggs
2 tablespoons milk
¾ cup white cheddar cheese, shredded
Crushed red pepper, as needed

1. Add butter and broccoli to your Ninja Foodi
2. Season with salt and pepper according to your taste
3. Set the Ninja to Medium Pressure mode and let it cook for about 10 minutes, covered, making sure to keep stirring the broccoli from time to time
4. Take a medium sized bowl and add crack in the eggs, beat the eggs gently
5. Pour milk into the eggs and give it a nice stir
6. Add the egg mixture into the Ninja (over broccoli) and gently stir, cook for 2 minutes (uncovered)
7. Once the egg has settled in, add cheese and sprinkle red pepper, black pepper, and salt
8. Enjoy with bacon strips if you prefer!

Onion And Tofu Scramble

Prepping time: 10 minutes| Cooking time: 5 minutes |For 4 servings

4 tablespoons butter
2 blocks tofu, pressed and cubed into inch pieces
Salt and pepper to taste
1 cup cheddar, grated
2 medium onions, sliced

1. Take a bowl and mix in tofu, salt, pepper. Set your Foodi to Saute mode
2. Add butter and onions, Saute for 3 minutes and add seasoned tofu
3. Cook for 2 minutes, add Cheddar cheese. Lock lid and cook for 3 minutes on Air Crisp mode at 350 degrees F. Transfer to a plate, serve and enjoy!

Quick Gouda Sauce

Prepping time: 10 minutes| Cooking time: 10 minutes |For 4 servings

1 zucchini, chopped
½ cup daikon, chopped
1 small cauliflower, cut into chunks
2 garlic cloves
1 and ½ cups of water
½ cup raw cashews, soaked
¼ cup nutritional yeast
1 tablespoon smoked paprika
2 tablespoons plum vinegar
2 courgettes cut into batons
2 carrots cut into batons
2 celery stalks cut into batons

1. Add the listed   to the Ninja Foodi and lock up the lid
2. Cook on HIGH pressure for 3 minutes. Naturally, release the pressure
3. Remove the lid and allow it to cool for 10-15 minutes more
4. Transfer to a blender and blend for 2 minutes until creamy. Enjoy with veggie dippers!

Quick And Easy Garlic Turkey Breasts

Prepping time: 5 minutes| Cooking time: 15 minutes |For 4 servings

½ teaspoon garlic powder
4 tablespoons butter
¼ teaspoon dried oregano
1 pound turkey breasts, boneless
1 teaspoon black pepper
½ teaspoon salt
¼ teaspoon dried salt

1. Season both turkey on both sides with garlic powder, dried oregano, dried basil, salt, and pepper. Set your pot to Saute mode and add breasts and butter. Saute for 2 minutes
2. Lock lid and BAKE/ROAST for 15 minutes at 355 degrees F. Serve and enjoy!

Creamy 5   Chicken Breasts

Prepping time: 5 minutes| Cooking time: 15 minutes |For 4 servings

1 small onion
2 tablespoons butter
1 pound chicken breasts
½ cup sour cream
Salt as needed

1. Season breasts with salt and keeps it on the side
2. Heat butter in skillet on medium-low heat, add onions. Saute for 3 minutes, add chicken breast. Lock lid and cook HIGH pressure for 10 minutes. Quick release pressure
3. Stir in sour cream and cook on SAUTE mode for 4 minutes more
4. Stir gently and serve. Enjoy!

Tasty Pepperoni Omelette

Prepping time: 10 minutes| Cooking time: 5 minutes |For 4 servings

4 tablespoons heavy cream
15 pepperoni slices
2 tablespoons butter
Salt and pepper to taste
6 whole eggs

1. Take a bowl and whisk in eggs, cream, pepperoni slices, salt, and pepper
2. Set your Foodi to Saute mode and add butter and egg mix. Saute for 3 minutes, flip
3. Lock lid and Air Crisp for 2 minutes at 350 degrees F. Transfer to serving plate and enjoy!

The Cool Scrambled Eggs

Prepping time: 10 minutes| Cooking time: 5 minutes |For 4 servings

½ cup milk
4 ounces bacon, chopped
7 whole eggs
½ teaspoon dried thyme
½ teaspoon dried basil
¼ cup fresh parsley, chopped
1 tablespoons cilantro, chopped
1 teaspoon paprika
¼ teaspoon salt

1. Beat eggs with milk, herbs, and spices. Set your Ninja Foodi to Saute mode
2. Add bacon and cook until crispy. Pour egg mixture over and cook for 5 minutes
3. Stir in chopped herbs and stir cook for 5 minutes more. Serve and enjoy!

Decisive Eggplant And Olive Keto Spread

Prepping time: 10 minutes| Cooking time: 10 minutes |For 4 servings

4 tablespoons olive oil
2 pounds eggplant
3-4 garlic cloves, skin on
1 teaspoon salt
½ cup of water
¼ cup lemon juice
1 tablespoon tahini
¼ cup black olives pitted
Sprigs of fresh thyme
Extra virgin olive oil

1. Peel the skin off your eggplant alternatively, meaning that you are skin parts of the eggplant and leave some parts with skin on
2. Slice the eggplant into large chunks and chop up the any remaining eggplant
3. Chop up the remaining eggplant
4. Set your Ninja Foodi to Saute mode and add the large chunks with the face facing down and caramelize for 5 minutes. Add garlic cloves (skin on) and cook for a few minutes
5. Flip the eggplant slices and add chopped eggplant pieces
6. Add water and season with some salt
7. Lock up the lid and cook on HIGH pressure for 3 minutes
8. Release the pressure naturally over 10 minutes
9. Take the inner pot out and discard the brown liquid, pour lemon juice to the pot
10. Add black olives and garlic cloves
11. Use an immersion blender to blend the whole mixture and puree
12. Serve with a sprinkle of thyme and a dash of olive oil

A Ballet Of Roasted Ham And Spinach

Prepping time: 10 minutes| Cooking time: 8 minutes |For 4 servings

3 pounds fresh baby spinach
½ cup cream
28 ounces ham, sliced
4 tablespoons butter, melted
Salt and pepper to taste

1. Set your Ninja Foodi to Saute mode and add butter, spinach
2. Saute for 3 minutes and top with cream, ham slices, salt, and pepper
3. Lock lid and bake on BAKE/ROASTED mode for 8 minutes at 360 degrees F
4. Remove from Foodi and serve. Enjoy!

Secret Indian Fish Curry

Prepping time: 5 minutes| Cooking time: 4 minutes |For 4 servings

2 tablespoons coconut oil
1 and ½ tablespoons fresh ginger, grated
2 teaspoons garlic, minced
1 tablespoon curry powder
½ teaspoon ground cumin
2 cups of coconut milk
16 ounces firm white fish, cut into 1-inch chunks
1 cup kale, shredded
2 tablespoons cilantro, chopped

1. Pre-heat your Ninja Foodi to by selecting the Saute mode and setting the temperature to HIGH heat. Add coconut oil and let it heat up, add ginger and garlic and Saute for 2 minutes until lightly brown. Stir in curry powder, cumin, Saute for 2 minutes until fragrant
2. Stir in coconut milk, reduce heat to low and simmer for 5 minutes
3. Lock lid and cook on LOW pressure for 4 minutes. Release pressure naturally over 10 minutes
4. Stir in kale and cilantro, simmer in Saute mode for 2 minutes. Serve and enjoy!

Magnificent Cauliflower Alfredo Zoodles

Prepping time: 10 minutes| Cooking time: 8 minutes |For 4 servings

2 tablespoons butter
2 garlic cloves
7-8 cauliflower florets
1 cup broth
2 teaspoons salt
2 cups spinach, coarsely chopped
2 green onions, chopped
1 pound zoodles
Chopped sundried tomatoes, balsamic vinegar, and cheese for garnish

1. Set your Ninja Foodi to Saute mode and add butter, allow the butter to melt
2. Add garlic cloves and Saute for 2 minutes
3. Add cauliflower, broth, salt and lock up the lid and cook on HIGH pressure for 6 minutes
4. Prepare the zoodles. Perform a naturally release over 10 minutes
5. Use an immersion blender to blend the mixture in the pot to a puree
6. Pour the sauce over the zoodles
7. Serve with a garnish of cheese, sun-dried tomatoes and a drizzle of balsamic vinegar. Enjoy!

Chicken Coriander Soup

Prepping time: 10 minutes| Cooking time: 10 minutes |For 4 servings

2 tablespoon of coconut oil
1 tablespoon of minced garlic
3-6 green chilies
2 tablespoon of grated ginger
1 cup of roughly chopped cilantro stems
1 pound of chicken breast
12 black peppercorns
1 teaspoon of salt
2 cup of chicken broth
1 cup of thinly sliced cabbage
1 cup of julienned carrots
3-6 tablespoon of arrowroot powder mixed
    in 1 cup of water
¼ teaspoon of fresh ground pepper
½ a cup of chopped cilantro
2 tablespoon of lemon juice

1. Set your Ninja Foodi to Saute mode and add 1 tablespoon of oil
2. Add garlic, green chilies, 1 tablespoon of ginger and cilantro stems. Mix well
3. Add chicken breast, salt, peppercorn, 2 cups of water, 2 cups of broth and give it a nice stir
4. Lock up the lid and cook on HIGH pressure for 10 minutes
5. Release the pressure naturally
6. Take a large sized bowl and take the breast out, shred the chicken and keep them on the side. Strain the broth into the bowl through a metal strainer and discard the stems
7. Reserve the broth. Rinse and dry your Ninja Foodie insert
8. Put it back and set your pot to Saute mode again
9. Add remaining oil, cabbage, ginger and carrots. Stir well
10. Add shredded chicken, broth and arrowroot mix. Mix well and bring the soup to a slight boil
11. Turn the Instant Pot off and add fresh ground pepper, chopped cilantro, and lemon juice
12. Enjoy!

Garlic And Mushroom Chicken Stew

Prepping time: 5 minutes| Cooking time: 10 minutes |For 4 servings

1 onion, sliced and halved
2 tablespoons olive oil
1 teaspoon salt
1 and ¾ pounds chicken breast, diced
7 ounces Swiss brown and white button
    mushrooms
4 large garlic cloves, diced
1-2 bay leaves
¼ teaspoons nutmeg powder
½ teaspoon pepper
½ cup chicken stock
1 teaspoon Dijon mustard
1/3 cup sour cream
1 teaspoon arrowroot
2-3 tablespoons parsley, chopped

1. Set your Ninja Foodi to Saute mode and add olive oil, allow the oil to heat up
2. Add onion and salt and cook for 3-4 minutes
3. Add chicken, mushroom, bay leaves, garlic, nutmeg, stock cube, pepper, water, and mustard and stir well. Lock up the lid and cook on HIGH pressure for 10 minutes
4. Release the pressure naturally over 10 minutes
5. Open the lid and scoop up a few tablespoons of liquid and mix with arrowroot, dissolve the liquid back and stir to thicken the gravy. Add sour cream and stir. Enjoy with a garnish of parsley

Spaghetti Squash In Sage And Butter Sauce

Prepping time: 5 minutes| Cooking time: 10 minutes |For 4 servings

1 medium spaghetti squash
1 and ½ cups of water
1 bunch fresh sage
2 tablespoons olive oil
1 teaspoon salt
1/8 teaspoon nutmeg

1. Halve the squash and scoop out the seeds
2. Add water to your Ninja Foodi and lower down the squash with the squash halves facing up
3. Stack them on top of one another. Lock up the lid and cook on HIGH pressure for 3 minutes
4. Release the pressure over 10 minutes
5. Take a cold Saute pan and add sage, garlic and olive oil and cook on LOW heat, making sure to stir and fry the sage leaves . Keep it on the side
6. Release the pressure naturally and tease the squash fibers out from the shell and plop them into the Saute Pan. Stir well and sprinkle salt and nutmeg. Serve with a bit of cheese and enjoy!

Ham And Hollandaise Delight

Prepping time: 10 minutes| Cooking time: 5 minutes |For 4 servings

2 whole eggs
2 tablespoons Hollandaise sauce
2 ham slices, chopped
1 and ½ cups + 2 tablespoons water

1. Add 1 and ½ cups water to Ninja Foodi. Lower trivet inside
2. Crack eggs into 2 ramekins. Add a tablespoon of water on top
3. Place ramekins in Ninja Foodi trivet and lock lid, cook on STEAM mode for 2-3 minutes
4. Quick release pressure and top with ham and hollandaise sauce. Serve and enjoy!

Delicious Ghee Carrots

Prepping time: 10 minutes| Cooking time: 5 minutes |For 4 servings

1 pound of baby carrots
1 cup of water
1 tablespoon of clarified ghee
1 tablespoon of chopped up fresh mint leaves
Sea flavored vinegar as needed

1. Place a steamer rack on top of your Ninja Foodi and add the carrots. Add water
2. Lock up the lid and cook at HIGH pressure for 2 minutes. Do a quick release
3. Pass the carrots through a strainer and drain them. Wipe the insert clean
4. Return the insert to the Ninja Foodi and set the pot to Saute mode
5. Add clarified butter and allow it to melt. Add mint and Saute for 30 seconds
6. Add carrots to the insert and Saute well
7. Remove them and sprinkle with a bit of flavored vinegar on top. Enjoy!

Simple Cheese Casserole

Prepping time: 2 minutes| Cooking time: 18 minutes |For 4 servings

16 ounces marinara sauce
10 ounces parmesan sauce, shredded
2 tablespoons olive oil
16 ounces mozzarella cheese, shredded
2 pounds sausage, scrambled

1. Grease your Ninja Foodi with olive oil, arrange half of the scrambled sausage
2. Layer with half or marinara, half mozzarella, and parmesan
3. Top with remaining half of sausage, marinara, and cheese
4. Lock lid and cook using "BAKE/ROAST" mode for 20 minutes at 360 degrees F
5. Remove from Foodi and serve. Enjoy!

Chapter 10: 5 Ingredients Or Less Ninja Foodi Recipes

Warm Avocado Chips

Prepping time: 10 minutes| Cooking time: 10 minutes |For 4 servings

4 tablespoons butter
4 raw avocados, peeled and sliced in chips
Salt and pepper to taste

1. Season avocado slices with salt and pepper
2. Grease pot of Ninja Foodi with butter and add the avocado slices
3. Air Crisp for 10 minutes at 350 degrees F. Remove from Foodi and transfer to a plate
4. Serve and enjoy!

Nutty Assorted Collection

Prepping time: 5 minutes| Cooking time: 15 minutes |For 4 servings

1 tablespoon butter, melted
½ cup raw cashew nuts
1 cup of raw almonds
Salt to taste

1. Add nuts to your Ninja Foodi pot
2. Lock lid and cook on "Air Crisp" mode for 10 minutes at 350 degrees F
3. Remove nuts into a bowl and add melted butter and salt. Toss well to coat
4. Return the mix to your Ninja Foodi, lock lid and bake for 5 minutes on BAKE/ROAST mode
5. Serve and enjoy!

Exquisite Mediterranean Cheese Spinach

Prepping time: 5 minutes| Cooking time: 15 minutes |For 4 servings

4 tablespoons butter
2 pounds spinach, chopped and boiled
Salt and pepper to taste
1 and ½ cups feta cheese, grated
4 teaspoons fresh lemon zest, grated

1. Take a bowl and mix spinach, butter, salt, pepper and transfer the mixture to your Crisping Basket of the Ninja Foodi. Transfer basket to your Foodi and lock Crisping lid
2. Cook for 15 minutes on Air Crisp mode on 340 degrees F
3. Serve by stirring in olives, lemon zest, and feta. Enjoy!

English Green Peas And Asparagus

Prepping time: 5 minutes| Cooking time: 3 minutes |For 4 servings

1-2 garlic cloves, minced
2 cups English Green Peas
2 cups asparagus
½ cup vegetable broth
1 lemon, zested
2-3 tablespoons pine nuts

1. Set the pot to Saute mode and add oil, allow the oil to heat up. Add garlic, cumin
2. Add the cut up bell pepper, potatoes, spices and give it a nice mix
3. Sprinkle water. Lock up the lid and cook on HIGH pressure for 2 minutes
4. Release the pressure naturally. Stir in mango powder, lemon juice
5. Mix and garnish with a bit of cilantro. Enjoy!

The Pecan Delight

Prepping time: 10 minutes| Cooking time: 2 hours |For 4 servings

3 cups of raw pecans
¼ cup of date paste
2 teaspoon of vanilla beans extract
1 teaspoon of sea salt
1 tablespoon of coconut oil

1. Add all of the listed   to your Ninja Foodi
2. Cook on LOW for about 3 hours, making sure to stir it from time to time
3. Once done, allow it to cool and serve!

Favorite Peanut Butter Cups

Prepping time: 5 minutes |Cooking time: 30 minutes |For 4 servings

1 cup butter
¼ cup heavy cream
2 ounces unsweetened chocolate
¼ cup peanut butter, separated
4 packs stevia

1. Melt peanut butter, butter in a bowl and mix, stir in chocolate, stevia, heavy cream
2. Mix well and pour in baking mold
3. Put mold in Ninja Foodi and lock lid, BAKE/ROAST for 30 minutes at 360 degrees F
4. Transfer to transfer plate and serve. Enjoy!

Crispy Mixed Up Nuts

Prepping time: 5 minutes |Cooking time: 15 minutes |For 4 servings

1 tablespoons butter, melted
½ cup raw cashew nuts
1 cup of raw almonds
1 cup Walnuts

1. Add nuts in Ninja Foodi, lock Air Crisping lid. Air Crisp for 10 minutes at 350 degrees F
2. Remove nuts into a bowl and add melted butter and salt
3. Toss well and return to Foodi. Lock lid and BAKE/ROAST for 5 minutes. Serve and enjoy!

Quick And Simple Pork Carnitas

Prepping time: 5 minutes| Cooking time: 23 minutes |For 4 servings

2 tablespoons butter
2 orange, juiced
2 pounds pork shoulder, with bone
Salt and pepper to taste
1 teaspoon garlic powder

1. Season pork with salt and pepper
2. Set your Ninja Foodi to Saute mode and add butter, garlic powder
3. Saute for 1 minute, add seasoned pork. Saute for 3 minutes, pour orange juice
4. Lock lid and cook on HIGH pressure for 15 minutes. Release pressure naturally
5. Add crisping lid and lock, broil for 8 minutes at 375 degrees F. Serve and enjoy!

Simple Teriyaki Chicken

Prepping time: 10 minutes| Cooking time: 8 hours |For 4 servings

2 and ½ pounds skinless chicken breasts
1 cup low sodium chicken broth
2 ounces pepperoncini, with liquid
2 tablespoons Italian seasoning

1. Add listed   to your Ninja Foodi
2. Stir and close the lid, cook on SLOW COOK mode (LOW) for 4 hours. Slice chicken and enjoy!

Lovely Yet "Stinky" Garlic

Prepping time: 5 minutes |Cooking time: 15 minutes |For 6 servings

3 large garlic bulb
A drizzle of olive oil
1 cup of water

1. Place your steamer rack on top of the Ninja Foodi. Add 1 cup of water
2. Prepare the garlic by slicing the top portion
3. Place the bulbs in your steamer basket and lock up the lid
4. Cook on HIGH pressure for about 6 minutes
5. Allow the pressure to release naturally over 10 minutes. Take the garlic out using tongs (very hot!) and drizzle olive oil on top. Broil for about 5 minutes and serve!

Simple Veggie And Bacon Platter

Prepping time: 10 minutes| Cooking time: 25 minutes |For 2 servings

1 green bell pepper, seeded and chopped
4 bacon slices
½ cup parmesan cheese
1 tablespoon avocado mayonnaise
2 scallions, chopped

1. Arrange bacon slices in Ninja Foodi, top with avocado mayo, pepper, scallions, cheese
2. Lock lid and Cook on "BAKE/ROAST" mode for 25 minutes at 365 degrees F
3. Remove from Foodi and serve, enjoy!

Cream Cheese And Zucchini Fries

Prepping time: 5 minutes |Cooking time: 10 minutes |For 4 servings

1 pound zucchini, sliced into 2 and ½ inch
Salt as needed
1 cup cream cheese
2 tablespoons olive oil

1. Add zucchini in a colander and add cream cheese. Add oil, zucchini to Ninja Foodi
2. Lock lid and Air Crisp for 10 minutes at 365 degrees F. Remove from Foodi, serve and enjoy!

Creamy Beef And Garlic Steak

Prepping time: 5 minutes + marinate time |Cooking time: 40 minutes |For 4 servings

½ cup butter
4 garlic cloves, minced
2 pounds beef top sirloin steak
Salt and pepper to taste
1 and ½ cup cream

1. Rub beef sirloin steaks with garlic, salt, and pepper. Marinate beef with butter, cream and keep it on the side. Place grill in Ninja Foodi and transfer the steaks to the Foodi
2. Lock lid and BROIL for 30 minutes at 365 degrees F, making sure to flip about after halfway through. Serve and enjoy!

Delicious Bacon Swiss Pork Chops

Prepping time: 5 minutes + marinate time |Cooking time: 15 minutes |For 4 servings

½ cup Swiss cheese, shredded
4 pork chops, with bone
6 bacon strips, cut in half
Salt and pepper to taste
1 tablespoon butter

1. Season pork chops with salt and pepper
2. Set your Ninja Foodi to Saute mode and add chops and butter, Saute for 3 minutes each side. Add Swiss Cheese. Lock lid and cook on MEDIUM-LOW pressure for 15 minutes
3. Quick release pressure. Transfer steaks to a platter and enjoy!

Hearty Baked Brisket

Prepping time: 10 minutes| Cooking time: 4 minutes |For 4 servings

20 garlic cloves, minced
2 bunch cilantro, chopped
1 and ¼ cups red wine vinegar
3 onions, sliced thinly
3 pounds beef brisket

1. Place reversible rack in your pot and attach crisping lid. Take a blender and add garlic, cilantro, red wine, onion, and pulse. Transfer mix to Ziploc bag and add beef brisket
2. Season with salt and pepper. Let them marinate for 2 hours
3. Transfer marinated beef to the rack and lock crisping lid, press "BAKE/ROAST" button and cook for 60 minutes
4. Take a pan and place it over medium heat, bring the marinade to simmer until reduced
5. Use sauce brush to brush the brisket halfway through. Serve and enjoy!

Nice Beef Fajitas

Prepping time: 5 minutes| Cooking time: 7 hours 8 minutes |For 4 servings

2 tablespoons butter
2 bell pepper, sliced
2 pounds beef, sliced
2 tablespoons fajita seasoning

2 onions, sliced

1. Set your Ninja Foodi to Saute mode and add butter, onion, fajita seasoning, pepper, and beef. Saute for 3 minutes, Lock lid and set SLOW COOK mode, cook for 7 hours. Serve and enjoy!

Divine Keto Nut Porridge

Prepping time: 5 minutes |Cooking time: 15 minutes |For 4 servings

4 teaspoons coconut oil, melted
1 cup pecans, halved
2 cups of water
2 tablespoons stevia
1 cup cashew nuts, raw and unsalted

1. Add cashews and pecans to a food processor, pulse until chunky
2. Add nuts mix to Ninja Foodi, stir in water, coconut oil, and stevia
3. Set your pot to Saute mode and cook for 15 minutes. Serve and enjoy!

Delicious Prosciutto Cane Wraps

Prepping time: 10 minutes| Cooking time: 5 minutes |For 4 servings

1 pound thick asparagus
80 ounces prosciutto, thinly sliced

1. Take a steamer rack/trivet and place it on top of your Ninja Foodi
2. Wrap up the asparagus sticks with prosciutto and prepare your spears
3. Place them in layers on your rack
4. Lock up the lid and cook for 2-3 minutes at HIGH pressure
5. Allow the pressure to release naturally over 10 minutes
6. Open up your lid and take out the steamer basket
7. Transfer the asparagus to your serving plate. Season with some salt if you prefer and enjoy!

Green Bean Mix

Prepping time: 5 minutes| Cooking time: 2 hours |For 4 servings

4 cups green beans, trimmed
2 tablespoons butter, melted
1 tablespoon date paste
Salt and pepper as needed
¼ teaspoon coconut aminos

1. Add green beans, date paste, pepper, salt, coconut aminos, and stir
2. Toss and place lid. Cook SLOW COOK MODE (LOW)) for 2 hours. Serve and enjoy!

5 ingredients Keto Choco Cheese Cake

Prepping time: 5 minutes + chill time|Cooking time: 15 minutes |For 4 servings

2cups cream cheese, soft
2 whole eggs
2 tablespoons cocoa powder
1 teaspoon pure vanilla extract
½ cup Swerve

1. Add eggs, cocoa powder, vanilla extract, cheese in an immersion blender and blend until smooth. Transfer mixture to a mason jar
2. Put the insert in Ninja Foodi and place mason jars on the insert. Lock lid and "BAKE/ROAST" for 15 minutes at 360 degrees F. Let them chill for 2 hours, serve and enjoy!

Helpful Raspberry And Peach Aid

Prepping time: 5 minutes| Cooking time: 5 minutes |For 4 servings

1 cup peaches, chopped
½ cup raspberries
1 lemon, zest and juiced

1. Place the above-mentioned   to a mesh steamer basket
2. Place the basket in your Ninja Foodi. Add water to barely cover the content
3. Lock up the lid and cook on HIGH pressure for 5 minutes
4. Once the cooking is done, quick release the pressure
5. Remove the steamer basket and discard the cooked produce
6. Allow the flavored water to cool and chill. Serve!

The Eldar Shrub

Prepping time: 5 minutes| Cooking time: 20 minutes |For 4 servings

1 cup dried elderberries
2 cups apple cider vinegar
2 cups of water
2 tablespoons agave nectar
½ cup oregano, chopped

1. Add the listed   to your Ninja Foodi
2. Lock up the lid and cook on HIGH pressure for 20 minutes
3. Release the pressure naturally over 10 minutes and strain the mixture into canning jars
4. Allow it to sit and chill and enjoy!

Cool "Cooked" Ice Tea

Prepping time: 5 minutes| Cooking time: 4 minutes |For 4 servings

4 teabags
6 cups of water
2 tablespoons agave nectar

1. Add the listed   to your Ninja Foodi and lock up the lid
2. Cook on HIGH pressure for 4 minutes. Release the pressure naturally
3. Allow it to cool and serve over ice. Enjoy!

Chapter 11: Holiday And Weekend Ninja Recipes

Extreme Choco Fudge Eatery For The Party

Prepping time: 20 minutes| Cooking time: 10 minutes |Freeze Time: 3-5 hours |For 24 servings

½ teaspoon organic vanilla extract
1 cup heavy whipping cream
2 ounces butter, soft
2 ounces 70% dark chocolate, finely chopped

1. Set your Ninja-Foodi to Saute mode with "Medium-HIGH" temperature, add vanilla and heavy cream. Saute for 5 minutes and select "LOW" temperature
2. Saute for 10 minutes more, add butter and chocolate. Saute for 2 minutes more
3. Transfer the mix to a serving dish and refrigerate for a few hours. Serve chilled and enjoy!

The Delightful Cauliflower And Cheese "Cake"

Prepping time: 10 minutes |Cooking time: 15 minutes |For 4 servings

2 cups cauliflower, riced
2 tablespoons cream cheese
½ cup half and half
½ cup cheddar cheese, shredded
Salt and pepper to taste

1. Take a heatproof dish and add all of the listed
2. Cover the dish with an aluminum foil. Add 1 and a ½ cup of water to your Ninja Foodi
3. Place a trivet or steamer basket on top. Transfer the covered trivet on top of your basket
4. Lock up the lid and cook for 5 minutes at HIGH pressure. Allow the pressure to release naturally over 10 minutes
5. Heat up your oven broiler and broil the cauliflowers a bit and broil them well until the cheese Is brown. Enjoy!

Fan-Favorite Aunt's Coconut Custard

Prepping time: 10 minutes |Cooking time: 5 hours |For 8 servings

1 tablespoon coconut oil
8 large eggs, lightly beaten
4 cups of coconut milk
1 cup Erythritol
2 teaspoons stevia powder
1 teaspoon coconut extract

1. Coat the inside of your Ninja Foodi with coconut oil
2. Stir in eggs, coconut milk, stevia, Erythritol, coconut extract to your Ninja Foodi
3. Stir and lock the lid. Cook on SLOW COOKER MODE (LOW) for 5 hours
4. Let it cool for 1-2 hours. Serve and enjoy!

The Christmas Strawberry Shortcake

Prepping time: 10 minutes |Cooking time: 15 minutes |For 4 servings

1 whole egg
½ cup almond flour
½ teaspoon vanilla extract
1 tablespoon agave nectar
1 tablespoon ghee
3 tablespoons strawberries, chopped
1 cup of water
3 tablespoons coconut whip cream

1. Add all   except whip cream to a heat resistant mug, add a cup of water to the Ninja Foodi pot. Place a steaming rack in your pot and place the mug in the rack
2. Lock lid and cook on HIGH pressure for 12 minutes. Quick release pressure
3. Remove lid and remove the mug. Top with coconut whipped cream and more strawberries.Enjoy!

Kid-Friendly Peanut Butter Cheesecake

Prepping time: 10 minutes |Cooking time: 10 minutes |For 4 servings

2 whole eggs
16 ounces cheese
2 tablespoons powdered peanut butter
1 teaspoon vanilla extract
1 tablespoons cocoa
½ cup stevia

1. Take a blender and add eggs, cream cheese and blend until smooth
2. Add rest of the   and blend well. Add the mixture into 4 ounces mason jars
3. Cover with aluminum foil. Add a cup of water to Ninja Foodi
4. Place mason jars and lock lid, cook on HIGH pressure for 15 minutes
5. Naturally, release pressure naturally over 10 minutes. Serve and enjoy!

Quick Lava Molten Cake For Keto Lovers

Prepping time: 10 minutes| Cooking time: 10 minutes |For 4 servings

1 whole egg
2 tablespoons extra virgin olive oil
3 tablespoons stevia
4 tablespoons coconut milk
4 tablespoons all-purpose almond flour
1 tablespoon cacao powder
Pinch of salt
Butter for grease

1. Take a ramekin and grease it up with clarified butter
2. Add 1 cup of water to your Ninja Foodi. Place a steamer rack or trivet on top of your pot
3. Take an e medium sized bowl and add all of the listed   , mix them well until you have a nice batter. Transfer the batter to your ramekins
4. Transfer the ramekins to the steamer rack and lock up the lid
5. Cook on HIGH pressure for 6 minutes
6. Allow the pressure to release naturally over 10 minutes and take the cake out. Serve and enjoy!

Grandmother's Pumpkin Carrot Cake

Prepping time: 10 minutes| Cooking time: 15 minutes |For 4 servings

1 tablespoon extra-virgin olive oil
2 cups carrots, shredded
2 cups pureed pumpkin
½ sweet onion, finely chopped
1 cup heavy whip cream
½ cup cream cheese, soft
2 whole eggs
1 tablespoon granulated Erythritol
1 teaspoon ground nutmeg
½ teaspoon salt
¼ cup pumpkin seeds, garnish
¼ cup of water

1. Add oil to your Ninja Foodi pot and whisk In carrots, pumpkin, onion, heavy cream, cream cheese, eggs, Erythritol, nutmeg, salt, and water. Stir and lock lid
2. Cook on HIGH pressure for 10 minutes Release pressure naturally over 10 minutes
3. Serve with a topping of pumpkin seeds. Enjoy!

Spiced Up Jack Cheese Muffin

Prepping time: 10 minutes| Cooking time: 10 minutes |For 4 servings

¼ cup pepper jack cheese, shredded
4 bacon slices
4 whole eggs
1 Green onion, chopped
Pinch of garlic powder
Pinch of pepper
¼ teaspoon salt
1 and ½ cups of water

1. Set your Ninja Foodi to Saute mode and add bacon, cook for a few minutes until crispy
2. Wipe bacon grease, pour water and lower rack
3. Take a bowl and beat eggs, pepper, garlic powder, salt. Crumbled bacon and add to the mixture
4. Stir in onion and cheese. Pour mix into 4 silicone muffin cups
5. Arrange on rack and lock lid. Cook on HIGH for 8 minutes
6. Quick release pressure. Serve and enjoy!

Early Morning Vegetable Stock

Prepping time: 10 minutes| Cooking time: 15 minutes |For 4 servings

2 small onion, chopped
2 stocks celery, diced
2 bay leaves
2 carrots, diced
1 dried shiitake mushroom
6 cremini mushrooms, sliced
4 crushed garlic cloves
1 teaspoon whole peppercorn
2 tablespoons coconut aminos
8 cups cold water
Dried herbs as needed

1. Prepare the   as mentioned above. Add all of the   to the Ninja Foodi
2. Lock up the lid and cook on HIGH pressure for 15 minutes
3. Release the pressure naturally over 10 minutes. Strain the stock through a metal mesh strainer
4. Allow it to cool and chill, serve!

Grandmother's Carrot Halwa

Prepping time: 10 minutes| Cooking time: 15 minutes |For 4 servings

2 tablespoons ghee
10 cups carrots, peeled and chopped
1 cup almond milk
1 tablespoon stevia
2 teaspoons cardamom powder
2 tablespoons raisins
½ teaspoons saffron
2 tablespoons almond

1. Set the Ninja Foodi to Saute mode and add ghee, allow the ghee to heat up
2. Add grated carrots and cook for 2-3 minutes. Add almond milk and lock up the lid
3. Cook on HIGH pressure for 5 minutes. Quick release the pressure
4. Add stevia, almond meal, raisins, saffron, and cardamom powder
5. Set the pot to Saute mode and add cook for 5-7 minutes more
6. Garnish with sliced almonds and enjoy chilled!

Lemon And Ricotta Party-Friendly Cheesecake

Prepping time: 10 minutes |Cooking time: 10 minutes |For 4 servings

8 ounces cream cheese
¼ cup Truvia
1 lemon – zested and juiced
1/3 cup ricotta cheese
½ teaspoon lemon extract
2 whole eggs

For topping
Natural sweetener as needed
1 tablespoon sour cream

1. Take your blender and add all the   except eggs, blend well
2. Add eggs and blend on low speed, making sure to not over beat the eggs
3. Add batter to pan and cover with foil. Add trivet to Ninja Foodi and 2 cups water
4. Place baking pan in trivet and lock lid, cook on HIGH pressure for 30 minutes
5. Release pressure naturally over 10 minutes
6. Blend in sweetener and sour cream in a bowl and decorate the cake with frosting. Enjoy!

Highly Sough-After Egg Devils

Prepping time: 5 minutes |Cooking time: 10 minutes |For 6 servings

8 large eggs
1 cup of water
Guacamole as needed
Sliced radishes as needed
Furikake
Keto-Friendly Mayo

1. Add 1 cup of water to your Ninja Foodi. Place the steamer insert in your Ninja Foodi
2. Arrange the eggs on top of the insert
3. Lock up the lid and cook for about 6 minutes at HIGH pressure
4. Allow the pressure to release naturally. Transfer the eggs to an ice bath and peel the skin
5. Cut the eggs in half and garnish them with dressings of Guacamole, sliced up radishes, Mayonnaise, Furikake, Sliced up Parmesan etc.!

Hearty Mushroom Stock

Prepping time: 10 minutes| Cooking time: 30 minutes |For 4 servings

1 ounce dried porcini mushrooms
1 ounce dried shiitake mushrooms
16 ounces white mushrooms, diced
1 large onion, diced
1 carrot, diced
1 cup dry white wine
2 tablespoons coconut aminos
1 bay leaf
3 sprigs fresh thyme
2 sprigs fresh parsley
1 teaspoon black peppercorn
12 cups water

1. Soak the porcini and shitake mushroom in 4 cups of hot water
2. Prepare your other
3. Add mushroom and onion to the Ninja Foodi and Set the pot to sauté mode
4. Saute for a while. Add leeks, garlic, carrots, red wine and stir until the wine has evaporated
5. Add the rest of the remaining
6. Lock up the lid and cook on HIGH pressure for 30 minutes. Naturally, release the pressure
7. Strain the stock through a metal strainer. Use as needed or store in the fridge

A Christmas-y Pot De Crème

Prepping time: 10 minutes |Cooking time: 3 hours |For 8 servings

6 egg yolks
2 cups heavy whipping cream
½ cup of cocoa powder
1 tablespoon pure vanilla extract
½ teaspoon stevia
Whipped coconut cream for garnish
Shaved dark chocolate for garnish

1. Take a medium sized bowl and whisk in yolks, heavy cream, cocoa powder, vanilla, stevia
2. Pour mix into 1 and ½ quart baking dish and place dish in the insert of your Ninja Foodi
3. Add just enough water until it reaches halfway up the sides of the baking dish
4. Lock lid and cook on SLOW COOK MODE (LOW) for 3 hours
5. Remove baking dish and let it cool
6. Chill the dessert completely and garnish with whipped coconut cream and shaved dark chocolate. Enjoy!

Creative Almond And Carrot Cake

Prepping time: 10 minutes |Cooking time: 50 minutes |For 4 servings

3 whole eggs
1 cup almond flour
2/3 cup Swerve
1 teaspoon baking powder
1 and ½ teaspoons apple pie spice
¼ cup of coconut oil
½ cup heavy whip cream (Keto friendly)
1 cup carrots, shredded
½ cup walnuts, chopped

1. Take a 6-inch pan and grease it up well
2. Take a bowl and add all of the listed   , mix them well until you have a nice and fluffy mix. Use a hand mixer if needed. Pour the batter into your pan and cover with a foil
3. Place a steamer rack/trivet on top of your Ninja Foodi
4. Add 2 cups of water and transfer the pan to the rack
5. Lock up the lid and cook for 40 minutes on BAKE mode at 350 degrees F
6. Once done, release the pressure naturally over 10 minutes
7. Enjoy the cake as it is or if you want, then add some Keto friendly frosting/toppings

Heavenly Zucchini Bread

Prepping time: 10 minutes| Cooking time: 3 hours 15 minutes |For 12 servings

1 cup almond flour
2 teaspoons cinnamon
1/3 cup coconut flour
½ teaspoon salt
½ teaspoon baking soda
1 and ½ teaspoon baking powder
1/3 cup soft coconut oil
3 whole eggs
2 teaspoons vanilla bean extract
1 cup sweetener
2 cups shredded zucchini
½ cup pecans, chopped

1. Take a bowl Add coconut and almond flour, salt, baking soda and powder, cinnamon and xanthan gum. Keep it on the side. Take another bowl and mix oil, vanilla, eggs, and sugar, mix well
2. Blend in shredded zucchini and nuts. Pour the baking soda into the bowl with zucchini and stir well. Pour the mixture into your prepared pan
3. Place your trivet/rack in your Ninja Foodi and place pan on top of the trivet
4. Cook on SLOW COOK MODE (HIGH) for 3 hours. Let it cool and wrap in foil, place in the fridge. Serve and enjoy!

Heart Melting Choco-Mousse

Prepping time: 10 minutes + 6 hours chill times |Cooking time: 10 minutes |For 4 servings

4 egg yolks
¼ cup of water
¼ cup cacao
½ cup Swerve
½ cup whipping cream
½ teaspoon vanilla
½ cup almond milk
¼ teaspoon of sea salt

1. Take a bowl and whisk in eggs. Add water, swerve, cacao in a saucepan and mix well
2. Stir in milk and cream, let the mixture warm over medium heat until it reaches a boil, remove heat. Measure 1 tablespoon of chocolate mix into the dish with eggs
3. Whisk and slowly empty the remaining chocolate into the mixture
4. Empty the mousse mix into 5 ramekins. Add 1 and ½ cups water to Instant Pot. Place a trivet
5. Place the trivets into the trivet and lock lid, cook on HIGH pressure for 6 minutes
6. Quick release pressure. Chill in the fridge for 6 hours, enjoy!

Chapter 12: Healthy Vegan/Vegetarian Ninja Foodi Recipes

Worthy Caramelized ONion

Prepping time: 10 minutes| Cooking time: 30-35 minutes |For 6 servings

2 tablespoons unsalted butter
3 large onions sliced
2 tablespoons water
1 teaspoon salt

1. Set your Ninja Foodi to Sauté mode and add set temperature to medium heat, pre-heat the inner pot for 5 minutes. Add butter and let it melt, add onions, water, and stir
2. Lock lid and cook on HIGH pressure for 30 minutes. Quick release the pressure
3. Remove lid and set the pot to sauté mode, let it sear in Medium-HIGH mode for 15 minutes until all liquid is gone. Serve and enjoy!

A Very Greeny Green Beans Platter

Prepping time: 10 minutes| Cooking time: 5 minutes |For 6 servings

2-3 pounds fresh green beans
2 tablespoons butter
1 garlic clove, minced
Salt and pepper to taste
1 and ½ cups of water

1. Add listed   to Ninja Foodi. Lock lid and cook on HIGH pressure for 5 minutes
2. Quick release pressure

A Mishmash Cauliflower Mash

Prepping time: 10 minutes| Cooking time: 5 minutes |For 3 servings

1 tablespoon butter, soft
½ cup feta cheese
Salt and pepper to taste
1 large head cauliflower, chopped into large pieces
1 garlic cloves, minced
2 teaspoons fresh chives, minced

1. Add water to your Ninja Foodi and place steamer basket
2. Add cauliflower pieces and lock lid, cook on HIGH pressure for 5 minutes
3. Quick release pressure. Open the lid and use an immersion blender to mash the cauliflower
4. Blend until you have a nice consistency. Enjoy!

Zucchini And Artichoke Platter

Prepping time: 10 minutes| Cooking time: 10 minutes |For 4 servings

2 tablespoon coconut oil
1 bulb garlic, minced
1 large artichoke heart, cleaned sliced
2 medium zucchinis, sliced
½ cup vegetable broth
Salt and pepper as needed

1. Set your Ninja Foodi to Saute mode and add oil, allow the oil the heat up
2. Add garlic and Saute until nicely fragrant. Add rest of the   and stir
3. Lock lid and cook on HIGH pressure for 10 minutes. Quick release, serve and enjoy!

Winning Broccoli Casserole

Prepping time: 10 minutes| Cooking time: 6 hours |For 4 servings

1 tablespoon extra-virgin olive oil
1 pound broccoli, cut into florets
1 pound cauliflower, cut into florets
¼ cup almond flour
2 cups of coconut milk
½ teaspoon ground nutmeg
Pinch of fresh ground black pepper
1 and ½ cups cashew cream

1. Grease the Ninja Foodi inner pot with olive oil. Place broccoli and cauliflower to your Ninja Foodi
2. Take a small bowl and stir in almond flour, coconut milk, pepper, 1 cup of cashew cream
3. Pour coconut milk mixture over vegetables and top casserole with remaining cashew cream
4. Cover and cook on SLOW COOK Mode (LOW) for 6 hours. Server and enjoy!

Spaghetti Squash Drizzled With Sage Butter Sauce

Prepping time: 10 minutes| Cooking time: 10 minutes |For 4 servings

1 medium-sized spaghetti squash
1 and a ½ cup of water
1 bunch of fresh sage
3-4 garlic cloves, sliced
2 tablespoon of olive oil
1 teaspoon of salt
1/8 teaspoon of nutmeg

1. Halve the squash and scoop out the seeds
2. Add water to your Ninja Foodi and lower down the squash with the squash halves facing up
3. Stack them on top of one another. Lock up the lid and cook on HIGH pressure for 3 minutes
4. Release the pressure over 10 minutes
5. Take a cold Saute pan and add sage, garlic and olive oil and cook on LOW heat, making sure to stir and fry the sage leaves. Keep it on the side
6. Release the pressure naturally and tease the squash fibers out from the shell and plop them into the Saute Pan. Stir well and sprinkle salt and nutmeg . Serve with a bit of cheese and enjoy!

Uber-Keto Caper And Beet Salad

Prepping time: 10 minutes| Cooking time: 25 minutes |For 4 servings

4 medium beets
2 tablespoons of rice wine vinegar

For Dressing

Small bunch parsley, stems removed
1 large garlic clove
½ teaspoon salt
Pinch of black pepper
1 tablespoon extra-virgin olive oil
2 tablespoons capers

1. Pour 1 cup of water into your steamer basket and place it on the side
2. Snip up the tops of your bits and wash them well. Put the beets in your steamer basket
3. Place the steamer basket in your instant pot and lock up the lid
4. Let it cook for about 25 minutes at high pressure. Once done, release the pressure naturally
5. While it is being cooked, take a small jar and add chopped up parsley and garlic alongside olive oil, salt, pepper and capers. Shake it vigorously to prepared your dressing
6. Open up the lid once the pressure is released and check the beets for doneness using a fork
7. Take out the steamer basket to your sink and run it under cold water
8. Use your finger to brush off the skin of the beets
9. Use a plastic cutting board and slice up the beets
10. Arrange them on a platter and sprinkle some vinegar on top

The Greeny And Beany Horseradish Mix

Prepping time: 5 minutes| Cooking time: 10-15 minutes |For 4 servings

2 large beets with greens, scrubbed and root ends trimmed
1 cup water, for steaming
2 tablespoons sour cream
1 tablespoon whole milk
1 teaspoon prepared horseradish
¼ teaspoon lemon zest
1/8 teaspoon salt
2 teaspoon unsalted butter
1 tablespoon minced fresh chives

1. Trim off beet greens and keep them on the side
2. Add water to the Ninja Foodi and place steamer basket, place beets in a steamer basket
3. Lock lid and cook on HIGH pressure for 10 minutes, release pressure naturally over 10 minutes
4. While the beets are being cooked, wash greens and slice them into ½ inch thick ribbons
5. Take a bowl and whisk in sour cream, horseradish, lemon zest, 1/16 teaspoon of salt
6. Once the cooking is done, remove the lid and remove beets, let them cool
7. Use a paring knife to peel them and slice them into large bite-sized pieces
8. Remove steamer from the Ninja Foodi and pour out water
9. Set your Foodi to "Saute" mode and add butter, let it melt
10. Once the butter stops foaming, add beet greens sprinkle remaining 1/6 teaspoon salt and cook for 3-4 minutes. Return beets to the Foodi and heat for 1-2 minutes, stirring
11. Transfer beets and greens to a platter and drizzle sour cream mixture
12. Sprinkle chives and serve. Enjoy!

Fully Stuffed Whole Chicken

Prepping time: 5 minutes| Cooking time: 8 hours |For 4 servings

1 cup mozzarella cheese
4 garlic clove, peeled
1 whole chicken, 2 pounds, cleaned and dried
Salt and pepper to taste
2 tablespoons lemon juice

1. Stuff chicken cavity with garlic cloves, cheese. Season with salt and pepper
2. Transfer to Ninja Foodi and drizzle lemon juice. Lock lid and SLOW COOK on LOW for 8 hours
3. Transfer to a plate, serve and enjoy!

Rosemary Dredged Green Beans

Prepping time: 5 minutes| Cooking time: 3 hours |For 4 servings

1 pound green beans
1 tablespoon rosemary, minced
1 teaspoon fresh thyme, minced
2 tablespoons lemon juice
2 tablespoons water

1. Add listed   to Ninja Foodi
2. Lock lid and cook on SLOW COOK MODE(LOW) for 3 hours . Unlock lid and stir. Enjoy!

Italian Turkey Breast

Prepping time: 5 minutes| Cooking time: 2 hours |For 4 servings

1 and ½ cups Italian dressing
2 garlic cloves, minced
1 (2 pounds turkey breast, with bone
2 tablespoons butter
Salt and pepper to taste

1. Mix in garlic cloves, salt, black pepper and rub turkey breast with mix
2. Grease Ninja Foodi pot and arrange turkey breast. Top with Italian dressing
3. Lock lid and BAKE/ROAST for 2 hours at 230 degrees F. Serve and enjoy!

Crazy Fresh Onion Soup

Prepping time: 5 minutes| Cooking time: 10-15 minutes |For 4 servings

2 tablespoons avocado oil
8 cups yellow onion
1 tablespoon balsamic vinegar
6 cups of pork stock
1 teaspoon salt
2 bay leaves
2 large sprigs, fresh thyme

1. Cut up the onion in half through the root
2. Peel them and slice into thin half moons
3. Set the pot to Saute mode and add oil, one the oil is hot and add onions
4. Cook for about 15 minutes
5. Add balsamic vinegar and scrape any fond from the bottom
6. Add stock, bay leaves, salt, and thyme
7. Lock up the lid and cook on HIGH pressure for 10 minutes
8. Release the pressure naturally
9. Discard the bay leaf and thyme stems
10. Blend the soup using an immersion blender and serve!

Elegant Zero Crust Kale And Mushroom Quiche

Prepping time: 5 minutes| Cooking time: 9 hours |For 6 servings

6 large eggs
2 tablespoons unsweetened almond milk
2 ounces low –fat feta cheese, crumbled
¼ cup parmesan cheese, grated
1 and ½ teaspoons Italian seasoning
4 ounces mushrooms, sliced
2 cups kale, chopped

1. Grease the inner pot of your Ninja Foodi
2. Take a large bowl and whisk in eggs, cheese, almond milk, seasoning and mix it well
3. Stir in kale and mushrooms. Pour the mix into Ninja Foodi. Gently stir
4. Place lid and cook on SLOW COOK Mode(LOW) for 8-9 hours. Serve and enjoy!

Delicious Beet Borscht

Prepping time: 5 minutes| Cooking time: 45 minutes |For 6 servings

8 cups beets
½ cup celery, diced
½ cup carrots, diced
2 garlic cloves, diced
1 medium onion, diced
3 cups cabbage, shredded
6 cups beef stock
1 bay leaf
1 tablespoon salt
½ tablespoon thyme
¼ cup fresh dill, chopped
½ cup of coconut yogurt

1. Add the washed beets to a steamer in the Ninja Foodi
2. Add 1 cup of water. Steam for 7 minutes
3. Perform a quick release and drop into an ice bath
4. Carefully peel off the skin and dice the beets
5. Transfer the diced beets, celery, carrots, onion, garlic, cabbage, stock, bay leaf, thyme and salt to your Instant Pot. Lock up the lid and set the pot to SOUP mode, cook for 45 minutes
6. Release the pressure naturally. Transfer to bowls and top with a dollop of dairy-free yogurt
7. Enjoy with a garnish of fresh dill!

Pepper Jack Cauliflower Meal

Prepping time: 5 minutes| Cooking time: 3 hours 35 minutes |For 6 servings

1 head cauliflower
¼ cup whipping cream
4 ounces cream cheese
½ teaspoon pepper
1 teaspoon salt
2 tablespoons butter
4 ounces pepper jack cheese
6 bacon slices, crumbled

1. Grease Ninja Foodi and add listed   (except cheese and bacon)
2. Stir and Lock lid, cook SLOW COOK MODE (LOW) for 3 hours
3. Remove lid and add cheese, stir. Lock lid again and cook for 1 hour more
4. Garnish with bacon crumbles and enjoy!

Slow-Cooked Brussels

Prepping time: 5 minutes| Cooking time: 4 hours |For 4 servings

1 pound Brussels sprouts, bottom trimmed and cut
1 tablespoon olive oil
1 -1/2 tablespoon Dijon mustard
¼ cup of water
Salt and pepper as needed
½ teaspoon dried tarragon

1. Add Brussels, salt, water, pepper, mustard to Ninja Foodi
2. Add dried tarragon and stir
3. Lock lid and cook on SLOW COOK MODE (LOW) for 5 hours until the Brussels are tender
4. Stir well and add Dijon over Brussels. Stir and enjoy!

Slowly Cooked Lemon Artichokes

Prepping time: 10 minutes| Cooking time: 5 hours |For 4 servings

5 large artichokes
1 teaspoon of sea salt
2 stalks celery, sliced
2 large carrots, cut into matchsticks
Juice from ½ a lemon
¼ teaspoon black pepper
1 teaspoon dried thyme
1 tablespoon dried rosemary
Lemon wedges for garnish

1. Remove the stalk from your artichokes and remove the tough outer shell
2. Transfer the chokes to your Ninja Foodi and add 2 cups of boiling water
3. Add celery, lemon juice, salt, carrots, black pepper, thyme, rosemary
4. Cook on Slow Cook mode (HIGH) for 4-5 hours
5. Serve the artichokes with lemon wedges. Serve and enjoy!

Well Dressed Brussels

Prepping time: 10 minutes| Cooking time: 4-5 hours |For 4 servings

2 pounds Brussels, halved
2 red onions, sliced
2 tablespoons apple cider vinegar
1 tablespoon extra-virgin olive oil
1 teaspoon ground cinnamon
½ cup pecans, chopped

1. Add Brussels and onions to Ninja Foodi. Take a small bowl and add cinnamon, vinegar, olive oil
2. Pour mixture over sprouts and toss
3. Place lid and cook on SLOW COOK MODE (LOW) for 4-5 hours. Enjoy!

Cheddar Cauliflower Bowl

Prepping time: 10 minutes| Cooking time: 5 minutes |For 8 servings

¼ cup butter
½ sweet onion, chopped
1 head cauliflower, chopped
4 cups herbed vegetable stock
½ teaspoon ground nutmeg
1 cup heavy whip cream
Salt and pepper as needed
1 cup cheddar cheese, shredded

1. Set your Ninja Foodi to sauté mode and add butter, let it heat up and melt
2. Add onion and Cauliflower, Saute for 10 minutes until tender and lightly browned
3. Add vegetable stock and nutmeg, bring to a boil
4. Lock lid and cook on HIGH pressure for 5 minutes, quick release pressure once done
5. Remove pot and from Foodi and stir in heavy cream, puree using an immersion blender
6. Season with more salt and pepper and serve with a topping of cheddar. Enjoy!

A Prosciutto And Thyme Eggs

Prepping time: 10 minutes| Cooking time: 5 minutes |For 4 servings

4 kale leaves
4 prosciutto slices
3 tablespoons heavy cream
4 hardboiled eggs
¼ teaspoon pepper
¼ teaspoon salt
1 and ½ cups of water

1. Peel eggs and wrap in kale. Wrap in prosciutto and sprinkle salt and pepper
2. Add water to your Ninja Foodi and lower trivet. Place eggs inside and lock lid
3. Cook on HIGH pressure for 5 minutes. Quick release pressure. Serve and enjoy!

The Authentic Zucchini Pesto Meal

Prepping time: 10 minutes| Cooking time: 10 minutes |For 4 servings

1 tablespoon olive oil
1 onion, chopped
2 and ½ pound roughly chopped zucchini
½ cup of water
1 and ½ teaspoon salt
1 bunch basil leaves
2 garlic cloves, minced
1 tablespoon extra-virgin olive oil
Zucchini for making zoodles

1. Set the Ninja Foodi to Saute mode and add olive oil
2. Once the oil is hot, add onion and Saute for 4 minutes
3. Add zucchini, water, and salt. Lock up the lid and cook on HIGH pressure for 3 minutes
4. Release the pressure naturally. Add basil, garlic, and leaves
5. Use an immersion blender to blend everything well until you have a sauce-like consistency
6. Take the extra zucchini and pass them through a Spiralizer to get noodle like shapes
7. Toss the Zoodles with sauce and enjoy!

Supreme Cauliflower Soup

Prepping time: 10 minutes| Cooking time: 5 minutes |For 4 servings

½ a small onion, chopped
2 tablespoons butter
1 large head of cauliflower, leaves and stems removed, coarsely chopped
2 cups chicken stock
1 teaspoon garlic powder
1 teaspoon salt
4 ounces cream cheese, cut into cubes
1 cup sharp cheddar cheese, cut
½ cup cream
Extra cheddar, sour cream bacon strips, green onion for topping

1. Peel the onion and chop up into small pieces
2. Cut the leaves of the cauliflower and steam, making sure to keep the core intact
3. Coarsely chop the cauliflower into pieces
4. Set your Ninja Foodi to Saute mode and add onion, cook for 2-3 minutes
5. Add chopped cauliflower, stock, salt, and garlic powder
6. Lock up the lid and cook on HIGH pressure for 5 minutes. Perform a quick release
7. Prepare the toppings. Use an immersion blender to puree your soup in the Ninja Foodi
8. Serve your soup with a topping of sliced green onions, cheddar, crumbled bacon. Enjoy!

Very Rich And Creamy Asparagus Soup

Prepping time: 10 minutes| Cooking time: 5-10 minutes |For 4 servings

1 tablespoon olive oil
3 green onions, sliced crosswise into ¼ inch pieces
1 pound asparagus, tough ends removed, cut into 1 inch pieces
4 cups vegetable stock
1 tablespoon unsalted butter
1 tablespoon almond flour
2 teaspoon salt
1 teaspoon white pepper
½ cup heavy cream

1. Set your Ninja Foodi to "Saute" mode and add oil, let it heat up
2. Add green onions and Saute for a few minutes, add asparagus and stock
3. Lock lid and cook on HIGH pressure for 5 minutes
4. Take a small saucepan and place it over low heat, add butter, flour and stir until the mixture foams and turns into a golden beige, this is your blond roux
5. Remove from heat. Release pressure naturally over 10 minutes
6. Open the lid and add roux, salt, and pepper to the soup
7. Use an immersion blender to puree the soup
8. Taste and season accordingly, swirl in cream and enjoy!

Summertime Vegetable Platter

Prepping time: 5 minutes| Cooking time: 3 hours 5 minutes |For 6 servings

1 cup grape tomatoes
2 cups okra
1 cup mushrooms
2 cups yellow bell peppers
1 and ½ cup red onions
2 and ½ cups zucchini
½ cup olive oil
½ cup balsamic vinegar
1 tablespoon fresh thyme, chopped
2 tablespoons fresh basil, chopped

1. Slice and chop okra, onions, tomatoes, zucchini, mushrooms
2. Add veggies to a large container and mix
3. Take another dish and add oil and vinegar, mix in thyme and basil
4. Toss the veggies into Ninja Foodi and pour marinade. Stir well
5. Close lid and cook on 3 hours on SLOW COOK MOD (HIGH), making sure to stir after every hour

The Creative Mushroom Stroganoff

Prepping time: 5 minutes| Cooking time: 10 minutes |For 6 servings

¼ cup unsalted butter, cubed
1 pound cremini mushrooms, halved
1 large onion, halved
4 garlic cloves, minced
2 cups vegetable broth
½ teaspoon salt
¼ teaspoon fresh black pepper
1 and ½ cups sour cream
¼ cup fresh flat-leaf parsley, chopped
1 cup grated parmesan cheese

1. Add butter, mushrooms, onion, garlic, vegetable broth, salt, pepper, and paprika
2. Gently stir and lock lid. Cook on HIGH pressure for 5 minutes
3. Release pressure naturally over 10 minutes
4. Serve by stirring in sour cream and with a garnish of parsley and parmesan cheese. Enjoy!

Garlic And Ginger Red Cabbage Platter

Prepping time: 10 minutes| Cooking time: 8 minutes |For 6 servings

2 tablespoon coconut oil
1 tablespoon butter
3 garlic cloves, crushed
2 teaspoon fresh ginger, grated
8 cups red cabbage, shredded
1 teaspoon salt
½ a teaspoon pepper
1/3 cup water

1. Set your Ninja Foodi to Saute mode and add coconut oil and butter, allow to heat up
2. Add garlic and ginger and mix. Add cabbage, pepper, salt, and water
3. Mix well and lock up the lid, cook on HIGH pressure for 5 minutes
4. Perform a quick release and mix. Serve and enjoy!

The Veggie Lover's Onion And Tofu Platter

Prepping time: 8 minutes| Cooking time: 12 minutes |For 4 servings

4 tablespoons butter
2 tofu blocks, pressed and cubed into 1-inch pieces
Salt and pepper to taste
1 cup cheddar cheese, grated
2 medium onions, sliced

1. Take a bowl and add tofu, season with salt and pepper
2. Set your Foodi to Saute mode and add butter, let it melt
3. Add onions and Saute for 3 minutes. Add seasoned tofu and cook for 2 minutes more
4. Add cheddar and gently stir
5. Lock the lid and bring down the Air Crisp mode, let the dish cook on "Air Crisp" mode for 3 minutes at 340 degrees F. Once done, take the dish out, serve and enjoy!

Feisty Maple Dredged Carrots

Prepping time: 10 minutes| Cooking time: 4 minutes |For 6 servings

2-pound carrot
¼ cup raisins
Pepper as needed
1 cup of water
1 tablespoon butter
1 tablespoon sugar-free Keto friendly maple
   syrup

1. Wash, peel the skin and slice the carrots diagonally
2. Add the carrots, raisins, water to your Ninja Foodi
3. Lock up the lid and cook on HIGH pressure for 4 minutes. Perform a quick release
4. Strain the carrots . Add butter and maple syrup to the warm Ninja Foodi and mix well
5. Transfer the strained carrots back to the pot and stir to coat with maple sauce and butter
6. Serve with a bit of pepper. Enjoy!

The Original Sicilian Cauliflower Roast

Prepping time: 10 minutes| Cooking time: 10 minutes |For 4 servings

1 medium cauliflower head, leaves removed
¼ cup olive oil
1 teaspoon red pepper, crushed
½ cup of water
2 tablespoons capers, rinsed and minced
½ cup parmesan cheese, grated
1 tablespoon fresh parsley, chopped

1. Take the Ninja Foodi and start by adding water and place the cook and crisp basket inside the pot. Cut an "X" on the head of cauliflower by using a knife and slice it about halfway down
2. Take a basket and transfer the cauliflower in it
3. Then put on the pressure lid and seal it and set it on low pressure for 3 minutes
4. Add olive oil, capers, garlic, and crushed red pepper into it and mix them well
5. Once the cauliflower is cooked, do a quick release and remove the lid
6. Pour in the oil and spice mixture on the cauliflower
7. Spread equally on the surface then sprinkle some Parmesan cheese from the top
8. Close the pot with crisping lid. Set it on Air Crisp mode to 390 degrees F for 10 minutes
9. Once done, remove the cauliflower flower the Ninja Foodi transfer it into a serving plate
10. Cut it up into pieces and transfer them to serving plates. Sprinkle fresh parsley from the top
11. Serve and enjoy!

Appendix 1
Measurement Conversion Chart

MEASUREMENT CONVERSION CHART

VOLUME EQUIVALENTS(DRY)

US STANDARD	METRIC (APPROXIMATE)
1/8 teaspoon	0.5 mL
1/4 teaspoon	1 mL
1/2 teaspoon	2 mL
3/4 teaspoon	4 mL
1 teaspoon	5 mL
1 tablespoon	15 mL
1/4 cup	59 mL
1/2 cup	118 mL
3/4 cup	177 mL
1 cup	235 mL
2 cups	475 mL
3 cups	700 mL
4 cups	1 L

VOLUME EQUIVALENTS(LIQUID)

US STANDARD	US STANDARD (OUNCES)	METRIC (APPROXIMATE)
2 tablespoons	1 fl.oz.	30 mL
1/4 cup	2 fl.oz.	60 mL
1/2 cup	4 fl.oz.	120 mL
1 cup	8 fl.oz.	240 mL
1 1/2 cup	12 fl.oz.	355 mL
2 cups or 1 pint	16 fl.oz.	475 mL
4 cups or 1 quart	32 fl.oz.	1 L
1 gallon	128 fl.oz.	4 L

TEMPERATURES EQUIVALENTS

FAHRENHEIT(F)	CELSIUS(C) (APPROXIMATE)
225 °F	107 °C
250 °F	120 °C
275 °F	135 °C
300 °F	150 °C
325 °F	160 °C
350 °F	180 °C
375 °F	190 °C
400 °F	205 °C
425 °F	220 °C
450 °F	235 °C
475 °F	245 °C
500 °F	260 °C

WEIGHT EQUIVALENTS

US STANDARD	METRIC (APPROXIMATE)
1 ounce	28 g
2 ounces	57 g
5 ounces	142 g
10 ounces	284 g
15 ounces	425 g
16 ounces (1 pound)	455 g
1.5 pounds	680 g
2 pounds	907 g

Appendix 2
Air Fryer Cooking Chart

Air Fryer Cooking Chart

Beef

Item	Temp (°F)	Time (mins)	Item	Temp (°F)	Time (mins)
Beef Eye Round Roast (4 lbs.)	400 °F	45 to 55	Meatballs (1-inch)	370 °F	7
Burger Patty (4 oz.)	370 °F	16 to 20	Meatballs (3-inch)	380 °F	10
Filet Mignon (8 oz.)	400 °F	18	Ribeye, bone-in (1-inch, 8 oz)	400 °F	10 to 15
Flank Steak (1.5 lbs.)	400 °F	12	Sirloin steaks (1-inch, 12 oz)	400 °F	9 to 14
Flank Steak (2 lbs.)	400 °F	20 to 28			

Chicken

Item	Temp (°F)	Time (mins)	Item	Temp (°F)	Time (mins)
Breasts, bone in (1 ¼ lb.)	370 °F	25	Legs, bone-in (1 ¾ lb.)	380 °F	30
Breasts, boneless (4 oz)	380 °F	12	Thighs, boneless (1 ½ lb.)	380 °F	18 to 20
Drumsticks (2 ½ lb.)	370 °F	20	Wings (2 lb.)	400 °F	12
Game Hen (halved 2 lb.)	390 °F	20	Whole Chicken	360 °F	75
Thighs, bone-in (2 lb.)	380 °F	22	Tenders	360 °F	8 to 10

Pork & Lamb

Item	Temp (°F)	Time (mins)	Item	Temp (°F)	Time (mins)
Bacon (regular)	400 °F	5 to 7	Pork Tenderloin	370 °F	15
Bacon (thick cut)	400 °F	6 to 10	Sausages	380 °F	15
Pork Loin (2 lb.)	360 °F	55	Lamb Loin Chops (1-inch thick)	400 °F	8 to 12
Pork Chops, bone in (1-inch, 6.5 oz)	400 °F	12	Rack of Lamb (1.5 – 2 lb.)	380 °F	22

Fish & Seafood

Item	Temp (°F)	Time (mins)	Item	Temp (°F)	Time (mins)
Calamari (8 oz)	400 °F	4	Tuna Steak	400 °F	7 to 10
Fish Fillet (1-inch, 8 oz)	400 °F	10	Scallops	400 °F	5 to 7
Salmon, fillet (6 oz)	380 °F	12	Shrimp	400 °F	5
Swordfish steak	400 °F	10			

Air Fryer Cooking Chart

Vegetables					
INGREDIENT	**AMOUNT**	**PREPARATION**	**OIL**	**TEMP**	**COOK TIME**
Asparagus	2 bunches	Cut in half, trim stems	2 Tbsp	420°F	12-15 mins
Beets	1½ lbs	Peel, cut in ½-inch cubes	1Tbsp	390°F	28-30 mins
Bell peppers (for roasting)	4 peppers	Cut in quarters, remove seeds	1Tbsp	400°F	15-20 mins
Broccoli	1 large head	Cut in 1-2-inch florets	1Tbsp	400°F	15-20 mins
Brussels sprouts	1lb	Cut in half, remove stems	1Tbsp	425°F	15-20 mins
Carrots	1lb	Peel, cut in ¼-inch rounds	1 Tbsp	425°F	10-15 mins
Cauliflower	1 head	Cut in 1-2-inch florets	2 Tbsp	400°F	20-22 mins
Corn on the cob	7 ears	Whole ears, remove husks	1 Tbps	400°F	14-17 mins
Green beans	1 bag (12 oz)	Trim	1 Tbps	420°F	18-20 mins
Kale (for chips)	4 oz	Tear into pieces,remove stems	None	325°F	5-8 mins
Mushrooms	16 oz	Rinse, slice thinly	1 Tbps	390°F	25-30 mins
Potatoes, russet	1½ lbs	Cut in 1-inch wedges	1 Tbps	390°F	25-30 mins
Potatoes, russet	1lb	Hand-cut fries, soak 30 mins in cold water, then pat dry	½ -3 Tbps	400°F	25-28 mins
Potatoes, sweet	1lb	Hand-cut fries, soak 30 mins in cold water, then pat dry	1 Tbps	400°F	25-28 mins
Zucchini	1lb	Cut in eighths lengthwise, then cut in half	1 Tbps	400°F	15-20 mins

Appendix 3
4-Week Ninja Foodi Plan

Plan for Week 1

	BREAKFAST	A.M SNACK	LUNCH	P.M SNACK	DINNER
Day 1	Tex-Mex Red Potatoes	Spicy Ranch Chicken Wings	Advanced Smothered Pork Chops	Tasty Brussels	Advanced Smothered Pork Chops
Day 2	Tex-Mex Red Potatoes	Spicy Ranch Chicken Wings	Advanced Smothered Pork Chops	Tasty Brussels	Advanced Smothered Pork Chops
Day 3	Tex-Mex Red Potatoes	Spicy Ranch Chicken Wings	Advanced Smothered Pork Chops	Tasty Brussels	Advanced Smothered Pork Chops
Day 4	Tex-Mex Red Potatoes	Spicy Ranch Chicken Wings	Parmesan Risotto with Herbs	Tasty Brussels	Saffron and Orange Rice Pilaf
Day 5	Tex-Mex Red Potatoes	Ultimate Layered Nachos	Parmesan Risotto with Herbs	Ultimate Layered Nachos	Saffron and Orange Rice Pilaf
Day 6	Sour Cream Scrambled Eggs	Ultimate Layered Nachos	Parmesan Risotto with Herbs	Spaghetti Squash And Chicken Parmesan	Saffron and Orange Rice Pilaf
Day 7	Sour Cream Scrambled Eggs	Ultimate Layered Nachos	Parmesan Risotto with Herbs	Spaghetti Squash And Chicken Parmesan	Saffron and Orange Rice Pilaf

Plan for Week 2

	BREAKFAST	A.M SNACK	LUNCH	P.M SNACK	DINNER
Day 1	Asparagus with Soft Boiled Eggs	Candied Maple Bacon	Lebanese Tabbouleh	Candied Maple Bacon	Black Bean and Sweet Potato Tacos
Day 2	Asparagus with Soft Boiled Eggs	Candied Maple Bacon	Lebanese Tabbouleh	Candied Maple Bacon	Black Bean and Sweet Potato Tacos
Day 3	Asparagus with Soft Boiled Eggs	Candied Maple Bacon	Lebanese Tabbouleh	Candied Maple Bacon	Black Bean and Sweet Potato Tacos
Day 4	Puffy Dutch Baby	Candied Maple Bacon	Lebanese Tabbouleh	Candied Maple Bacon	Black Bean and Sweet Potato Tacos
Day 5	Puffy Dutch Baby	Candied Maple Bacon	Lebanese Tabbouleh	The Kool Poblano Cheese Frittata	Black Bean and Sweet Potato Tacos
Day 6	Puffy Dutch Baby	Candied Maple Bacon	Lebanese Tabbouleh	The Kool Poblano Cheese Frittata	Black Bean and Sweet Potato Tacos
Day 7	Puffy Dutch Baby	Candied Maple Bacon	Black Bean and Sweet Potato Tacos	The Kool Poblano Cheese Frittata	Black Bean and Sweet Potato Tacos

Plan for Week 3

	BREAKFAST	A.M SNACK	LUNCH	P.M SNACK	DINNER
Day 1	Gooey Candied Bacon	Spice Lover's Jar Of Chili	Maple-Glazed Carrots	Easy To Swallow Beet Chips	Cauliflower Steaks
Day 2	Gooey Candied Bacon	Spice Lover's Jar Of Chili	Maple-Glazed Carrots	Easy To Swallow Beet Chips	Refried Black Beans
Day 3	Gooey Candied Bacon	Spice Lover's Jar Of Chili	Maple-Glazed Carrots	Easy To Swallow Beet Chips	Refried Black Beans
Day 4	Gooey Candied Bacon	Spice Lover's Jar Of Chili	Maple-Glazed Carrots	Easy To Swallow Beet Chips	Refried Black Beans
Day 5	Gooey Candied Bacon	Easy To Swallow Beet Chips	Maple-Glazed Carrots	Easy To Swallow Beet Chips	Refried Black Beans
Day 6	Giant Omelet	Easy To Swallow Beet Chips	Maple-Glazed Carrots	Bacon Samba Bok Choy	Refried Black Beans
Day 7	Giant Omelet	Easy To Swallow Beet Chips	Cauliflower Steaks	Bacon Samba Bok Choy	Refried Black Beans

Plan for Week 4

	BREAKFAST	A.M SNACK	LUNCH	P.M SNACK	DINNER
Day 1	Chinese Ginger Chicken Congee	Delicious Bacon-Wrapped Drumsticks	Avocado and Spinach Pasta	A Hot Buffalo Wing Platter	Avocado and Spinach Pasta
Day 2	Chinese Ginger Chicken Congee	Delicious Bacon-Wrapped Drumsticks	Avocado and Spinach Pasta	A Hot Buffalo Wing Platter	Fried Rice with Vegetable
Day 3	Chinese Ginger Chicken Congee	Delicious Bacon-Wrapped Drumsticks	Avocado and Spinach Pasta	A Hot Buffalo Wing Platter	Fried Rice with Vegetable
Day 4	Chinese Ginger Chicken Congee	Delicious Bacon-Wrapped Drumsticks	Avocado and Spinach Pasta	The Original Braised Kale And Carrot Salad	Fried Rice with Vegetable
Day 5	Chinese Ginger Chicken Congee	Delicious Bacon-Wrapped Drumsticks	Avocado and Spinach Pasta	The Original Braised Kale And Carrot Salad	Fried Rice with Vegetable
Day 6	Chinese Ginger Chicken Congee	Delicious Bacon-Wrapped Drumsticks	Avocado and Spinach Pasta	The Original Braised Kale And Carrot Salad	Fried Rice with Vegetable
Day 7	Chinese Ginger Chicken Congee	A Hot Buffalo Wing Platter	Avocado and Spinach Pasta	The Original Braised Kale And Carrot Salad	Fried Rice with Vegetable

Appendix 4 Index

Made in United States
North Haven, CT
26 October 2022